LOOKING LIKE THE ENEMY

MY STORY OF IMPRISONMENT IN JAPANESE-AMERICAN INTERNMENT CAMPS

MARY MATSUDA GRUENEWALD

NEWSAGE PRESS
Troutdale, Oregon

LOOKING LIKE THE ENEMY:
My Story of Imprisonment in Japanese-American Internment Camps
Copyright © 2005 by Mary Matsuda Gruenewald
Paperback Original ISBN 0-939165-53-8

All rights reserved. No part of this book may be reproduced or used in any form or by any means without permission from the publisher.

NEWSAGE PRESS
PO Box 607
Troutdale, OR 97060-0607
503-695-2211

website: www.newsagepress.com

Cover Photo: The cover photo was taken on March 30, 1942 by a *Seattle Post Intelligencer* photographer as the Hayashida family was being evacuated from Seattle. Holding the flag is Hiro Hayashida. Beside him stands his sister Susan. Behind them stands their mother, Nobuko Hayashida. Another sister (not shown) stands at Susan's left. Hiro Hayashida and Susan Hayashida Furuta still live in the Seattle area. Photo courtesy of Frank Kitamoto, a nephew to Hiro and Susan.

Cover & Book Design by Sherry Wachter.
Printed in the United States on recycled paper.

Library of Congress Cataloging-in-Publication Data

Gruenewald, Mary Matsuda, 1925-
  Looking like the enemy / by Mary Matsuda Gruenewald.-- 1st ed.
     p. cm.
  Includes bibliographical references.
  ISBN 0-939165-53-8
  1. Japanese Americans--Evacuation and relocation, 1942-1945. 2. Gruenewald, Mary Matsuda, 1925- 3. Japanese Americans--Biography. I. Title.
  D769.8.A5G78 2005
  940.53'1779635--dc22

                                                      2005004076

7 8 9 10

*For the Isseis whose courage, devotion, and faith in the United States
and in their children made it possible for our people to triumph
over the internment experience. The values they passed on
laid the foundation for the ultimate fulfillment of their dreams
by the Nisei and future generations.*

The Matsuda Family, 1933.

ACKNOWLEDGMENTS

I wish to thank the countless people who helped to make this book possible. First and foremost are the members of my original family: my mother, father and brother, all of whom died long ago, but whose memory remains vivid and central to this story. My children, Martha, David and Ray, and my nieces, Marlene, Kathryn, Marguerite and Sheila, formed the primary motivation for me to write my story late in life. My sister-in-law, Miyoko, provided inspiration, support, and specific mementos from my brother's collection of books and papers.

I am indebted to Tok Otsuka and Augie Takatsuka, who served in the 100th / 442nd Regimental Combat Team with my brother. From them, I gained a better perspective of the ferocity of the battles they fought on behalf of the Allied forces and for the freedom of our people.

I will always be grateful to my special friend, Haru Ishikawa, who inspired and helped me with numerous discussions, meals shared, and books from her collection. Her untimely death deprived her of the pleasure of seeing this book come to fruition.

I wish to acknowledge Pam Woodroffe who, in writing about farming on Vashon Island in her book, *Vashon Island's Agricultural Roots: Tales of the Tilth as Told by Island Farmers,* devoted a chapter to my family's early years as strawberry farmers. It includes a part of my story of the internment process.

I am indebted to Mr. Ivar Nelson, formerly of the University of Idaho Press, who provided support and guidance as I moved through the initial phases of the writing of my story.

I wish to extend my special thanks to Jo Cripps, who worked with me during my initial, limited attempts at writing.

I want to formally acknowledge the crucial role of my writing teacher, Brenda Peterson. It was through her unfailing support and wise counsel that I was finally able to come to terms with my Japanese background that had been the source of unexamined confusion and pain during much of my life. Members of her writing group made major contributions to clarifying and writing my story. They include: Leigh Calvez, Claire Dederer, Liz Gruenfeld, Leslie D. Helm, Susan Little, J. Kingston Pierce, Trip Quillman, John Runyan, Dori Jones Yang, Denise Benitez, Jordan Buck, Kristina Danilchik, Cathy Englehart, Laurie Greig, Anne Hayden, Donna Kelleher, Susan Knox, Tara Kolden, Anne Mize, Trish Murphy, Ginny NiCarthy, Kimberly Richardson, Ward Serill, Julie Stonefelt, and Louise Wisechild.

I am deeply grateful for the support of Robert S. Fisher of the Wing Luke Museum and Carolyn Marr of the Museum of History and Industry in Seattle, Washington. They made it both possible and pleasant for me to include valuable photographs from their collections.

I am indebted to Liz Nesbitt, Ph.D., Curator of Paleontology, Burke Museum of Natural History and Culture. She provided invaluable information about the shells I found at the Tule Lake Internment Camp.

I wish to give special thanks to my son, Ray, who has given his heart, soul, expertise, and energy to my writing of this book. His contributions have helped me to complete this narrative that has been my focus for most of the last decade. While his time and efforts have been indispensable, it has been his interest, passion, and support that have meant so much to me. I can think of no greater gift that he could have given to our whole family and to me.

I would also like to acknowledge NewSage Press' book designer, Sherry Wachter. Her exquisite design sensibilities helped bring my story to life on these pages. And finally my profound thanks must go to Maureen R. Michelson, publisher of NewSage Press, for the extraordinary editing and personal support she provided. She recognized the potential in my story and helped to transform my initial manuscript into a polished work.

MARY MATSUDA GRUENEWALD
Seattle, Washington

CONTENTS

BREAKING THE SILENCE

One sunny day my brother, Yoneichi, and I sat on a log floating in front of our home at Shawnee Beach on Vashon Island, Washington. I was four years old and he was six.

That day in 1929 as we peacefully rode the gentle tide of Puget Sound we could not know about the impending tsunami of World War II. Thirteen years later a wave of anti-Japanese prejudice swept across the United States and forced my family to leave our secure island home and succumb to the will of a hostile and turbulent world at war. Little did I know the political storms and social upheavals that would beset my family, tear us away from our home, and confine us in internment camps simply because we looked like the enemy.

During World War II Japanese-Americans endured the wholesale violation of our civil and human rights as residents and citizens of the United States. Many would lose their homes, livelihoods, and dreams, and be left with pain, confusion, and shame. This legacy has shadowed my entire adult life.

Some seventy-five years later I gaze long and hard at this photo, recalling my innocence, joy, and security. With what I know now, how I wish I could have held that little girl in the photo and reassured her, "Have faith in your family and the ultimate goodness of people. Especially have faith in

yourself to survive the catastrophic events yet to come. In spite of all the terror, pain, depression, and tears in your future, you will reach a final hopeful conclusion."

With the hindsight of age, I have learned faith, hope, and love in a world gone crazy. Over the years I have carved out a life marked by reason and patience for myself and for my three children. I also learned the importance of speaking, telling my story, in the hope that history will not repeat itself.

Historians have referred to the interned Japanese-Americans as the "silent generation" because most of us did not speak about our experiences—even to our children. Years after the end of World War II, whenever I met someone whom I suspected of having been a prisoner at an internment camp, I might ask, "Were you in one of the camps during the war?"

If the response was "Yes," I continued. "Which one?"

He or she would answer: "Amache, Gila, Heart Mountain, Jerome, Manzanar, Minidoka, Poston, Rohwer, Topaz, or Tule Lake."

After a pause one of us might say, "That was a long time ago, wasn't it?" We would both nod and then fall silent. We understood each other. This might seem strange to people who had not shared this experience, but for those of us who did, we knew what the experience was like. At the time, it seemed as if there was no need for words.

In the decades following the internment I managed to suppress feelings and memories of this painful period. I thought the only way I could achieve normalcy was to forget about the evacuation, and work diligently to get on with my life. To speak or even to think of those times meant to revisit what had happened, and that was too painful to consider.

The penalty I paid for being silent for years—even to myself—seems perplexing even now. I complied and endured, albeit begrudgingly, but never had the nerve to fully break out of those self-imposed "barbed-wire fences" built around my experiences in the camps. For most of my life I was afraid to deal with those years of repressed shame and anger and the unknown depth of those feelings.

As I reflect on all that happened, I am reminded of a book, *The Trial*, by Franz Kafka. In this story a man is accused of some crime about which he is unclear. The elements of the trial are fearful and unpredictable, and it is difficult to foresee the conclusion of the ordeal. I, too, had a sense of guilt for a crime I had supposedly committed, but I never understood what that crime was.

My three children had to discover for themselves what the Japanese-American internment was about. I kept a few relics from that era such as the three, one-gallon jars of shells I gathered from the grounds of Tule Lake Camp. These would stimulate occasional conversations, but I matter-of-factly told the same safe anecdotes over and over again. As a parent, I did not want to show my children how vulnerable I felt at that time, nor did I want to get into the emotional part of my experience that could lead me to tears.

In 1967 when my oldest child, Martha, tried to write a research paper on the internment, she could not find a single book that mentioned it. But a few years later, books and films such as *A Farewell to Manzanar* finally broke the silence. This is how my children and the rest of the public began to learn about this regrettable chapter in American history. More recently the best seller, *Snow Falling on Cedars,* by David Guterson, and the subsequent film showed the evacuation of the first group of Japanese from a fictional island in Washington state. As I watched the part of the movie when the FBI searched the home of a Japanese-American family who were later forced to evacuate under armed U.S. soldier escorts, I broke down and wept. Vivid memories of my own experience swept over me.

When I was seventy-four years old I was invited to participate in a writing class and began writing about those war years. The dam broke loose when emotions and tears I had repressed for decades burst through, at times seemingly uncontrollable. At last, I was telling my story—a *Nisei* no longer willing to be silent.

Now as I near my eightieth birthday and the completion of my book in 2005, my tears come more easily and with them understanding and acceptance. I weep for all Japanese-Americans who could not acknowledge that it was all right to be angry and confused about our identity in the face of the mass rejection by American society. At the same time, I am profoundly grateful for the open-minded, compassionate, and humane fellow citizens who helped Japanese-Americans make the difficult transition back to normal life.

I yearn for the day when the general American public will read, listen, and understand the implications of what the United States did to Japanese-Americans—and what we must do differently and far better in today's world torn by terrorism and war.

The Matsuda family's new home on Vashon in the winter of 1931.
Mary was six years old.

CHAPTER ONE

An Island in Darkness

In the midst of the complicated jumble of waterways and islands of Puget Sound, there is a slice of rural America called Vashon Island, just a twenty-minute ferry ride from Seattle. In the 1920s Vashon had large-scale industrial logging, substantial greenhouse operations, and farms specializing in diverse products such as poultry, dairy, vegetables, and berries. Today Vashon is home for thousands of people commuting to work in Seattle and Tacoma.

Vashon may be only a few water miles from two large cities, but it is protected from their influence by a salt-water channel that is more than six hundred feet deep. Building a bridge across these waters has been studied many times but never accomplished because of the fierce desire by many residents to preserve a particular lifestyle. Vashon maintains the character of a small town where neighbor helps neighbor and the sense of community is strong.

In 1927 my parents, Heisuke and Mitsuno Matsuda brought my brother, Yoneichi, and me to Vashon. Yoneichi was four years old, I was two. My parents leased a small berry farm and worked long days to secure a livelihood and a future for their family. Like many others, we grew strawberries and lived a quiet, self-sufficient life. By 1936, we were one of thirty-seven Japanese families living on Vashon Island.

I attended Vashon Grade School with eight grades in one building, two classes per room per teacher. The majority of the students were Caucasian but in my grade level there were two Chinese students and three Japanese-Americans out of a class of seventy-eight.

My life in that idyllic setting was one of innocence and pleasure, just being one of the island kids. My parents chose Vashon to raise their family in order to protect us from the corrupting influences of modern life. But nothing could protect us from the events following December 7, 1941, the day Pearl Harbor was bombed.

That December morning Yoneichi and I walked through a light rain to the Vashon Methodist Church as we had for the past eight years. The Sunday service was in English so my parents didn't attend, opting for Methodist services in Japanese often held in our living room. My brother and I knew everyone in the church so we always looked forward to singing the familiar hymns and feeling a part of the congregation. As usual, we arrived early to dust the pews and distribute church bulletins and hymnals in the sanctuary. Sunday services were a part of the rhythm of our week and that day felt like years of Sundays on Vashon.

After church my brother and I wished everyone a good week ahead and left for home. As we walked I studied the Bible verse I had received and repeated it until I memorized it for next Sunday. It was my last carefree morning preoccupied with all the trivial cares and worries of a sixteen-year-old American teenager. It was also the last time I fully believed I was an American.

When we got to the house, we cheerfully announced our arrival. My father, whom we always called Papa-san, was sitting at his usual place at the kitchen table, eyes downcast, silent. Normally, Papa-san would have been working outdoors, only returning when lunch was ready. Our mother, Mama-san, always greeted us with a smile whenever we came home, but that day she looked pale as she leaned against the counter and stared out the window.

"Papa-san, why are you home early?" my brother asked. When there was no response, Yoneichi's wide smile vanished as his eyes darted back and forth between the two of them. Then he turned to our mother. "Mama-san, is something wrong? What's going on?"

I put my things down, suddenly frightened. I had never seen this look on my father's face. I wondered, *Why won't they look at us?*

After a long silence Papa-san looked up and answered quietly in Japanese, "Mr. Yabu called. Japanese airplanes bombed Pearl Harbor in Hawaii early this morning." Yoneichi whirled around and snapped on the radio sitting on the kitchen counter.

We didn't have to wait long. The booming voice of an urgent reporter burst out the news of the attack. We listened with horror as he hurriedly spit out information about the heavy losses sustained by the United States Navy.

All stared at the radio in stunned silence. *This can't be,* I thought. *There must be some mistake.* I didn't want to hear about all the ships that had been

2

hit or that more American servicemen had been killed. But the loud, blaring voice of the announcer kept interrupting the scheduled programs with more news about the attack. I couldn't catch my breath.

After awhile I turned from the radio and looked at my parents. They understood enough English to grasp the meaning of this announcement. As the gravity of the news sunk in, Papa-san's head dropped to his chest, and his shoulders slumped forward. He looked defeated.

Little did we know that Sunday afternoon how much our lives would change, but Papa-san knew enough to be afraid. He realized what could happen if public opinion turned against him. Some forty years earlier, shortly after his arrival in the United States, my father and several other Japanese men were working in the coal mines in the Alaskan Klondike. One day a white friend sought him out and said, "Harry, there's a bunch of guys who don't like you fellows and they are planning to raid your camp tonight. You'd better get out of town right away." The Japanese men scrambled to gather their things, hurriedly broke up camp, left their jobs, and escaped before the vigilantes arrived. At the time Papa-san told us about this incident, he also described learning first hand about prejudice and how important it was to develop good relationships with everyone wherever he went. Now all those good relationships with neighbors and business associates would be tested.

My mother, Mitsuno Horiye Matsuda, was the perfect Japanese wife—obedient and devoted. She had been cooking fried chicken for our Sunday meal, but now it was set aside and forgotten in the midst of the unfolding crisis. Ordinarily she was lighthearted, gracious, and very practical about life. The pride she felt in Yoneichi and me was something we understood even though she always modestly protested whenever others complimented us. Now her eyes filled with tears as she sank into the chair. I heard her whisper to herself in Japanese, "This is terribly distressing. What will happen to us?"

Yoneichi and I looked at each other, stunned. We still couldn't believe what was being said on the radio. The blaring, bitter news report was suffocating but I couldn't stop listening. I thought, *This can't really be happening. Are they insane coming thousands of miles from Japan to attack United States territory? Why did they do this? How will this affect us because we are Japanese-Americans?*

Even though Papa-san had lived in America since 1898, and Mama-san since 1922, they could not become naturalized citizens because of immigration laws and could not own land because of the anti-alien land laws in many Western states. We had lived in our home for eleven years, had cordial relationships with our neighbors, and participated in the Vashon community, but my parents were still vulnerable. Yoneichi and I had been born in the United States, which made us American citizens. We were sure our citizenship would protect us, but still, we were afraid.

As the news sank in, Mama-san remarked thoughtfully, "Now I understand why my brother, Moichi-san, wrote me those letters urging us to come back to Japan. I wonder if he might have suspected that something like this was going to happen."

Mama-san moved aimlessly about the kitchen, touching different items on the counter. After awhile she stopped in front of the kitchen sink and stared blankly out the window at the front yard. Her usually erect body sagged. Her eyes, which were usually bright and generated smiles from others, looked sadder this day than I had ever seen them. As though trying to remove cobwebs from her face, she moved her hands across her eyes and over her graying hair as she sighed.

Papa-san did not move from the kitchen table. He kept turning his teacup around and around, lost in fearful thoughts that deepened the crease between his eyes. Periodically he took a deep breath and turned his sad eyes toward the window and the sky beyond.

Never before had I seen my parents so self-absorbed and troubled. A big knot doubled, then tripled in the pit of my stomach. Thoughts and feelings collided, trying to make sense of what had just happened and how this would affect my family—and the world.

Many times my parents had told Yoneichi and me, "What you think about yourself is not nearly as important as what *other* people think about you." Every once in awhile my parents would ask me what image I thought I was projecting and what people might think about me as a result of my behavior. They were thinking about my future. Now I had a gnawing feeling of guilt—guilt for being Japanese. I didn't want to think about the possibility that now American people would consider me as the enemy.

I picked up our cat, Kitty, and sat down on a kitchen chair. Repeatedly I stroked her lean silky body and held her close. Our dog, Frisky, sensing that something was amiss, stood near and stared at me with his searching gaze. I patted him on his head and rubbed his ears. In turn, he licked my hand and comforted me as he leaned his body against my legs.

4

Yoneichi paced about the house, going in and out of the kitchen, listening to the radio reports. Whenever he sat down, his right leg nervously jiggled up and down, unable to contain himself. His lips were pursed, his brows knitted in a perpetual frown. He kept raising his right hand to rub his neck as though he had a pain there. *What could my brother possibly be thinking?* Yoneichi was a recent high school graduate and was working on the family farm while he thought about his future. Suddenly, his future seemed suspended.

I looked at my family and thought, *What beautiful people they are. What will happen to us now?*

We spent the rest of the day near each other, tense and silent. Our telephone was ominously quiet. We tried to brace ourselves against some nameless premonition of trouble, which we each intuitively knew would overtake us. Radio reports brought more bad news—additional ships destroyed, growing casualties, more disasters wrought. Yoneichi kept going outdoors to search the sky for any evidence of airplanes. In time the rest of us joined him, unable to listen any longer to the devastating news that hammered away at our fears. That night we had very little appetite for dinner and we stayed up later than usual. Each of us spent a restless night.

The following morning I reluctantly went to school at Vashon High. I felt guilty, ashamed that the Japanese government—to which my parents tied me—had done this terrible deed to our United States. As I went through the halls from one class to another, every time anyone looked at me, I imagined hatred in their eyes. I assumed that everyone was prejudiced and didn't want to have anything to do with me. In one of my classes, I began to cry as much from confusion as frustration. Crying seemed to be the only thing I could do. I thought, *I am an American yet I don't look like one. I am Japanese but ashamed that I am.*

It seemed as if an unknown penalty awaited my family, yet I didn't know what, when, or how. Even though all of my classmates and teachers were kind and behaved the same towards me, everything had changed inside of me. It was clear non-Japanese students shared my fear of the future and the shock of the sudden turn of events, but no one did anything to single me out or blame me.

One friend came up to me and linked her arm with mine as we went to English class together. My classmates offered their silent support, and I was grateful, but my perception had changed. Now, I felt like an outsider. Ever since the third grade, when one of the white kids called me a "Jap," I knew I was different. But still, we got along pretty well. Only now, things were not the same.

All the years we lived here, our parents had stressed the importance of our being good citizens of the community and nation. "America is made up of people from all walks of life from many countries of the world," they declared. "The equality of all of the people, and tolerance, are keys to living peacefully together." We had tried so hard to promote favorable relations between the Japanese community and our neighbors, but I assumed that all our efforts had been ruined. My parents had taught us to be stoic, brave, serene, respectful of authority, and in total control of our emotions. But on that Monday after Pearl Harbor, in place of my usual serenity, I felt incredible tension building inside of me. Afraid and helpless, I couldn't do the thing that I most wanted—to change things back to the way they were.

That evening as we ate dinner near the radio, an announcement by the Civil Defense Authority declared: "Beginning this evening at 7:00 p.m. all citizens in the Puget Sound area are required to implement a complete, dusk-to-dawn visual blackout to prevent an attack on our defense industries." The blackout was to last every night until further notice. Cooperation from the entire community was mandatory. If we had questions we were supposed to call the local Civilian Defense office.

We briefly discussed what we had to do to be sure no light was visible outside of our home. Mama-san got up from the table and said to me, "Mary-san, help me gather up some blankets to cover our windows. We'll have to bring out the old kerosene lamps, too."

As I got up to help, my arms felt heavy and my hands were clammy. And the lump in my throat wouldn't go away no matter how often I tried to clear it. Mama-san quietly commented, *"Kowai desu ne*—This is frightening, isn't it?"

Yoneichi got a stepladder and helped drape the blankets over every window. He voiced what was running through my mind. "I wonder what will happen next. You don't suppose more Japanese planes will come over and bomb us here, do you?" After a few moments, he added, "And what about us? Surely it will make a difference because we have been good citizens in our community, and Mary and I are Americans, not Japanese, won't it?" His questions trailed off. No one could answer them.

A few days later when I was in the living room doing my homework, I overheard snatches of conversation between my parents. They had lingered at the dinner table long after we had finished our meal. Papa-san said with a worried tone, "I wish Japan hadn't attacked Pearl Harbor. Our lives will certainly become more difficult."

"Yes, I'm afraid they will," Mama-san replied, distressed. "It's hard to tell who will still be our friends and who will turn against us. I hope our neighbors will still be friendly."

"I won't feel as comfortable coming and going as I have in the past," Papa-san confessed. "And doing the business for our farm will become more complicated, I'm sure. We'll just have to wait and see how things unfold to know how to proceed."

"Yes, I agree," Mama-san said. "Even though you and I have never been able to become citizens, we've raised our children to be good members of the community. We must have faith that this will all work out eventually."

"Yes, and I think it is important for us to cooperate with the civil defense efforts," Papa-san added. "We'll do whatever we can to show that we are good citizens in spite of everything."

They continued talking in Japanese in hushed voices as if to protect Yoneichi and me from their private concerns and fears. Sometimes one of them spoke rapidly with a quick response from the other. Much later, I recognized the anguish they must have felt knowing the country of their birth was at war with their adopted country.

In the fall of 1941 before the bombing of Pearl Harbor, there was no way we could have known how close the United States was to an imminent war with Japan. Neither could we have known about a U.S. government study conducted a decade earlier that examined the loyalty of Japanese-Americans living on the West Coast and Hawaii. Years later Michi Weglyn would reveal in her book, *Years of Infamy*, that an investigation by the U.S. State Department "certified a remarkable, even extraordinary degree of loyalty [to the United States] among this generally suspect ethnic group." Yet, in spite of thoroughly researched conclusions by U.S. intelligence that "there is no Japanese problem," this information was not disclosed to the public prior to World War II, during the war years, or in the years shortly thereafter.

I, of course, knew nothing of this. All during my childhood I had believed that I was "one of the group" in America. It was wonderful.

One of my *Nisei* first-grade classmates on Vashon, whose family spoke only Japanese at home, had a different experience. Occasionally the teacher left the classroom for a minute, leaving the children on their honor. One of the mischievous boys shot spit wads around the room and created havoc among the kids. When the teacher returned and wanted to know who the culprit was, the troublemaker pointed to my *Nisei* friend as the offender. The teacher disciplined him with many swats on the hand with a wooden ruler. He did not know how to defend himself from the teacher nor the offending classmate until much later.

When Yoneichi started first grade, he too had a difficult time understanding his teachers. He almost flunked the first grade because we spoke only Japanese at home. But with additional tutoring, he caught on quickly and eventually graduated as the salutatorian of his high school class. Because he was two years ahead of me, I learned English from him and had a much easier time starting school.

In the weeks following the bombing of Pearl Harbor, high school proceeded as though things were unchanged. The elaborate junior prom being planned by my classmates for the end of the school year did not interest me. Instead, I was struggling to understand what was happening and the implications for our future. I attended Latin I and U.S. history classes but I did not remember anything. In English III we studied poetry and that caught my attention. I began collecting poems, made my own poetry book, and included illustrations. The poems took me outside myself, comforting me in a way that nothing else could. A poem by Rudyard Kipling foreshadowed what was in store for us.

IF

If you can keep your head when all about you
Are losing theirs and blaming it on you;
If you can trust yourself when all men doubt you,
But make allowance for their doubting too:
If you can wait and not be tired by waiting,
Or being lied about, don't deal in lies,
Or being hated don't give way to hating,
And yet don't look too good, nor talk too wise...

As the war in the Pacific progressed that winter following Pearl Harbor, Guam, Hong Kong, Manila, and Singapore fell to the advancing Japanese forces. This brought increased attention to the Japanese and Japanese-Americans in Hawaii and on the West Coast. Many non-Japanese-

Americans began to see us as conspirators responsible for the attack on Pearl Harbor. There were false stories in local newspapers and on radio broadcasts that Japanese "sympathizers" in Hawaii cut arrows into the cane fields, directing Japanese planes to Pearl Harbor. There were reports of Japanese-American sabotage on the West Coast and of an impending attack on our continent. Although these rumors were never substantiated, General John L. DeWitt, the Western Defense Commander, insisted that "no proof of sabotage was indeed proof that sabotage was imminent." California's Attorney General Earl Warren, who later became Chief Justice of the Supreme Court, supported General DeWitt's assessment.

As the anti-Japanese propaganda machinery kicked into full gear, I began to withdraw more and more. I started to drop my eyes whenever anyone approached me. Never much of a talker, I spoke even less in those months following Pearl Harbor.

Japanese people such as my parents had come to the United States to make a better life for themselves and their families, and to be good upright citizens in their new country. Having already experienced discrimination earlier, my parents were not surprised at the severe degree of distortion in the press and elsewhere. However, this was my first real exposure to discrimination and I could not believe nor accept what was happening. I also knew the negative claims against Japanese-Americans were not true.

A couple years before, Papa-san had told us his story of leaving Japan for Hawaii. "From the time I set foot in the Territory of Hawaii in 1898, I saved my money to pay off my debt for my passage from Japan. Going into debt was the only way most of us could afford to make the trip. Then I began saving to settle down somewhere in this land that held so much promise."

"Did you like Hawaii?" I asked him, enthralled with his brave adventures and how courageously he handled adversity.

"Yes, the weather was nice but after a couple of years working in the sugar cane, I decided to go to the Territory of Alaska to see another part of the world. I found work in a coal mine in the Klondike. That was very hard work and so dirty but the pay was pretty good for that time. You already know about that harrowing time when we barely escaped the vigilantes who came to raid our camp."

"Yes," I affirmed. "That must have been a terrible experience for you."

"Yes it was, but I learned a lot. I learned firsthand about prejudice and I'm grateful for the friendship of some of the *hakujin*, white men. From that

9

experience I learned to be more aware of others and to always strive to develop good relationships wherever I went.

"From there I decided to go to another place. I found work in another coal mine in Cle Elum in our state of Washington. But wherever I worked, I saved my money. At one point another *hakujin* friend advised me to invest in a one thousand dollar New York Life Insurance policy as well as put my earnings into a savings and loan bank. That money would earn interest and grow for me. Later when I was ready I could take the money out of both accounts and buy a piece of property and build a house. So that's what I did. I was saving for the future when I could have a family."

I wanted to have my father's courage in the face of adversity, but I continued to worry about what all of this would mean for us. Intimidated by all of the propaganda, I felt increasing self-reproach for being who I was. Every time a newscaster blasted the Japanese army for the "shameful attack on Pearl Harbor and the destruction and loss of lives that resulted," I cringed. The caricatures of Japanese soldiers featured on the covers of such widely circulated magazines as *Time* showed them as jaundiced bespectacled men with squinty, slanted eyes. They had huge, white buckteeth framed by a sardonic grin. The tiny button nose with high prominent cheekbones, and large pointed head under a miniature, grotesque military cap made the Japanese soldier look like a crazed monkey or an insane degenerate.

The December 22, 1941 issue of *Time* magazine contained an article, "How to Tell Your Friends From the Japs." It discussed how even an anthropologist has difficulty telling the difference between Chinese and Japanese people. Some examples were that Chinese are taller and slimmer, not as hairy, and their facial expressions are more placid, kindly, and open. In Washington, D.C., a journalist wore a large badge on his lapel reading "Chinese Reporter—NOT Japanese—please."

I hated what I heard and read but I couldn't help but pay attention to what was printed and broadcast over the radio. *Is that how people see me?* I wondered. I wished I had never been born.

Following Japan's sweeping early victories, the perception emerged of the Japanese soldiers as evil supermen. Many editorial cartoons and other propaganda reinforced this image. I recoiled every time I saw these caricatures. I wanted to run away and hide but there was no place to go. I had a terrible feeling of guilt by association, but there was no way I could change my skin color, my eyes, my straight black hair, or my name. Shame and self loathing framed my sense of myself. Yet, that's the way it was—I looked like the enemy.

I began to have frequent stomach pains. Food didn't taste good even though Mama-san's cooking was always delicious. I began having nightmares with a constant theme of trying to run but my legs wouldn't work right. In some nightmares I was running down stairs and falling but never hitting bottom. Many nights I would wake up in a cold sweat, my heart pounding, gasping for breath.

Am I Japanese? Or am I American? This became the defining question I ruminated over daily. From my earliest memories, I had been both. I grew up playing hopscotch and jacks, learning *kendo* and *ikebana*. I studied U.S. history at school and Japanese on Saturday. For breakfast I ate scrambled eggs and *mochi*. Dinner could include fried chicken and sushi. I always felt that I was Japanese-American and I belonged in America, that I was part of the group. Before December 7, 1941, it never occurred to me that I was not.

Mitsuno and Heisuke Matsuda, Mary's parents. The photo was taken in 1922 shortly after Heisuke returned to the United States from Japan with his bride.

BEING JAPANESE IN AMERICA

The Japanese who came to America were, in many ways, just like every other group of people who emigrated seeking a better life. Many came to escape problems in their homeland, such as famine, religious persecution, war, or a particular way of life that was not satisfying. Others, like my parents, came because they were drawn to the promise of opportunities and an exciting new life in America.

The problems facing newly arrived Japanese as well as other immigrants were daunting, especially grappling with a new language in a foreign land. How do you eat when you can't find the foods you are familiar with, and you can't even ask questions about the food that is available? How do you land a job when you can't speak the same language as your boss or customers? How do you work and support yourself and a family?

In order to survive in a different setting, many immigrant groups established cultural centers, such as Japantown, Little Italy, or Chinatown. These cultural communities made it easier to survive financially and socially, but these centers also isolated the immigrant population from neighbors outside of their cultural group, prolonging the assimilation process.

In all immigrant populations, the parents worked hard to establish a firm foothold in the new country. My parents were the epitome of hardworking immigrants, sacrificing for their family's future in America. To a large degree they continued with old country customs, spoke traditional Japanese, ate Japanese food, and celebrated Japanese holidays such as Girls' Day and Boys' Day.

Before 1941 the Japanese in America were culturally isolated, a people without a future. Even *Nisei* who were American citizens and fluent in English could not expect professional careers. Who would hire them, except for other Japanese? Most took menial jobs far below their capabilities, working in Japantowns up and down the West Coast or in their *Issei* parents' businesses. My parents ran their own farm and berry business, and

Vashon Methodist Church.

it looked as if their future in America was secure—they had not imagined the fate that awaited them.

⊰◉⊱

Like many children of immigrants, Yoneichi and I often found ourselves in the awkward position of serving as translators for our parents when interacting with the larger community. Inevitably, as the second generation, the *Niseis,* we became more American through our school activities, friendships with non-Japanese students, and exposure to the media.

One Sunday when I was in first grade, shortly after we moved into our new house, Papa-san took Yoneichi and me by the hand and walked us toward the town of Vashon until we happened upon a church. It was the first church we came to, and it looked inviting, so he dropped us off, leaving us in the capable hands of the minister and Sunday school staff. While Papa-san did not attend the service, because it was held in English, he and Mama-san ended up becoming devout Methodists. They were very adaptable people, and could appreciate the need for a solid spiritual foundation for all of us.

Along with the influences of our new Protestant foundation, our family was also strongly influenced by the world that streamed into our home every evening via the radio. Our first radio was a gift from an old neighbor, Mr. Shereen, who gave it to Yoneichi when he was six years old in 1929. My parents regarded it as a novelty item and didn't have much interest in it, especially since all of the broadcasts were in English. But it immediately became Yoneichi's favorite toy, and he listened to the radio every night, often acting out what he heard. Because only one person could listen at a time, I had to beg for my turn to listen, especially when we first got it.

One night when we were supposed to be asleep, a week or so after we got the radio, Yoneichi had the headphones on and was listening intently to a radio program. I kept waving my hands in front of his eyes, nagging him to let me listen. He kept saying to me, "Wait a minute, just wait another minute, okay?" I continued to insist with the persistence of a four-year-old. Then all of a sudden Yoneichi grabbed the headphones from his head and in one swift movement clamped them over my ears. In that moment my four-year-old mind expanded to unimagined worlds.

"CHANDU the Magician," BONG! Then a deep, menacing, male voice barked, "Twelve o'clock at Midnight! Even walls have ears!" An earsplitting, ominous laugh cackled in my head. I flung the headphones off and plunged under the covers crying hysterically. Mama-san came rushing in and gave us heck for still being awake and making so much noise.

By the time I was ten, the radio was like another member of the family. I liked to listen to "Jack Benny" and "Amos 'n' Andy," and read the Sunday funnies with Flash Gordon, Dick Tracy and Little Orphan Annie. Once I persuaded Papa-san to buy some Ovaltine advertised on the "Little Orphan Annie" radio program because I wanted to mail the inside seal for a ring to decipher secret messages given during the show. It was fun comparing the messages with my classmates. My brother and I, with the help of the radio and all of our other outside activities, were typical American kids in many ways.

Throughout childhood and our teen years, Yoneichi and I found ourselves caught between the traditions of our parents and the influences of our thoroughly American friends. As the obedient daughter, I never complained, but I longed to go with my friends to buy candy and ice cream, or wear makeup, or go to movies and dances. When the carnival came to Vashon with the merry-go-round, Ferris wheel, and other kids' rides, we did not go. I could hear the carousel music from our house, and I wished I could go, but I never asked because I knew my parents would frown upon such a suggestion. They would have considered the carnival frivolous.

While my parents wanted us to adapt to some American ways, they were also sure about the importance of Japanese values. Traditional Japanese culture emphasizes family and group-centered activities. Unlike the dominant American culture, which emphasizes individuality first, in Japanese families children are reminded continuously how their behavior is a reflection on the whole family.

Several important concepts are essential in a traditional Japanese family, and they were the foundation of our family life on Vashon. The Japanese expression *on*, pronounced like a cross between "on" and "own," means a powerful sense of loyalty, respect, and gratitude toward others, especially one's parents. Our *on* for one another was expressed daily through our family duties to one another and through respectful verbal communication.

In most Japanese families, the suffix *san* was used after a person's name only in formal situations, as a form of respect. Children were usually addressed using the informal *chan* at the end of their names as a form of endearment. My parents always called me "Mary-san," not "Mary-chan" because our family members were more formal in their spoken Japanese.

Mama-san was always the first to get up in the morning and the last to go to bed at night. She and Papa-san showed complete devotion to one another, and worked hard for our benefit. Before starting every meal, Yoneichi and I would invariably say, "*Itadaki masu*" to Mama-san in a respectful tone of voice with a slight nod of the head. It means, "I am about to eat this meal you have prepared for us." Mama-san's traditional response would be, "*Dozo*—By all means" or "*Itadaki masho*—Let us all partake." She, too, would look at us and respond with a smile and a slight nod of her head. After each meal we would say, "*Gochisosama deshita*—It was very delicious," a compliment of respect and appreciation going deeper than the flavor of the meal.

Every time we left home for any reason, we would always say to our folks, "*Itte kimasu*—I am going to...." We would include where we were going. Their response was always, "*Itterashai*," meaning "Please be on your way." Our greeting when we returned home was "*Tada ima kaeri mashita*—We have just returned."

In the spirit of *on*, we would never think of doing things without going through these short but respectful rituals with our parents. It was our way of maintaining closeness in our family. Some of my Caucasian friends said our conversations sounded so formal, and indeed they may have been.

Yoneichi and I also learned *giri*, which means a sense of duty, obligation, and loyalty to one's family or group. There is nothing comparable to this word in the English language. A common statement Papa-san and Mama-san offered to Yoneichi and me in the spirit of *giri* was, "You will always want to conduct yourself properly because you don't want to bring *haji*—shame—on our family and the other Japanese families on Vashon Island." Throughout my childhood my parents admonished me to be polite, respect others, study hard, and get the best grades possible. Hand-in-hand with this Japanese value was another Japanese principle, *enryo*, which implies restraint, modesty, and humility in our daily actions. We were never to brag or to take excessive credit for anything.

Although my parents never used the word "love," in Japanese or in English, they clearly communicated it. Their love was in the softness around their eyes and the spontaneous smiles that broke on their faces whenever they spoke to us. Papa-san wasn't as verbal as Mama-san, yet he had his own ways of letting us know how much he cherished us. Whenever he had to travel to Seattle for business, he brought each of us our favorite foods; wonderful fruits for me, such as persimmons, pomegranates, watermelon, and peaches; for Yoneichi he brought cakes, pies, cookies, and candy. For Mama-san, he found special Japanese goodies. My father was like a Japanese Santa, joyfully bringing home enormous overstuffed bags, carrying them long distances on the bus.

The Japanese children on Vashon all attended Japanese language school every Saturday during the regular school year. Most of us students protested silently against the parental requirement that we learn to read and write Japanese, especially all day on Saturday. The Japanese kids in Seattle had to attend Japanese language school five days a week after their regular school day.

Yoneichi, being the first born and male, felt a familial obligation to learn Japanese and study hard to master the language. I felt compelled to learn, too, but I wasn't as conscientious as he was. I learned enough and years later this skill was an important asset because I could write to my parents in Japanese.

In our family we usually did things together, in large part because we lived on a farm that demanded our group effort. Except during the severest winter days, there was almost always something to do outdoors. During the months when it rained daily, we donned our boots and raingear, and trudged outdoors anyway. There were times when we had to take shovels and pick axes and make trenches or dig ditches to redirect excess water. We had to keep a close eye on the ditches to make sure dirt didn't fall in and obstruct the flow of the water. During overly rainy summers the strawberries didn't have a chance to ripen properly, and we lost much of the potential crop to mold and fungus. Other years when rain was scarce, the plants dried up and the berries, though sweet, were small and withered.

Leisure time within our family was spent doing light tasks around the property. We planted or weeded flower beds, pruned fruit trees, tended bee hives, experimented with grafting apples on a common tree, and tried our hand at propagating rhododendron plants. We were successful with almost all of them except the rhododendron plants. During the winter months, Mama-san made futons with cotton batting covered with colorful cotton covers. She and I also made jams and jellies, pickles, cookies, and pies. We liked to try making different kinds of food to the delight of the family.

A few days before January 1 each year, eight to ten Japanese families on Vashon would come to our home to make *mochi,* which is steamed rice pounded into cakes. Papa-san had made an *osu* out of a large tree stump, which stood about thirty inches high and twenty inches in diameter. He made a smooth bowl in the center of the stump, about sixteen inches wide and fourteen inches deep. For years we used this *osu* for our annual *mochi*-making event. Every year Mama-san scrubbed the bowl with a brush and plenty of soap and hot water before the guests arrived.

On the appointed day Mama-san had water boiling in a big copper pot on the stove as the guests arrived. Women brought special rice and spread it along the bottom of bamboo-slotted trays. Mama-san stacked these trays, three at a time, over the boiling water. While the rice cooked, the kids played games like kick the can, red rover, hide 'n' seek, or whatever else we felt like doing.

When the rice in the bottom tray was cooked, Mama-san lifted the top two trays while the bottom tray was rushed outdoors and the rice dumped into the *osu*. Two young men stood opposite each other and took turns pounding the steamed rice with wooden mallets. The woman whose rice was being pounded would turn the rice over and over, just like kneading bread dough. Of course, she had to be quick and watchful so the descending mallets wouldn't strike her. As the mallets pounded in turn, someone would count out or chant with the rhythm of the strokes, a raucous, primitive-sounding chant that made my insides smile. "*YOI-sho, YOI-sho, YOI-sho, Yo!*" Soon all the adults would join in clapping hands or stomping their feet in time to the rhythm as the men pounding the rice hurled out the words.

To prepare for the next step, Mama-san put rice powder on a clean table. Women placed the freshly pounded hot *mochi* on the table, rolled it a few times in the rice powder to reduce stickiness, and pinched off small pieces. All of us kids would run to the bathroom and scrub our hands really clean. Then we'd come to the table, put some of the powder on our hands and mold the *mochi* into a mound. If the rice belonged to a Buddhist family, the mother would take the whole batch and shape the *mochi* into three flattened mounds of different sizes. The largest one was used at the base representing a strong, firm foundation. The second largest mound stood for happiness, and the smallest on top represented good health and long life for the family. At home the mother would stack the *mochi* in front of the family's Buddhist shrine. Since my family was Methodist, we made all the *mochi* the same size. There was a respectfulness and tolerance that the Buddhists could do things their way, and the Methodists could do the *mochi* their way. We saw no reason for disagreement.

After all the rice had been cooked and pounded, Mama-san always had some kind of nourishing lunch for everyone to eat with the *mochi*.

Each family's mounds of *mochi* would be firm by the time they were ready to go home.

On December 31, we always stayed up until midnight to wish each other a happy New Year and have a special hot dish of sweet dark beans and *mochi* soup. The next day the Japanese men and boys would visit each Japanese household on Vashon to eat sushi, tempura, and other delicacies, and give the women and girls in each home their greeting. This ritual gave everyone in our community a chance to visit with each other during the dark winter months.

While I am sure that the Japanese "city kids" had somewhat different traditions than we did on Vashon, those Japanese traditions were just as important in maintaining a sense of community. One important difference between Japanese living in rural America and Japanese in urban areas was the degree to which families assimilated into the larger American culture. In the city, it was possible for Japanese families to stick to their own groups and limit interaction with the larger American society. However, Japanese families on Vashon were scattered throughout the island, so we had a more integrated Americanized lifestyle.

As a carefree teenager about to be thrown into the chaos and devastation of World War II, I had no idea how these Japanese values would sustain me and my family and give us the strength to endure. In some cases these same cultural values, completely misunderstood by the U.S. government, would create incredible dilemmas for our family as well as for most Japanese-American families in the internment camps. And it would be these same values that caused many *Isseis* and *Niseis* to suffer in silence for decades afterwards, including me. But the events about to unfold could have destroyed us and many other Japanese-American families. Instead, the wisdom of our heritage—*on, giri,* and a strong sense of community—enabled us to weather the storm of internment and emerge stronger.

U.S. soldier posting a Civilian Exclusion Order.

MUSEUM OF HISTORY & INDUSTRY

EVACUATION ORDERS

On February 19, 1942, President Franklin Delano Roosevelt issued Executive Order #9066, which directed the Secretary of War to begin the mass evacuation of Japanese residents from the Washington, Oregon, and California coasts. The president issued this order in spite of data collected for years by naval intelligence and the FBI documenting that residents of Japanese descent were not a threat.

I pored over the newspaper stories with a mixture of dread and relief, finally getting answers to questions I had dared not ask. Unfortunately, for every question that was answered there were ten new questions to be asked, and no government specifics given regarding where, when, or how the evacuation would happen. My mind raced considering the possibilities.

After dinner on the evening of the nineteenth, the four of us sat around the dinner table to discuss the new order. "Now we know that we will be evacuated," Papa-san said.

"Yes," Yoneichi replied. "At least we now have an official notice. It will allow us to plan a little bit, anyway."

"It defines the limits of our freedom," Mama-san noted.

"There are a lot of questions that will have to be answered," Papa-san said. "For instance, when will we have to leave? How can we care for our property while we're away?"

"And where will we be going?" Mama-san asked. "How long will we be gone? I'm sure there will be many more questions as time goes on."

The notice replaced my free-floating anxiety with something concrete, even if I didn't like what I heard. It was better than all the vague fears that plagued my waking hours and gave me stomach pains.

At school my teachers were kind and understanding. They called on me in class only when I raised my hand. One day after Latin class my teacher, Mrs. Keyes, pulled me aside and said, "Mary, I've been wanting to ask you how you're doing these days. This must be a terrible time for you and your family. Is there anything I can do for you?"

"Thanks Mrs. Keyes, you're already doing what I need the most, just treating me normally. Just keep doing what you've been doing." Then I added, "Yes, these are very difficult times for my family and me, but everyone has been great—the teachers, students, and all of our neighbors. That helps more than you will ever know. If something comes up, I'll be sure to let you know."

Despite any evidence to the contrary, my family still clung to our belief that perhaps the evacuation orders might spare Yoneichi and me because we were American citizens. Rumors continued to fly among the Northwest Japanese community. One evening after dinner, Yoneichi said to me, "According to the newspaper, if there is an evacuation order, it would apply only to *Isseis* [first generation] and the *Kibeis* [those born in the U.S., educated in Japan, and returned to the U.S. again]. That would mean you and I would stay here with other U.S.-born Japanese, and the folks would be taken somewhere else." He put the paper down angrily. "There's no way we can run the farm and take care of the folks when they get sent away to some godforsaken place. I don't like that at all."

"Me neither," I replied. "How are they going to get along without us to help them understand what will probably be told to them in English? That isn't the way we do things in our family. That's contrary to *on.*"

One Saturday morning in late February, Mama-san received an alarming phone call from Mrs. Yamamoto on nearby Bainbridge Island. She was shouting so loud I could hear her as I stood nearby. Agitated, she spoke so rapidly her words tumbled into a stream of sentences.

"Two men from the FBI were here this morning to search our place," Mrs. Yamamoto began. "And do you know what those men did? One of them looked all around the yard before coming inside. They asked all kinds of questions about guns and short wave radios, all sorts of things. They took out some of our books, flipped through them and asked what they were about. Then they ran their hands through our rice bin, our sugar, and rummaged through most of our kitchen and bedroom drawers and closets. It was awful, just awful. I felt like a common thief."

Mama-san tried to respond but Mrs. Yamamoto continued.

"At Fuji's place they took some books on radios, but over at Tadashi's they found some dynamite. They sure grilled him about what he was going to use it for. Tadashi told them that he used it years ago to clear his land and had forgotten that he had any left. I don't know if they believed him or not. They took it away with them anyway. You folks on Vashon Island are probably going to be next," Mrs. Yamamoto warned. "Get rid of anything that can incriminate you, anything that can tie you too closely to Japan. That's what they're looking for—and if they find anything, they might take your husband and send him off somewhere far away, or some other terrible thing."

We were shaken by the call but grateful for the warning. Immediately we started looking at everything in our home. We went through every drawer, closet, cupboard, and shelf looking frantically at everything that could possibly threaten our future. Papa-san and Yoneichi went through the barn and woodshed, too. We gathered all our mementos of Japan and put them together in several boxes, ready to burn after dark. We had to get rid of these things because the risk of being labeled even faintly "disloyal" was just too great.

That evening after dusk while we still had our work clothes on, we brought out the boxes with all of our treasures. The vigorous fire in the oil stove hurled ominous shadows against the white walls of our living room. Papa-san took out all the special Japanese phonograph records and placed them together on one side of the dining room table. Next to that Mama-san placed all the family pictures from both sides of their families in Japan. Then she brought out our beautifully crafted Japanese dolls she used to display for celebrations of *Hina Matsuri*, Girls' Day on March 3, and *Tango no Sekku*, Boys' Day on June 5. These ceremonial dolls did not indicate any sense of emperor worship in our family, yet we feared they would be seen by the FBI as symbols of loyalty to Japan. Silently Mama-san set up the tiered platform, covered it with red cloth, placed the folding screen in the background, and gently placed each of the delicate dolls of the imperial court in their places. Finally, she reached into the bottom of the last box and brought out her treasured books of Japanese classic literature and Japanese history, along with magazines, books of fairy tales, and children's books.

We stood in front of the table looking at all of our cultural treasures. Papa-san took a deep breath and said, "This is it. Let's get this difficult task done." He picked up the first phonograph record, read the label and said to Mama-san, "This one, 'Sakura,' is my favorite. Yoshiko-san's voice is so clear and beautiful and the words evoke such feeling in me." With doleful eyes he handed it to Mama-san who also read the label. With teary eyes she broke it into small pieces, stepped over to the stove and slipped it into the flames. One by one they looked over each record and took turns breaking them, silently feeding their beloved music into the stove until every record was destroyed. The flames illuminated my parents' sad but determined faces.

Our photographs of relatives in Japan came next. Together Mama-san and Papa-san looked at each picture with tired eyes, and talked about each person. Then they tossed the family photos into the burning stove, one by one, imploring each image as it burned.

"*Gomen nasai ne*—Forgive me for what I am doing."

"*Gomen nasai ne*—Forgive me for what I am doing."

With increasingly heavy hearts we turned our attention to the display of the emperor and empress sitting in regal splendor with several ladies in waiting and samurai warriors on the tier below. Each of us looked at them for a long time, noticing how delicate and perfect these dolls were in every detail. The heaviness in my chest made breathing difficult. I was powerless to stop what we had to do.

Heaving a big sigh, Yoneichi picked up a samurai warrior and studied it carefully. He gently touched the warrior's garb, the sword by his side, and hair. Then, taking a deep breath he looked at Papa-san and Mama-san. At their nod, he walked over to the stove and flung the warrior into the flames. He quickly bowed his head and turned away from us.

Then Papa-san looked at me and nodded for me to take my turn. Reluctantly I looked at the remaining dolls to see which one I should take. I could scarcely breathe as I carefully picked up one of the ladies in waiting. She was my favorite. Her kimono was a shimmering delicate light pink. Her *obi* was simple and elegant, red with gold threads and tied with a large bow in back. Her face was calm and composed—nothing like what I was feeling. I slipped the doll behind my back and quickly grasped another lady in waiting. Moving to the front of the stove, I flung the second one into the roaring fire. I couldn't bear to watch the hungry flames consume the beautiful doll.

As each one of us took turns throwing the dolls into the burning fire, I looked away but I could still hear the roar of the flames feeding on our precious possessions. Papa-san's jaws were set, his lips pursed, and a deep crease remained between his eyebrows. He flung the emperor doll into the bright fire. Mama-san kept wiping the tears away with the edge of her apron as she did the same with the empress.

Finally it was time for me to part with my favorite doll. Papa-san looked at me with misty, understanding eyes, nodded slowly and waited. Slowly I walked to the front of the stove, gave my doll one final squeeze, then flung her into the inferno that seared my heart like some fierce dragon destroying all that I loved. With tears streaming down my face, I turned away but I could still feel the heat and hear the roar of the flames as they consumed her delicate body in a matter of seconds. I thought about the last time Mama-san carefully set up the display for us. She said, "These are very special dolls just like you and your brother are so special to us." I wondered, *Is she worrying about the possibility that something equally terrible might be in store for her children?*

Now it was time to turn our attention to Mama-san's Japanese books. They had been such treasures in our home. When she came to our favorite fairy tale of Momotaro, the Peach Boy, I asked her, "Mama-san, would you read it to us for the last time, please?" And she did as Yoneichi and I sat down nearby to listen.

> Long, long ago there lived an old man and an old woman who longed to have a child but were never successful. They were peasants and had to work hard to earn their daily rice. One day the old woman found a large peach floating down the river as she was washing their clothes. She brought it home and set it aside for her husband who was away gathering wood for the home. After he came home he admired it and took a knife to cut it. It suddenly split in half and out stepped a beautiful child. They named him Momotaro, Peach Boy....

This boy grew up to become an extraordinary soldier who took leave from his parents to fight a band of devils that were plundering the countryside. Taking a large dog, a monkey, and a pheasant, he conquered the devils, freed the prisoners, and brought home the treasures that had been stolen from the people. Momotaro returned to a hero's welcome, and the treasures he brought back allowed the old couple to live in peace and plenty to the end of their days.

After this fifteen-minute story Mama-san closed the book and placed her hand on top of it. We were silent for awhile holding on to this final moment. Yoneichi remarked wistfully, "That is such a great fairy tale. I wish we could have such a wonderful thing to look forward to." Little did we know at the time that Yoneichi would, in fact, go with many other *Nisei* young men, literally to assume the role of Momotaro, and go off to fight for democracy and freedom for all of us.

As Mama-san sadly took the book over to the stove and forced herself to throw the exquisitely illustrated book into the fire, I echoed Yoneichi's thoughts in my heart, *I wish we could have such a wonderful thing to look forward to.*

That fateful day we burned all of our cultural treasures in the oil-burning stove in the living room. We tried to make our house and yard appear untouched, careful not to disturb the cobwebs in the corners of each room or the dust on the picture frames. We didn't want it to look as if we had hidden anything. The only Japanese book we didn't burn was the Bible.

The day after we burned our treasures, I saw Yoneichi dig a deep hole in the ground on the side of our house. "Yoneichi, what are you doing?" I asked.

"I've spent a lot of time on this story that I wrote in Japanese. If I put it into this can and bury it, I hope I can save it," he explained.

Years later I realized how rash we were in destroying our Japanese mementos but at that time we acted out of an understandable panic. We thought if we destroyed those things that represented some of our most precious cultural gems, then Papa-san wouldn't be taken away from us. Perhaps we wouldn't be evacuated either. In the end it would make no difference to the authorities, but for our family we began to feel the little deaths that would haunt us for years as we faced our fate as Japanese-Americans during World War II.

One evening when I was doing the dinner dishes, I noticed that a very beautiful Japanese vase was not in its usual place. The set of silver was gone, too. I didn't need to ask to understand that Mama-san had quietly given her prized possessions to someone she knew would value them.

Later, I had a shocking thought as I caught a glimpse of myself in the mirror. *After all we have done to protect ourselves, nothing has changed.* My hair was still coarse, straight, and black. My skin was yellow, and my bespectacled eyes were small and slanted. We tried to erase our Japanese history by destroying all those precious things, but we couldn't escape from the way we looked. Nothing could change that. And in the end, all that mattered to the United States government was what we looked like.

On a Saturday morning several weeks after we burned our treasures, I was washing the breakfast dishes before going out to the fields to work with my brother and parents. From the kitchen window I saw a shiny, black car pull slowly into the driveway. *Oh, oh. This doesn't look good!* I thought. Two tall, clean-shaven, grim-faced white men dressed in black suits got out. They came to the back door and asked, "Is this the residence of Heisuke Matsuda?"

Gripping the door handle to keep my hand from shaking, I answered, "It is."

Each man revealed his badge and said, "We're from the FBI. We would like to talk with him. Is he at home?"

Trying to keep my voice calm, I said, "My father and the rest of the family are out in the field. I will go out there and have them come home."

My breathing quickened at the thought of why they were here. The president of our Japanese association on Vashon had been picked up by the FBI and taken away after Pearl Harbor. *Now are they here for my father, too?* I wondered. Papa-san had been the secretary of the association for years, and I was almost certain they had come to take him away. For a split second I imagined a big arm, representing the United States government, reaching all the way from Washington D.C. and grabbing Papa-san away from us. The agents began to look around the yard and I briefly saw one of them kneel down to peer into the crawl space under the house. A wave of nausea settled over me as I headed toward the fields.

My legs felt weak and wobbly from the weight of what I had to tell my family. The sun was out but it felt cold and chilly. I wanted to run and blurt the news quickly to get it over with, but at the same time, I just wanted to sit down at the edge of the field and not tell them anything at all. I thought, *Perhaps I could yell and scream and wake myself up from this bad dream.* But it was no dream; I had to go get Papa-san right away. When I finally forced myself out to the field where everyone was hoeing, my mouth felt full of cotton. "Papa-san, two men from the FBI have come to the house, and they want to talk with you."

Everyone's face blanched. No one moved. No one said a thing for a long time. They had the pained look of being "caught." Papa-san heaved a big sigh and said, "It looks like the time has finally come. Mama-san, you stay here. Yoneichi-san and I will go to the house with Mary-san." Mama-san and I exchanged fearful glances.

As the three of us returned to the house, I thought about a lot of things: *Have they come to take Papa-san away from us? How will we get along without him? Will they take our farm, too?* My parents had worked so hard since those early days and now I feared it would all be for naught. This farm held so much of our history and our hopes.

Now these two strangers from the FBI were here to search our beloved home. My heart pounded as I led them through the utility room into the familiar, homey kitchen. The kitchen was the heart of our home. Mama-san had decorated it in white and soft lime-green. The kitchen window, framed in white cottage curtains, looked out onto the lawn, which was surrounded by a short evergreen hedge, annuals, and a camellia bush ready to bloom. Across from the wood stove was our kitchen table and four chairs. This was our family's touchstone, our daily gathering spot for Mama-san's nurturing meals and family conversations.

While the agents examined the kitchen, I stared out the two, full-sized windows by the table framed by soft, white curtains with lime-green polka dots. I could see the men's car parked in the front yard. Suddenly, I looked at this familiar setting with a new intensity, trying to burn every detail into my memory.

The men stood in the middle of the room. I was to their right, Yoneichi to their left, and Papa-san stood behind us. The men slowly looked at everything from one side of the room to the other, up above at the ceiling, and along the linoleum-lined floor below. When they asked us to open specific drawers or cupboards, we complied promptly. They began taking notes.

One of the men said to me, "Would you pull out that drawer please?" indicating the one to the right of the sink. Holding my breath, I did as he asked. He pointed to a well worn, little book lying there and asked, "What is that book?"

I opened it and showed it to him, saying, "This is my parents' New Testament in Japanese. They read from it often. We are Methodists." I thought this fact might make us seem less foreign. He nodded. I put it back and closed the drawer. The minister from the Japanese Methodist Church in Seattle came occasionally to Vashon to hold services in Japanese for *Issei* Protestants like my parents. The services were always held in our home. The New Testament was the only book we had refused to burn or hide.

Next he asked to look in the broom closet. I had butterflies in my stomach as I saw them looking at Yoneichi's .22 caliber rifle that he used to shoot pellets at the crows that raided our strawberries in the springtime. They didn't say a word but they wrote something in their notebook.

We proceeded into the living room. The agents saw our matching sofa and chair, the oil burning stove over to the right, my piano to the left, and a small table beside it with a record player on top. The dining room table occupied the center of the room. I held my hands tightly together as I saw them taking special note of the console radio standing against the wall, its face resembling an old-fashioned dial phone.

"Can you get Japanese broadcasts through that?" one of the agents asked.

Yoneichi replied, "We can occasionally when the weather condition is clear, but most of the time there is so much static that the folks can't understand most of it."

"What capabilities do you have for sending messages to Japan?" the same agent asked.

"None. We don't have any equipment to do that," Yoneichi replied.

Their eyes scanned everything in my parents' bedroom and closet, the bathroom, and the spare bedroom and closet on the main floor. There was nothing that caught their attention. When we went upstairs to Yoneichi's and my bedrooms, their big shoes clomped up the wooden stairs behind me. I held my breath as they looked in my room. Nothing of mine interested them. They opened the little doors off of each room into the unfinished crawl spaces beyond and took their time looking all around with their flashlights. There was nothing up there except a few old pictures of movie stars that I had clipped and saved in a flat box. They seemed satisfied.

Throughout the extensive search of our simple farmhouse, the men were not disruptive or condescending in any way. They were clear about their task, did it respectfully and quietly, and seemed satisfied with our responses. However, they did take away two items: my brother's .22 caliber rifle and the large console radio.

When they finally left, I put my hand on Papa-san's shoulder and gave him a squeeze. I felt tears on my cheeks. A broad smile of relief crossed Papa-san's face bringing color back to his cheeks. We hurried out to the field to share the good news with Mama-san who had been waiting anxiously. She relaxed when she saw our faces. I, too, was relieved, thinking, *They didn't take my father away.*

CHAPTER FOUR

Leaving our Home

In mid-March the government established a curfew that required all Japanese on the West Coast to stay in their homes from 8 p.m. to 6 a.m. This curfew was probably easier for us on the farm than for those with urban businesses such as restaurants and hotels, which depended on customers for their livelihood. In addition, the U.S. government restricted the Japanese to traveling no more than fifteen miles from their homes. This meant we could not get off the island for any reason. Our bank assets had been frozen by order of the government for several weeks right after Pearl Harbor, but eventually we were allowed to withdraw up to one hundred dollars per month to cover our expenses.

These increasing restrictions created a psychological pall as well as a general fear about what the government would do to us. Whenever I went out to the main highway to get our mail, I cautiously peered both ways before I dared to step out to the mailbox and grab the contents. Then I would run home with the mail. Even when I went to church on Sundays, I searched everyone's faces fearfully—not even sure what I was afraid of, but still watching carefully.

The first official order for the evacuation from the Puget Sound area arrived on March 30, 1942. Bainbridge Island residents would be the first to go, probably because they lived close to the strategic Bremerton navy yards. We knew we would not be too far behind with our proximity to Boeing Field and other strategic assets in the Puget Sound area. When we learned each person would be allowed to carry only two suitcases of belongings, we ordered eight large suitcases through the Sears & Roebuck catalog.

One night our family huddled around the kitchen table and tried to plan what we should take. We talked in a matter-of-fact manner, as if we were planning an extended vacation. We decided each of us would take one pair of sheets, a pillowcase, and one blanket. Clothes included one heavy winter overcoat, several sweaters, two blouses or shirts, two slacks or skirts, a week's worth of socks and underwear, one pair of shoes, and a flannel nightgown or pajamas. In addition to personal toilet articles, we would include silverware, a cup, and a plate. I wanted to take my English Bible and a small radio. As we packed, questions swirled in my head: *Will this be enough? How long will we be gone? What kind of weather will we have to live through? Will there be anything to buy if we don't have the right things and will we have enough money to buy things if we need them?* There were many questions but no answers.

While we anxiously waited for the government's order to evacuate, we kept working the farm. There was always weeding, planting, replacing sickly strawberry plants with healthy ones, and fertilizing to ensure healthy fruit in the coming months. Digging and planting and tending to our berry crop kept our minds occupied, stimulated our appetites, and kept us fatigued so we slept better at night. Perhaps this was our way to keep believing in the future even though great uncertainty encased us.

On the evening of May 8, Papa-san got a phone call. As he listened, Papa-san turned and stared intently at Mama-san for a few moments, then turned away. Fear rose in my chest as Papa-san asked a few brief questions in Japanese. When he hung up the phone and turned to us, resigned and somber, he said, "That was Hiroshi Morita. He said we have to leave in eight days." Papa-san paused and looked at each of us, almost apologetically. "So now we know when we have to go. We don't have much time."

The inevitable had finally happened. Suddenly, my future had shrunk to eight precious days, followed by—what? The unknown was overwhelmingly and terrifyingly unimaginable. So many questions whirled around in my head that I could scarcely focus on any one thought. For the rest of the evening I stayed close to my family as we discussed this sudden development and tried to figure out what needed to be done.

The next day Yoneichi walked the half mile to Hiroshi's place to see the official order nailed to a telephone pole near Hiroshi's home. It read:

WESTERN DEFENSE COMMAND AND FOURTH ARMY WARTIME CIVIL CONTROL ADMINISTRATION
Presidio of San Francisco, California
May 8, 1942

Instructions
TO ALL PERSONS OF JAPANESE ANCESTRY

Living in the Following Area: All that portion of the Island of Vashon, State of Washington.

Pursuant to the Provisions of Civilian Exclusion Order No. 18, this Headquarters, dated May 8, 1942, all persons of Japanese ancestry, both alien and non-alien, will be evacuated from the above area by 10 o'clock P.W.T. May 16, 1942.

Government instructions listed what each evacuee must carry, including bedding, toilet articles, extra clothing, plates, bowls, silverware, cups, and essential personal effects. No pets of any kind would be permitted. Government storage at the sole risk of the owner was available if the belongings were properly marked.

Yoneichi came home and told us what he saw. "You and I, Mary, are called 'non-alien.' They don't call us citizens, which is what we are!" He frowned and flung himself in the nearby chair. Mama-san looked at him in dismay, but said nothing. It did not matter that Yoneichi and I by birthright were U.S. citizens. In one fell swoop, the government robbed us of our rights. Now, because of our Japanese heritage, we were the "non-aliens" and our parents were the "aliens."

I was puzzled by that official designation. *Aren't I a citizen?* I asked myself. *Why do they have to call us non-aliens? What does that mean?*

Papa-san worried about the farm and our strawberry crop, which he planned to begin harvesting in late May. The timing was terrible. "Couldn't they have waited until after we harvested our crop?" asked Papa-san. Then he sighed in resignation and said, "Let's check with Mack and see if he would be willing to oversee the harvest."

Mack Garcia was a Filipino farm worker who had helped us for six years. He was one of thousands of Filipino men who came to the United States looking for work, just as the Chinese and Japanese men had done earlier. The Chinese came to the United States in the mid-1800s to work on the railroads and do other menial or dangerous jobs, such as mining. But when the railroads were completed and they began competing for jobs with the rest of the population, Congress passed the Chinese Exclusion Act in 1882 barring further Chinese immigration. The Japanese later followed suit until the Exclusion Act of 1924, which was aimed at limiting Japanese workers. Then in the early 1930s the U.S. government allowed Filipino workers to immigrate.

Mack was in his mid-twenties when he started working on our farm. Papa-san welcomed him and was glad to have an extra pair of hands. He was fairly short, about Yoneichi's height, with a dark complexion and a quiet but pleasant demeanor. Mack didn't talk much, but whenever anyone spoke to him, his face lit up with a shy smile before he responded.

We had a barn near the main house, and Papa-san converted it into a home for Mack. Papa-san paid him a fair wage, and Mama-san shared fresh produce from our garden with him.

"We should ask Mack to move into our home," suggested Mama-san. Mack knew when things had to be done on the farm especially during the harvest and afterwards. "I know he will do a good job making sure the berry picking is done properly." And then she began to worry: "But he can't do that and all the administrative tasks that go with running the farm. Look how much it has taken all of us to run our place."

Yoneichi agreed. "Mack can't handle everything. Let me check with some of the other Japanese farmers and see what they plan to do."

The following evening at dinner, Yoneichi reported his findings. "There is a deputy sheriff on the island named G. H. Hopkins. He is willing to manage up to six farms. Ours will be one of them. Each farmer will work out his own arrangement with Hopkins regarding the terms of the relationship. In our situation, we should make Mack our boss in residence."

The deputy sheriff had been serving for years and had a good reputation. The Japanese people always respected authority and there was no reason to doubt Hopkins's integrity, but Yoneichi and Papa-san decided that a legal contract might be the best way to document the agreement—just in case. That would later turn out to be a wise decision.

Yoneichi got help from an older *Nisei* resident on Vashon who knew lawyers in Seattle, and he had a contract developed. The terms of the document clearly established that Hopkins would oversee our farm, and all costs and income would be split fifty-fifty when the time came for fulfilling the terms of the contract. If we returned to the farm before December 31 of that year, the following spring harvest earnings would belong to our family. If we returned after that, the crop earnings would go to the deputy sheriff.

Papa-san and Yoneichi reviewed the plan with Mack, who agreed to his position as the boss in residence. "We will give you an additional bonus when we return. How does this sound to you?" asked Papa-san.

Mack respectfully accepted. "I'll do the very best I can while you are gone." We all felt relieved and thanked him.

By this time we were resigned to the inevitable. I longed for a sense of stability and calmness in my life. How I wished I had paid more attention when at age ten I had the opportunity to take *ikebana* from an expert hired by the *fujinkai*, the Japanese women's group. The tranquility and simple beauty of *ikebana* would have helped in the midst of all the chaos.

I could not quell my resentment and bitterness about the whole situation. The daily newspaper headlines continued to blast the Japanese for the death and destruction in the Far East. The war was not going well for the Allies. Radio reports repeatedly aired rumors of treachery and sabotage by Japanese and Japanese-Americans on the West Coast. *Will all of this increasingly inflammatory propaganda incite riots against us in the streets of America?* I grew more terrified considering this possibility. The world beyond Vashon Island seemed so dangerous, and now I would have to leave our harbor of safety. I didn't want to admit that some white people considered me unworthy of living. I couldn't accept they might hate me because I looked like the enemy.

I was American in my feelings. Therefore, I felt totally unprepared for the turmoil that came from feeling American yet being punished for being born of Japanese parents. I loved and honored my parents—to blame them for my misery was consciously unacceptable, though it occurred to me in the fleeting recesses of my mind.

All I wanted was for Japan and the United States to stop fighting and we could get back to living normally again. But that was not going to happen. The whole evacuation process had been planned and would grind on to the bitter end. The crisis just kept escalating.

As the actual evacuation day approached, the threat loomed so large I could not envision any future for myself. *Will I ever be able to finish eleventh grade, let alone graduate from high school?* I wondered. While I felt numb and in despair, I took heart in observing my parents. Their enduring Christian faith as well as previous experiences dealing with life's crises gave them strength and thereby gave me the cues I would need to survive in the larger world beyond.

On May 14 before lunch, we had an urgent telephone call from Mr. Yamano. "Shizuko Ota died this morning. The funeral service must be held tomorrow afternoon before we leave on the sixteenth."

The news of Shizuko's death was unbelievable. *Surely this can't be happening!* I told myself. *She is only fourteen years old.* Everything around me seemed unreal, as numbness stepped in like a great protector in the face of shock.

The Otas were farmers, too. In addition to Shizuko they had a son Bill, age sixteen. Shizuko had Downs Syndrome and whenever I saw her at community gatherings I was put off by her unusual appearance and behavior. I would shy away from her, but I certainly took note of how kind Mama-san was and how gently she spoke to Shizuko.

Mrs. Ota treated Shizuko tenderly with the matter-of-fact efficiency of a busy farmer's wife. I didn't know what Mr. Ota's relationship with his daughter was like since I rarely saw them together. But as in so many other settings, the men would visit with each other in one room and the women and children were in another. Usually I saw Shizuko either beside her mother or aimlessly wandering in and out among the assembled people. There seemed to be a quiet acceptance of this daughter who obviously was different from the rest of us young girls.

One time I heard Mama-san say that whenever Shizuko needed new clothes, her brother and father traveled to a department store in Seattle where Bill made the selections. Shizuko was always dressed immaculately, like an exquisite doll. Mama-san often commented to Bill, "You select lovely dresses for your sister. It is so wonderful that you would do that for her."

Mrs. Ota cried bitterly at the funeral. All of us were in such turmoil, so overwhelmed with dread of the future. In the end all we could do was gather close together as the men used ropes to lower Shizuko's coffin into the ground. As I watched the family drop clumps of earth into the grave, this haunting sight seared a memory that would last a lifetime. We buried this innocent girl with aching hearts as the Japanese families prepared to bury and leave behind their homes and their culture.

When we walked home after the funeral the sky was clear and the warm air hinted of summer. After eating dinner and completing the evening chores, we went off in pairs, Mama-san and me, and Yoneichi and Papa-san. Silently we walked along the eastern and southern boundaries of our farm. We admired majestic Mount Rainier off to the southeast bathed in pink reflections from the sunset. We walked half way along the west side, then down through the middle of our field, admiring the plump red strawberries almost ready to be picked. Each of us found a ripe one, bit into it, and savored the sweetness of the fruit. How we longed to be part of the hustle and bustle of the harvest. It was always so much work, but it was wonderful to look forward each year to seeing the same pickers work and laugh together during the intense picking season. We would not be here for it this year. *Will we be back next year?* I wondered. *And if not next year, when?* My heart ached.

Next we stopped at the vegetable garden that Mama-san had planted. The lettuce was almost ready to eat and the peas were growing tall along the fence. We hoped Mack would enjoy the carrots and radishes. We lingered by the pink and white carnations, and I closed my eyes while inhaling the sweet fragrance of the blossoms. Mama-san examined the fruit trees; the apple trees were beginning to bud, the nectarine tree looked as though it would bear profusely, and so would the fig vines.

We went to the barn to pat and brush Dolly and thank her for all the years she had worked so faithfully for us. Next to the barn was the chicken coop. We threw some extra corn to the hens, who came clucking and scrambling to pick the choice grain. At the front of the house near the kitchen window was Mama-san's favorite rose bush covered with scarlet blossoms. Mama-san gently touched their smooth petals in a gesture of farewell. Finally, we sat on the front porch in the deepening twilight, savoring our last evening of peace and home.

When Papa-san and Yoneichi came back from their survey of the farm, Mama-san made a pot of tea. Each of us was lost in his or her own thoughts as we sipped in silence on our front porch. Papa-san held his cup in his left palm and slowly turned it as he gazed around the property. We found comfort in each other's presence. Frisky, our beloved watchdog, and Kitty, Mama-san's cat, huddled beside us while we talked. I wondered, *Do they sense that something is different?*

Finally Mama-san said, "Hasn't this been a wonderful home that Papa-san built for us eleven years ago? I have enjoyed living here so much. We've been incredibly blessed with so many things to make us comfortable and happy here. Now tomorrow we will begin a new experience. Who knows what that will be like but let us remember all the blessings that we've enjoyed here."

When we finally got up to go inside to sleep for the last time in our own beds, I asked the great unknown, *How long will it be before we can come back? Will our farm still be here when and if we return?*

◂ ◉ ▸

May 16, 1942, evacuation day, came early after a fitful night's sleep. When I awoke I lay still for a moment and took a deep breath, thinking, *This is the day.* I could hear Mama-san stirring downstairs and smelled the coffee. Reluctantly I got out of my comfortable bed, smoothed the covers, and puffed up the pillow.

After I got dressed, I pulled up the shade and looked outdoors. The sky was gray—a good reflection of how life appeared to me that morning. Across the fields ripening berries peered out here and there from rows of green and lush strawberries plants. *Why do we have to go?* I asked no one. *Where are we going? When will we come back?* My vision blurred. Slowly I turned from the window and went downstairs.

"*Ohaiyo gozaimasu,* good morning, Mama-san. This is the day, isn't it?"

Mama-san nodded her head. "*Ohaiyo gozaimasu,* Mary-san. Yes, this is the day we have been planning for. Let's all sit down and have a good breakfast together before we leave."

All of us gathered for the last time around the kitchen table. We bowed our heads as Mama-san raised a brief prayer. "*Kamisama,* God, thank you for the wonderful life we have shared here. We look to you as we begin another part of our lives. Guide us, sustain, and strengthen us as we move ahead. Amen. Now, *itadaki masho,* let us eat."

Filled with foreboding, I had little appetite. We ate scrambled eggs, toast with strawberry jam, cocoa for Yoneichi and me, and coffee for our parents. Mama-san talked about how happy she had been in our home. As she talked, I wondered, *Why is she talking about happy times now?* But Yoneichi and Papa-san joined in, and soon we were all talking about the fun times we had shared on our farm. Perhaps Mama-san remembered the time when she and her new husband left Japan for America many years ago. She knew our bodies needed fortification for the demands of each new day.

We enjoyed our meal, then carefully tidied up the kitchen and our bedrooms. Then we laid out our suitcases side-by-side in the living room. We had already checked them over repeatedly, but we felt the need to do it one last time.

Finally it was time to leave. Mama-san put on her hat, something she did only when going somewhere special. Instead of slacks and a shirt, she wore a pretty, navy blue dress with a white crocheted collar along with hosiery and dress shoes. She carried a coat and purse. Papa-san wore his navy blue suit, white shirt, dress shoes, and a hat. Yoneichi dressed in a nice pair of slacks, a long sleeve dress shirt, Sunday shoes, and he carried a jacket. I wore a skirt and blouse, a sweater, and bobby sox with black oxfords.

We picked up our luggage and shut the door behind us. One last time I patted Frisky and Kitty on their heads as I told them, "Help Mack and watch the house, okay?" Then silently, numbly, we moved away. The cat and dog sat on the back stoop, watching us. The four of us walked along our quarter-mile gravel driveway to the highway, silent. At the edge of our property we turned and took one final look through our tears at our beloved home.

MUSEUM OF HISTORY & INDUSTRY

Japanese-Americans and soldiers at an assembly point on Bainbridge Island.

FAMILY NUMBER 19788

Evacuation day changed my life forever. Each of us carried two heavy suitcases as we walked down the road. Anger and fear held a nauseous grip on my stomach. My thighs tightened as my toes grabbed at the earth, our earth, through the soles of my shoes—a futile attempt to stay rooted in my home. Above, barnyard swallows dipped and soared through the gray, still sky, twittering sporadically. Turbulent thoughts and feelings swirled through my mind and heart. *Why is this happening to us? What have we done to justify such a drastic order?*

I turned to Mama-san and asked, "Why do we have to leave? Why are they making us go?"

Mama-san turned her sad eyes towards me and quietly said, "Japan has attacked Pearl Harbor. There is fear that she will attack the West Coast. It is best that we leave."

Somehow, her answer didn't feel very satisfying. I had never been away from home, even to a friend's house, for more than one night. Now I was leaving against my wishes, perhaps forever, and I didn't even know where we were going. Having lived on a berry farm on an isolated island, I was totally unprepared for any disruption to my life, much less one as big as this. We were among 120,000 Japanese and Japanese-Americans living in Western Washington, Oregon, and California ordered to leave our homes.

I looked at Papa-san, who moved steadily forward, his eyes staring straight ahead, shoulders squared, lips pressed tightly together. A resolute look on his face belied the realization that he could not protect his family from this looming threat. Yoneichi mirrored our father, moving ahead with firm steps, his face sober, his jaws set firmly together. Mama-san followed several paces behind, her sad eyes cast down. Dragging my feet I walked beside Mama-san, feeling empty and confused. I was old enough to know that something was dreadfully wrong, but still frightened, like a lost child. We said nothing. Much of our family communication was done silently through a glance or a body posture.

I looked south to our neighbor's berry farm with its neat rows of currant bushes loaded with blossoms. I thought, *It's going to be a good crop this year for the McDonalds. That's great because they're good people.* Eleven years earlier when we first moved into our new home the McDonalds were the first to greet us. That evening they gathered several neighboring families to surprise us with a shivaree. We didn't know until then that the loud pounding of pots and pans and shouting was the typical way of welcoming newcomers in this rural community. We were overwhelmed by all of the good food and drink they brought us. This confirmed what my parents had told Yoneichi and me many times: "This is a wonderful country to live in." Although my parents were from a different country, it didn't matter to our Vashon neighbors. Their friendly welcome reinforced their assurances that tolerance and acceptance of people's differences were real in this community. Every spring after that shivaree Mama-san took boxes of big, sweet, sun-ripened strawberries, the first and best of the season, over to the McDonalds and our other neighbors. That morning as we left our home I wondered wistfully, *Will such a time come again?*

As we passed by the Peterson's home and their chicken ranch, I thought about how kind and understanding these neighbors had always been. Mr. Peterson was tall and lanky, but slightly stoop-shouldered from hunching over all the time tending to his chickens or their eggs. I used to buy eggs when our hens were not laying because his chickens' eggs were always fresh and good. I often found Mr. Peterson in a special little room located in the midst of the chicken houses where he sized the eggs. I loved to watch him as he showed me how he sorted and cleaned the best ones for market. Mrs. Peterson would invite me in for a cookie and a glass of milk whenever she saw me come.

One morning in the fifth grade I missed the school bus and was running down the highway as fast as I could. Before I got a quarter of the way to school, Mr. Peterson came along in his pickup truck and stopped. "Missed the bus, huh? Jump in." Away we went, getting to school before the bus. These simple kindnesses loomed large as we walked away from our community, following government orders against our will.

When we were still about a quarter of a mile from the Morita's, we were startled to see covered army trucks lined up along the street. Soldiers stood at attention with rifles and fixed bayonets. We all stopped. I couldn't believe what I was seeing. *Are we going to be treated as prisoners of war and executed?*

Papa-san set his suitcases down without taking his eyes off the trucks. His eyes narrowed and his jaw tightened. "Army trucks." His shoulders slumped. Under his breath I heard him whisper, "I wonder what this means." This was the first time I ever saw my father broken. Seeing him defeated terrified me.

Yoneichi's body stiffened and his face turned ashen. He tightened his grip on his suitcases. He answered Papa-san in a clipped voice, "Yeah, looks bad." He lowered his face, but his eyes remained fixed on the trucks, as if to ask, "Those guns, are they going to finish us off before we leave the island?"

Mama-san sucked in her breath and held it as all the color drained from her face. Slowly she exhaled as if she had only enough breath to say, "*Kowai na*—This is scary, isn't it?" My throat tightened, my heart started pounding, and I broke out in a cold sweat. Seeing my family's reaction terrified me. I had to force myself to resume walking, asking myself repeatedly, *What have we done to deserve this?*

As we neared the designated area, it looked as if the soldiers were ready for any disorder, any disturbance, any disruption, as if they thought some of us might resist or get out of hand. One soldier in particular watched my family. His piercing dark look searched our faces, evaluating the seriousness of the threat we posed. With his glare and his rough actions he communicated, "No bullshit from you Nips. I mean business!" Holding his weapon in his right hand, his finger on the trigger, he pointed with his left to the place to deposit our luggage. "Over there," he shouted, his upper lip curled into a snarl. His words exploded contempt and scorn. I couldn't let myself consider the possibility that he might take us away somewhere to shoot us. I wanted to cry but I didn't dare. I had to force myself to follow instructions.

We put our luggage together on the ground behind the trucks as directed. Another soldier with a much softer tone of voice gave us tags and our family number, 19788. He looked at each of us and said, "Be sure to put that number on these tags and put them on each piece of luggage. You'll be identified as members of the same family, so be sure to put it on your coat or sweater, too, where we can see it." The tag was to dangle clearly in view wherever we were. Now I had become just a number, counted and labeled as the enemy.

While we waited for the others, Mrs. Watanabe arrived. I groaned inwardly when I saw her. Whenever she came over to our place she always chattered endlessly about things that held no interest to me. Mama-san was always polite, but I knew Mrs. Watanabe was looking at me to evaluate my potential as a future good wife for some Japanese boy. I was annoyed with that. Incredibly, given the circumstances, Mrs. Watanabe was her usual inane self. She talked non-stop, this time complaining about the situation. I just wanted her to shut up. Mama-san acknowledged her with a slight bow and a faint smile, but her face remained impassive. This was no time for chatter about trivial things.

More families arrived. At the sight of the armed soldiers, they all looked frightened and whispered to each other. The children fell silent, huddling close to their parents. The adults were tight-lipped, their eyes darting from the soldiers to the guns to the line of army trucks nearby. I stood close to Mama-san and found comfort in our shared silence.

We had no idea where we were going that fateful day as we waited. I did not know what the bigger picture was, and I didn't know if the government did either. All I knew was that all of us of Japanese descent would be affected.

.: ◉ :.

By 10:00 a.m. the Japanese families on Vashon Island—126 people in all—had gathered at specified assembly sites. The soldiers dispassionately directed us to climb aboard the trucks and insisted that we crowd close together. A sturdy box was in place for us to use as a step stool to climb aboard. Yoneichi helped the older women as they took the gigantic step into the truck. Most were dressed in their finest Sunday clothes with silk stockings and nice shoes. One by one we silently and grimly climbed aboard and sat along the sides of the truck and then on the benches placed along the middle. The soldiers piled our luggage around us before we started for the Vashon Heights dock. I took my place on the uncomfortable bench, avoiding eye contact with those across from me. I felt ashamed and dirty despite my tidy appearance. No one said a word, not even Mrs. Watanabe.

The caravan of trucks snaked through the small town, past the Methodist Church that had been such a part of Yoneichi's and my life. Through tear-filled eyes I caught a glimpse of the newly painted theater, the post office with the American flag fluttering, the Alibi, a restaurant with its sign painted boldly above the doorway, the well-stocked hardware store and Tim Clark's drugstore. I thought about the day in 1933 when there was a fire in downtown Vashon. They dismissed church service and Sunday school so the adults and older boys could help remove merchandise from the store. The owners of the drugstore gave away free ice cream cones to everyone because they knew it would melt without electricity. In my childish innocence, I felt lucky that day to get one.

We passed Vashon Grade School and the gymnasium where I played with my friends. From inside the dark, noisy truck that memory seemed a long time ago. Now we all rocked back and forth in unison as the truck lumbered along the bumpy road, twisting around tight turns in the final descent to the ferry terminal.

The ferry dock was familiar yet strange. Hundreds of people milled around with a sense of foreboding. I was stunned to see many of our non-Japanese neighbors and friends from church and school at the dock. They had gotten word of the evacuation and had come down that Saturday morning. As each of my classmates came up to me for final words, I found it hard to say anything.

Bob came up and said, "Mary, I don't know what this is all about, but it all seems so unfair. I will really miss you. Do you know where you are going?"

"No, I have no idea."

Even Shirley, one of the most popular girls in our class, approached me and said, "Boy, this is terrible. Will you write to us so we can stay in touch?"

"I promise to do that," I responded, surprised that she would take the time to come to see me off. I didn't know she cared that much.

One of my closest Sunday school friends, Angie, said, "Take good care of yourself and your folks. We'll be praying for you."

"Thanks, Angie. I'll miss you." What I wanted to say to Angie was, *I'll always remember that time you and your brother took me out on Puget Sound in your sailboat. It was so quiet and peaceful out there with the light warm breeze moving the boat gently through the smooth water. That was the only time I have ever been out on a sailboat and it was so much fun.* But I couldn't bring myself to say it out loud for fear that I would cry uncontrollably.

A ferry finally arrived, but this was not the usual ferry we sailed on all the time. It was smaller, old, and gray. Slowly it moved into place, then the workers tied it off and positioned a gangplank. I hugged my friends and said my tearful goodbyes. As I started down the gangplank, I had to blink several times to see where I was going. We descended into the unknown. It was now about 12:30 p.m.

The soldiers followed us aboard, then a worker raised the gangplank with a loud clang. As the ferry began to move out into the Sound, everyone on the dock began to wave. Angie had one arm around her dad's waist as she waved her handkerchief with the other. She kept wiping her eyes with the handkerchief, calling out, "Goodbye, goodbye." The words floated across the waves as the ferry moved farther away.

My legs felt heavy, glued to the deck. I thought my lungs would burst from holding back my sobs. The voices from the dock became fainter and fainter until I could no longer hear them. The dock and the people grew smaller, but I couldn't stop looking until they disappeared.

The ferry made another stop to pick up more families on the west side of Puget Sound at Kingston. It was late afternoon before we arrived at Pier 52 in Seattle. By then I was exhausted from standing and staring for hours at the water.

Soldiers directed us toward a waiting train not far from the ferry landing. People gathered on the streets and the overpass nearby to watch us being escorted by armed soldiers. We had to walk past the silent glaring crowd. I noticed a long string of cars parked along both sides of the street where we had to walk. My stomach knotted up when I saw a group of restless, angry-looking men with dirty coveralls standing along the sidewalk, each nervously fingering a shotgun. One ruddy-faced, tall, heavyset man with deep vertical lines between his eyebrows acted like the leader. His steel gray eyes bulged as he lifted his gun with one hand and shook his clenched fist with the other. "Get outta here, you God damn Japs!" he shouted. "I oughta blast your heads off."

Dropping my eyes and head, I walked quickly past him. The other men didn't say anything, but they spat at us as we passed. Most of the crowd just stood and watched. Hurrying past, a thought crossed my mind. *Maybe it's a good thing we're leaving. Maybe hysteria over the war news and the media frenzy could make it too dangerous for us to remain here. Maybe the government is trying to protect us.* I was too frightened to make any sense out of it.

Silently we walked to the train about one hundred yards from the dock. We boarded and looked for a place where we could sit together. Making my way down the aisle, I realized immediately these cars had not been used in a long time. There was a strong musty, acrid smell and the seats and floors were dusty and dirty. All the windows were shut and smoked to block the view outside. There would be no way of knowing where we were going. A sense of isolation and impending doom rose.

Families tried to stay together and for the most part, this was possible. Eventually, everyone was aboard, including the soldiers. The train lurched forward into the night toward an unknown destination.

I had never ridden on a train before. Occasionally Papa-san and I took a streetcar to downtown Seattle to go to the optometrist. On those days, Papa-san and I would get all dressed up, catch the bus out on the highway, and ride to the ferry. After the twenty-minute crossing, we walked down the long dock to the streetcar station nearby and rode into Seattle. I enjoyed looking at all the houses built so close together with such small yards compared to ours in the country. As we approached downtown, Papa-san usually pointed to the one tall thin building and said, "See that building over there? That's the Smith Tower, the tallest building west of the Mississippi River." I was impressed.

After the doctor's visit, Papa-san and I always went to Japantown to my favorite restaurant, Maneki's, to have buta-dofu, pork and tofu with rice and miso soup. The waitresses always recognized us and welcomed us for lunch. Having to change my glasses almost annually was a nuisance, but those trips to Seattle with Papa-san were such a treat. I always felt special being with him. I also saw how Papa-san moved easily among business people, both white and Japanese, and noticed how comfortably he could engage in conversation with friends and strangers alike. I was proud of my Papa-san.

This train ride was nothing like those trips. Looking around at everyone's grim and stoic faces, I felt afraid and frustrated that no one could say where we were going or why. People spoke only in brief and hushed tones to one another. Even the children were subdued. There were so many people in our car, some standing in the aisles, we had to squeeze by one another to get to the restroom. Once when I tried to get back to my seat, I found that someone else had taken it. When I went looking for another place to sit, I found one on the top bunk of a sleeper car. There were many girls sprawled up there, none of whom I knew.

One of the tall, good looking soldiers laughingly said to us as he walked down the aisle, "Hey, why don't some of you beautiful girls come three cars back to our car. There's plenty of room, and we've got some great grub, booze, and music. It'd be a heck of a lot more fun than being cramped up there."

One of the girls giggled and said, "Hmm, I wonder what that would be like."

Another answered, "Do you think we should go or not?"

"It sounds like it could be fun," the first girl replied. "It'd sure beat what we got here."

"Do you want to go for a little while, just to see what's back there?" Something inside of me said, *No, that's not a good idea. I may be seventeen years old but I'm not ready for doing that sort of thing yet.* Finally two of the girls did get down and the last I saw of them they were worming their way toward the back. I have no idea what happened to them.

The girls on the bunk talked about how hot and stuffy the air was becoming. I dozed off and on. I did not like being crowded together with so many strangers, even if they were Japanese. The one comfort I had was that our little family, Papa-san, Mama-san, Yoneichi and I were all on the same train. We were all going to the same place—or were we? Then I began to worry. I got down from the bunk and when I found my parents, I asked Papa-san, "Do you think we are all going to the same place?"

He dropped his eyes, thought a minute before he looked at me and replied, "I don't know, Mary-san. We'll do everything we can to stay together."

Fear gripped my heart. *What would I do if we were separated from each other? What would become of my parents and what would become of me?* I wanted to grab his hands and never let go. I broke out in a cold sweat. I couldn't shake this foreboding thought. I stood in the aisle beside his seat for a long while before I found a place to sit down.

We rode on the train for about three days, punctuated by occasional unexplained stops of various lengths. At regular intervals, soldiers distributed bagged meals, consisting of tasteless sandwiches, apples, and water. Some of us thought we must have been going south because it kept getting hotter. At one point I felt hot and cold simultaneously and slightly nauseated, then I only saw blackness. A short time later I awakened to see Mama-san and other people scurrying around me, wiping my face with a cool, damp cloth. Someone even got a window cracked open and we finally had some air circulating through the car. That was the only time in my life I ever fainted.

≾ ◎ ≿

We could not have known at that time that some families initially would be housed in hastily modified "assembly centers," including livestock stalls and stables. Evacuation centers would include fairgrounds in Portland, Oregon, and Puyallup, Washington and the Santa Anita Race Track and the Tanforan Race Track in California. Years later we would learn through word of mouth that some of the people who were sent to these foul places became very ill, with vomiting and diarrhea caused by the urine and feces-saturated environment of the livestock stalls in which they had to live.

Our train rumbled towards an unknown destination, carrying us to some place, somewhere, for some unknown length of time, and possibly to our death. Uncertainty was all we knew.

CHAPTER SIX

THE FIRST INTERNMENT CAMP

Our train came to a stop shortly after noon on the third day of traveling. Soldiers with rifles walked down the aisles and ordered us to get off. I was startled to see that the landscape was entirely different from the lush green surroundings back home. Hills in the distance were mauve and shades of brown. Wispy white clouds floated lazily in a stark blue sky. A faint sweet fragrance, unlike anything I had smelled before, wafted through the hot dry air. *Where are we?* I wondered. *Where are we going and how far is that?*

There was no time for conversation. Soldiers barked orders to move ahead and climb aboard the covered army trucks. About twenty of us wedged in tightly in a truck. I was thirsty and had to go to the bathroom, but too fearful to ask, and too focused on surviving the unknown.

As the truck moved away from the train we could see miles of medium-sized trees in orchards. They were not like any trees we had ever seen before. Someone guessed they might be olive trees. We rode in silence for what seemed like hours, then the truck slowed down, turned, moved forward a short distance and stopped. Someone shouted, "This is the end of the line." Later I would learn that we had arrived at Pinedale Assembly Center, a hastily built internment camp located eight miles north of Fresno, California.

When I got off the truck I couldn't believe what I saw. Soldiers with machine guns stood in twenty-foot-high guard towers situated at strategic points along the perimeter of a huge camp. The area was encased in steel-wire fencing topped by three rows of barbed wire. Large searchlights next to the towers rotated continuously. Black tar-papered barracks were laid out in regimented form along the flat terrain. Gray dirt or lava gravel completed the menacing scene. Impatient soldiers yelled at us to move forward, into the camp as a stream of Japanese families flowed in behind us. As we entered the camp I stared at the barbed wire. *Why is the barbed wire facing inward?* I thought. *Isn't the government putting us here for our protection?*

Stunned by the sight, I stopped. My feet were riveted to the ground. Papa-san put his arm across my shoulder and gently guided me forward as he said softly, "Let's move ahead and find the place where we are to be."

Everywhere I looked there were hundreds of people with brown eyes, black hair, and yellow skin, just like mine. On Vashon Island where we had come from, the majority of the people were white with a generous sprinkling of Japanese, Chinese, and a few Filipino men. I had never lived in a place where everyone looked the same. People already living at the camp briefly glanced at us new arrivals with curiosity, disinterest, or sympathy. Then they quickly dropped their eyes and moved on about their business.

Internees who had arrived much earlier escorted us, helping us find the space we would try to make into a "home." All the barracks were identical, obviously constructed in a hurry. They had been framed up, the outsides sheeted with crude wooden siding, then covered with tar paper. No additional siding was put over the tar paper. The inside was plain wood sheeting. There was no plaster, paint, or insulation—just a blank, drab tan room with four walls, a peaked roof, and an off-white concrete floor. A cow had obviously walked across the concrete floor before it had hardened, leaving her hoof prints.

Our living space was a bare twenty foot by twenty-four foot room in the middle of a 120-foot-long barrack. Ours had six army cots and a pile of blankets left in the middle of the room. Nothing else. No other furniture, no running water, no storage space, and nothing to use to prepare a meal. Only a single, bare light bulb screwed into a ceramic socket on the end of a long electrical cord hung from the ceiling. We would later learn there were five different sized living spaces in the building, all of them small and bare.

An older couple who had arrived just ahead of us was to share this same space with us. We were strangers to each other. Upon meeting we looked at each other and silently nodded in acknowledgment. That nod between my parents and the older couple spoke volumes. The simple, nonverbal communication said how much we would see and not see, hear and not hear, smell and not smell, as we lived four feet from each other. The nod meant, *We will honor your privacy.*

Partitions between the living spaces were only about seven feet high, leaving a four-foot triangular opening from the top of the partitions to the peak of the ceiling. This opening extended the full length of the barrack. While we could not see our neighbors, we could hear everything that went on anywhere in the barrack regardless of the time of day or night. We could hear family quarrels, babies crying, laughter, hushed giggles, and at night snoring, coughing, and grinding teeth. I was mortified as I gradually realized that nighttime moans, sighs, and repetitive thumps meant that some couple was having sexual intercourse. All the sounds of humanity became background noise in the barracks.

We would soon begin to refer to these living spaces, about the size of storage rooms, as "apartments." All of the internees quickly adapted to euphemisms when describing their imprisonment, perhaps as a way of coping and maintaining some dignity. We were in "camps," not a prison.

On that first day Papa-san and Yoneichi went off to find straw and ticking to make mattresses for each of our cots. Mama-san and I tried to figure out with the older couple how we should divide the space to accommodate our needs. We decided to hang army blankets to form walls so we could have some privacy. Years later I would be unable to remember anything about the older couple we shared the same space with—not their faces, names, or anything else about their lives. I was overwhelmed and too distraught.

Totally bewildered, I asked, "Mama-san, how can they do this to us?"

Mama-san looked at me, her eyes revealing a great grief. "Japan attacked Pearl Harbor, Mary-san. And because we are Japanese, we have to take this. *Shikata ga nai, desu yo*—It can't be helped, that's the way it is."

Mama-san had always been a practical and optimistic person. Whatever her emotions were during our internment, she could adapt her frame of mind and feelings to the demands of the moment. In her characteristic manner, knowing that this was to be our "home," she matter-of-factly suggested we explore the immediate environment to find out what was available to meet our basic needs. Silently I followed her outside to look around.

The central California sun was already very hot by late May. As we walked, a slight wind kicked up the fine dirt creating dust clouds. We found the mess hall, the men's and women's latrines, showers, laundry room, and the recreation hall. Aside from these structures that had the same kind of construction as our barracks, there was nothing else in sight: no grass, trees, or flowers blooming anywhere. Even the birds seemed to vacate the skies above our prison camp. People wandered about, all looking preoccupied, lost in disbelief of this barren environment.

≈◎≈

Pinedale was one of fifteen assembly centers; all but three were in California. The government selected these sites because they had pre-existing facilities, including water, power, and sewage. This minimized the

Internment camp barracks were all similar. This photo was taken at Minidoka.

amount of construction required. Fairgrounds and racetracks were often used for this reason. Substandard construction practices were the norm, including the conversion of animal stalls into living spaces for human occupancy. We would later learn that Pinedale Assembly Center was actually better than some, built on vacant land eight miles north of Fresno near an existing mill workers' housing area. From May 7 to July 23, 1942, 4,823 people lived in five blocks, each block containing forty barracks with five apartments each. There were two mess halls to each block, equipped to feed five hundred people in three shifts.

That first night we learned it was mealtime when a kitchen crewmember made a horrendous clatter by whirling a thick metal rod around the inside of a large triangle hung outside the mess hall door. Initially my family didn't know what all that racket was for, but we soon found out when we saw everyone going toward the mess hall with their plates and utensils brought from home.

My family and I got in line outside the mess hall door. The line moved slowly. Once inside I was amazed to see this huge hall packed with Japanese people of all ages. It seemed as though everyone was talking at once, a loud mixture of Japanese and English. Inching along I finally got to the place where hot rice was plopped onto my plate followed by hot spicy chili and tossed salad—not what I would have chosen given the 100-degree heat. The salad was mostly lettuce and cabbage, some spinach, a few slices of radish, and slivers of grated carrots. Someone had blanched the salad and poured vinegar over it for flavor. As I waited for the rest of my family to get their food, I looked around to find a place for the four of us to sit at one of the picnic tables lined up throughout the mess hall.

Mama-san got her food and she and I looked back to wait for Papa-san and Yoneichi. We both noticed a hunch-backed *oba-san*—an old lady, behind us. She was followed by a young woman who I assumed was her daughter. The kitchen crew dishing out the food seemed annoyed with the *oba-san* for shuffling along so slowly and holding up the long line of people behind her. We found a table for all of us and saved places for her and her daughter. Mama-san took the *oba-san's* plate and put it on the table for her. Bracing her arms on the table the old lady slowly lifted one leg and slid it into the high, bench-like seat. She lifted the other leg with difficulty and finally sat down heavily. She slumped for a moment and took a deep breath before she finally looked up at her plate.

Mama-san said to her gently, "These seats are high, aren't they?" The *oba-san* nodded. After a few moments she picked up her fork and took a bite of food. I saw her put her hand up to her mouth as she swallowed the spicy chili. She quickly took a mouthful of rice and chewed it awhile.

Mama-san said, "We are the Matsuda family from Vashon Island, Washington. I am Mitsuno Matsuda. This is my *shujin*, husband, Heisuke, my son, Yoneichi, and daughter, Mary. And you are?"

"I am Yasuko Okimoto from Kent, Washington and this is my daughter, Kimi. I am glad to meet you and thank you very much for helping us. My, this is very confusing, isn't it?"

"Yes, it is," Mama-san answered as she bowed her head for a brief moment in agreement.

I found it reassuring that Mama-san found this environment confusing, too.

The noise around us in the mess hall was deafening. Some small children cried, older ones yelled to others across the hall trying to persuade their friends to join them. Mothers and fathers called to their children to sit with the family and some of the youngsters resisted.

With all the noise and the turmoil of moving into this incredibly strange place and the hot mess hall, I had no appetite. I took a little of the salad, chewed it a long time, and finally swallowed, but it lodged in my throat and felt like it would go no further. Mama-san said gently, "It's hard to eat, isn't it? But let's try to eat something—this may be all we will have today."

"Hey, lady, let's have some tea over here," a man at the next table demanded as he stood and waved his cup at a young *Nisei* working as a waitress passing nearby with a big white pitcher.

Someone else called out, "Coffee over here, please."

"Sumi, come over here and eat with the family," a shrill voice pierced the air. I wanted to put my hands over my ears to shut out the pounding on my eardrums. Up to this point, the biggest crowd I had ever seen on Vashon was at our farm during holiday celebrations, and at school assemblies.

Our life on Vashon seemed so far away and long ago that first night at Pinedale. I had a great deal of trouble getting to sleep. The room felt like an oven, with not one cool breeze throughout the night. I could hear people tossing and turning on their cots, coughing persistently, and a tired baby wailing somewhere in our barrack. Every few seconds the sweep of the searchlight lit up the inside of our room. Each one in my family turned over repeatedly trying to find a comfortable spot on the straw mattress that lay on the hard, unyielding canvas cot.

The next morning Mama-san and I went to the showers. They were located in a building that was divided in half: one end for men and the other for women. The shower building was unlike anything either of us had ever seen before. It had been hastily thrown together like all the other structures to accommodate a large number of people. Multiple shower spigots hung from the ceiling. Privacy was not even a consideration. All of us girls and women would have to bathe in front of each other.

The first couple of times Mama-san and I took our showers, I felt very self-conscious. After turning the water on and waiting for it to heat up, I stood with my arms across my chest to hide my budding breasts. The exposure was difficult to adjust to, but I had no choice. Later we learned that some boys outside liked to press their faces to the knotholes to peek at us while we showered. We quickly fixed that by standing watch for each other and holding our hands over these peepholes.

I thought about the conversation Mama-san and I once had about how she took baths in Japan. "The bathtub in my childhood was located at the back of our home. A deep wooden tub filled with water sat on a wooden platform. There was a small black door open at the bottom of the tub where coal was burned in an iron container to heat the water in the tub.

Beside it was a stool for us to sit on, a barrel of cool water, soap, and washcloth, and a dipper to pour water over our bodies after we had soaped and scrubbed thoroughly."

"Oh," I said, "you washed before you washed."

"Yes," Mama-san continued. "By doing it that way all the dust and grime from the day is completely rinsed off and the hot water for soaking could be used by more than one person."

"Everyone used the same water?"

"Yes, but it was clean and hot. When one stepped into the tub and sat down, the hot water would come up to one's chin. By sitting very still for a few minutes the body adjusted to the heat. The steam would rise and the smell of cedar was so relaxing. It was the favorite time of the day for me," Mama-san recalled. "Some people would go to public baths where men and women bathed together in large tubs, but we had our own so we didn't need to do that. Baths were a wonderful part of our lives." She smiled at these pleasant memories.

How different and strange these public showers were from what I had known before. Bathing was a nightly ritual at our home on Vashon and it was done leisurely and with such pleasure, similar to how they bathed in Japan. Every evening after the dishes were washed, the paper read, and the kitchen tidied up, my folks would take a bath together. Mama-san would get the hot water running in the bathtub. Papa-san would undress in the living room beside the stove. Carrying his *yukata*, a cotton kimono, he would walk naked through the kitchen to the bathroom and step into the tub. Mama-san would undress in their bedroom next to the bathroom and join him.

Each of them would slowly sink into the hot water, sit, look at each other, and relax with deep sighs while they adjusted to the heat. The air was always warm and moist, the light dim, and the atmosphere peaceful. Eventually they would bathe themselves as they talked over the events of the day, and end by washing each other's backs.

It was in this setting that I could occasionally spend some special time with my parents. There was a naturalness to Japanese bathing that made it okay for me to talk with them while they bathed and soaked. I often sat on the toilet seat cover and asked all kinds of questions:

"How come Yoneichi gets to do things I can't do?"

"Beverly and Mary Jane are so popular with the other kids. Why can't I be, too?"

"What's the difference between boys and girls and why can't girls come and go like boys do?"

At the internment camp bathing wasn't "bathing" at all. It was a quick wash while someone stood guard against peeping toms. I quickly learned that every routine activity took extra thought and energy. Using the bathroom was one such activity. I figured out that I should get up early in the morning and hurry to the bathroom to brush my teeth. There was a long galvanized sink with water faucets located about every three feet for washing the hands and face. I went to the farthest end of the trough away from the drain so I did not have to watch dozens of other people's frothy, yellowish saliva flow by me before going down the drain at the far end.

The bathrooms were divided similarly to the building for showers—one end for men, the other for women. The toilets were raised platforms with holes to sit over. There were partitions separating the stalls but no doors for privacy. A faucet at one end of the row of toilets dripped water constantly into a trough. The water ran below and slightly behind the toilet holes. I quickly learned to recognize when the sound of the dripping water got to a certain pitch; this meant enough water had accumulated to make the trough tip. That would force enough water to "flush" the contents down to the other end and into the sewer below. The first time I had to go to the bathroom I didn't know this. I got an unwelcome splash of cold water all over my bottom. Never again.

One day I came into the bathroom and noticed all the spaces were taken. There was an *oba-san*, a grandmother, sitting in the first spot hunched over and grunting. Then there were two young women in their twenties and one in her sixties all sitting on toilets reading magazines or newspapers. The last two holes were taken by two young girls who kept trying to stifle their giggles as they passed gas. As I stood waiting I started having abdominal cramps. I had put off going to the bathroom as long as I could. It was so embarrassing for me to go to the toilet in such a public place that I would put it off until I really had to go.

On this particular day the air inside was humid and the sound of people's voices walking past the building was clearly audible. Still, everyone inside paid close attention to the sound of the dripping water while they sat on the toilets. When it reached that certain pitch, everyone silently raised their rear ends in unison while the contents were flushed away. Solemnly everyone resumed their previous postures. That moment made me chuckle in spite of the circumstances.

The laundry room was a large common room. There were no washing machines, just scrub boards, deep sinks, soap, and lots of elbow grease. I often went with Mama-san to help with our weekly washing. She always greeted people pleasantly and knew the fine art of small talk without seeming trivial. Throughout the laundry room pairs of women talked quietly to each other, gesturing, bowing, and nodding their heads. The laundry provided a place for them to gather to meet new people, share gossip, and complain. All conversation among the *Isseis* was in Japanese.

One day Mrs. Sato, a recent acquaintance, came in. Mama-san asked her how she and her family were getting along. In a loud, high-pitched, whiny voice Mrs. Sato began wailing and gesturing wildly: "I can't stand the heat, the awful food, the dust storms, the lack of privacy, and I can't sleep and get any relief at night. I hate everything about this place."

Mama-san kept scrubbing Papa-san's pants, nodding in understanding and looking at her new friend from time to time as she quietly responded, *"Ah, ah"* in acknowledgment. Occasionally Mama-san would say, "It is hard isn't it? I want things to get better, too. *Gaman shimasho*—Let us persevere."

We had to eat all of our meals in the mess hall. There were no cooking facilities or running water in the barracks and no way for us to prepare any food in our room. How I missed our home-cooked meals and family time around the dinner table. Mama-san was an excellent cook, but being a traditional mother, she never bragged about her delicious meals. I enjoyed working beside her in our farm kitchen, whether it was shelling peas, cutting up vegetables, or making a special dish for dinner.

In the internment camp I spent a lot of time savoring food memories and time spent cooking with Mama-san. One time when I was about eight years old, I decided to make my first pie. We were growing loganberries at the time and the crop was at the peak of the season. We didn't have a cookbook with a recipe for loganberry pie, so Mama-san and I made it up. We gathered the darkest, ripest berries we could find, washed them thoroughly, and put them into the crust I had made. I put in some flour, butter, a touch of salt, and some sugar. The pie looked wonderful when I put it into the oven. After taking such pains to make it look so delicious, I was disappointed to see the startled looks on Papa-san and Yoneichi's faces when they took their first bite. Struggling to control their expressions, they nodded solemnly while chewing and finally swallowing. "Very good," they both said. Papa-san bravely took another bite. "Maybe just a little more sugar next time. Okay?" he said. I quickly cut myself a piece and tasted it. It was so sour I shivered.

~⊙~

The days became hotter. Those of us from the cool Pacific Northwest were not used to the one hundred to one hundred fifteen-degree heat. The desert sun sapped our energy, and we suffered especially when we had to line up outside the mess halls for meals.

Every single activity at the internment camp that required my venturing out into the open seemed strange and threatening. The only safe place was with my parents and brother in our small living space. But even there we still had to contend with the other couple living with us.

All the privacy that I had taken for granted in my past was gone. It was the constancy of Mama-san's reassuring smile, nod, and gentle words, conveying understanding and patience, that gave me strength and kept me stable.

One afternoon while we waited for dinner, an *oba-san* fainted. Mama-san and I recognized her from the first day at the mess hall. It was Mrs. Okimoto from Kent. We gently lifted her up under the arms and guided her to the shade of the closest barrack. I fanned her with my plate, hoping to offer some relief from the stifling heat. Mama-san gently wiped the perspiration off her forehead. Our efforts seemed to revive her. *"Ah, mata domo arigato gozaimasu*—Thank you very much again," Mrs. Okimoto replied. "It was so hot inside our apartment I had to get outside. But it's so hot out here too. What are we to do?"

Mama-san's reply was, "Yes, it is very hot. We will suggest to your daughter to put your cot out in the shade of the barrack and you will be cooler than inside. We've done that with ours and we are much more comfortable. Be sure you drink enough water and take some salt pills, too."

When Mama-san and I returned to the mess hall line, she said with a worried look on her face, "Mrs. Okimoto seems so frail. I'm afraid life here is too hard on her."

Fainting was a common occurrence. Some people showed concern when someone fainted, others did not unless it was a relative. The extremely hot climate and the strange, controlled environment of the camp added to everyone's agitation. People complained everywhere, every day. "This is terrible. I wonder how long we'll have to stay here," a teenage girl said in a worried voice to a friend.

An old lady was complaining in the mess hall, "I can't stand the food. Don't they know Japanese people need more fresh vegetables and fruit?"

Nearby a young mother holding her baby added, "I'm worried my baby isn't getting enough milk and the vitamins she needs to grow properly."

People continuously asked questions to government authorities that went unanswered. "What about our fishing boats? The nursery? Our berry fields?" My parents wondered about those very things, but they were more philosophical. Their responses were, "Yes, it is difficult, isn't it? I have those same concerns. All we can do now is hope that all this will end soon and we can all go home. *Shikata ga nai*. It can't be helped. *Gaman shimasho*—Let us be patient."

I often wondered, *How can they be so endlessly stoic?* On reflection much later, I realized that was the way they had always looked at life—with thoughtful planning, patience, faith, and hope.

I gradually became accustomed to seeing only Japanese people around me. But being a part of the majority in the internment camp did not give me a feeling of well-being at all. To the contrary, it felt humiliating since our common ancestry was the reason that all of us had been rounded up against our will. I was ashamed to be part of the Japanese majority.

Once around 4:00 in the morning I had to go to the bathroom. I put my coat on over my pajamas and slid my feet into my shoes. Once outside a huge, bright light flashed on me. As I thrust my hands in front of my eyes I realized immediately that the searchlight at the nearby watchtower was focused on me. In the darkness the searchlight had grabbed my privacy and exposed it to the camp guards. Blinded and stunned, I felt invaded. Powerless to stop the searchlight from bearing down on me, I fled back to the barracks. The light followed me and waited at the doorway as I hid, pressing my body against the inside wall of my family's living space. Finally the searchlight resumed its automatic circuit. Shaking in the darkness I realized, *At seventeen, I am a prisoner of war in my own country.* I vowed to wait until morning to go to the bathroom.

In the morning I told my family what happened. Everyone looked grim. Yoneichi struck the bed with his fist. If he had been a swearing man, he would have cursed. A shadow of pain flitted across Mama-san's face. After a long silence, she spoke. "After this whenever you have to go to the bathroom in the night, awaken me. I will go with you. I don't want you to go alone."

"And I will go with you, too, Mama-san," I replied. "Thank you. I was really scared."

Yoneichi and Papa-san looked at me and nodded their heads. I felt reassured by their understanding and their support, but Papa-san looked frustrated and powerless, unable to protect his daughter from the relentless searchlight.

⋋◉⋌

At the internment camp we got snippets of news that the war in the Pacific and Southeast Asia was going badly for the Allies. I didn't want to think about the possibility that the camp soldiers might kill us all because we looked like the people they were fighting. I could not let myself think that this is what some people in the U.S. government might want to do. Everything held a potential threat and I lived in a constant state of fear. It was a surprise whenever someone laughed or more so when I laughed. Jokes or funny stories were not a part of daily conversation.

Back home Yoneichi had always been the clown in our family. Periodically he would make us all laugh by imitating different characters he had heard on the radio or seen in the movies. He sounded and looked like Donald Duck when he quacked and waddled around the house. He would flex his biceps like Popeye as he sang, "I'm Popeye the Sailor Man, I'm Popeye the Sailor Man, I fights to the finish 'cause I eats my spinach, I'm Popeye the Sailor Man. Toot! Toot!" Or he would imitate Woody Woodpecker's famous laugh: "hahaHaHAha!"

There was no one laughing at Pinedale Assembly Center. Black tar-papered barracks with the barbed-wire fence, manned guard towers, and continuously rotating searchlights were somber reminders of our imprisonment. I saw all the other Japanese people wandering around trying to make the best of each day. The most sobering realization was that the U.S. Army and government could do this to American citizens. An executive order could take us away in shame and we had no recourse. Our government held the ultimate power. I began to question, *If this could happen to us, couldn't it happen to anyone?*

During the first month I developed a detachment from my surroundings at Pinedale. I lived from day to day, eating the same kind of food, living in the same kind of conditions, and resigned to there being very little opportunity for individual initiative or creativity.

In the midst of the bleak, monotonous routine I had frequent fantasies of picnics at a beautiful green park or playing on the beaches of Puget Sound. I also worried about what was going on back at the farm. My future seemed immobilized. I could not bring myself to think too far into the future. My life at Pinedale had become totally formless in a meaning-less routine. Even the thought of cool rain, sweet strawberries, and hot baths only brought sorrow and tears. Daily I struggled to understand, *Why are we in such a despicable place? Why are we treated like criminals and outlaws?* My soul wept silently because it was safe only if I was silent, obedient, and cloaked in numbness.

We had been at Pinedale a month and a half when the soldiers told everyone to pack up their things because we were leaving the next day for a "permanent camp." Startled, I said to Papa-san, "A permanent camp? Was this only a temporary place? I wonder where we'll have to go this time? And how permanent is permanent?" I wondered, *Does permanent mean dead?*

Papa-san looked down and was silent. Finally he raised his tired eyes and said, "I don't know, Mary-san. We'll just have to wait and see what happens."

By now, I was starting to get exasperated that Papa-san didn't have the answers either. In the past he had always known what to expect, and it was frightening to see him as helpless as I was. I hoped desperately that wherever we were going we could be together.

We slept little during our last night at Pinedale. The next morning we were all up, dressed, and packed before the breakfast triangle clanged. Afterwards we carried our luggage to the departure gate and climbed aboard waiting army trucks. Soldiers drove us to the same train depot we had arrived at a month and a half before.

The four of us spoke little during the train trip, but I overheard many of the adults complain quietly to one another. The laments were familiar to all of us. The trouble was, it just made things feel darker to me.

Wing Luke Asian Museum

Tule Lake guard tower.

CHAPTER SEVEN

THE LAST DANCE IN THE SEARCHLIGHT

The train ride out of Pinedale, though stressful, was at least a break from the monotonous routine of one and a half months in the camp. The old train cars were musty, dirty and creaky, just like the last train. As before, the windows were smoked and we could not look at the passing landscape. How I wished we could have seen signs of normal life.

Rocking back and forth on the decrepit seats, we were lost in our thoughts. Papa-san sat erect most of the time, occasionally leaning his head against the headrest while he intermittently sighed deeply and stared into space. Periodically his eyes glazed over and a frown creased his forehead. I imagined, *He is feeling the loss of all he and Mama-san have worked so hard to establish.* I turned away, unable to tolerate his loss on top of my own.

When I looked across at Mama-san she nodded her head and smiled as though to reassure me, yet I could see the sadness in her eyes. At times she sat with her hands clasped in her lap, her lips pressed tightly together, as she discreetly looked around at those who rode with her to the next unknown destination.

Papa-san, Mama-san, and I remained seated most of the time, but Yoneichi moved about the train car talking with people. When he came back to sit with us, his foot jiggled nervously up and down. Others dozed or looked about with dull eyes. We were all preoccupied with questions of the future.

My periodic trips to the restroom took me past several families from Vashon huddled together in somber silence. The Aoyama family sat with bowed heads. Mrs. Aoyama, one of Mama-san's closest friends from home, nodded to me each time I passed. The Ohashis and their three boys sat together looking grim and preoccupied. I raised my hand slightly and tried to smile at Ardith Kumamoto sitting with her parents and her three sisters. Ardith was a petite, pretty girl with big, dark eyes and long eyelashes. She and I had become good friends because we used to perform Japanese dances together back home. From the time she was in the fifth grade and I was in the fourth grade, we went weekly to Mrs. Nakamura's Japanese dance class. We would practice for performances in Japanese community events. It was the only time I could dress up and wear a touch of lipstick.

One time Ardith's father took us for a ride in their black, shiny touring car with the top folded down. In the 1930s, cars were still a novelty on the island, and getting a ride was a real treat. Ardith and I giggled as we sat together in the back seat anticipating our ride. First Mr. Kumamoto adjusted the levers on the steering column that controlled the fuel and ignition. Then he walked around to the front, rested his left hand on top of the radiator, and grasped the crank with his right. He gave it a brisk, firm turn, then another. After several cranks the motor took hold, belched, sputtered, and shook as Mr. Kumamoto sprang into the driver's seat. Black smoke spewed out the tail pipe then gradually changed to white as he readjusted the levers. The motor settled down into a rhythmic clatter and the car began to move forward in low gear. Releasing the hand lever and removing his foot from the pedal, the car shifted into high gear. The car leapt forward amid our cheers and we sat back to enjoy the wind on our faces. What an incredible sense of freedom! Ardith and I raised our arms and cheered wildly.

Seeing my neighbors' faces on the train took me to thoughts of Vashon and home. How I missed the island lush with evergreens, surrounded by the pristine waters of Puget Sound. I closed my eyes and inhaled deeply, imagining the crisp, clean air of Vashon. How I longed for a drink of pure, cool water from our well. How innocent I had been in that peaceful environment with the warm and satisfying relationships of neighbors, friends, and classmates. But in the midst of my reverie, no matter how hard I tried, I could not shake the dread. *We are going to a "permanent" camp. Does permanent mean we will be "permanently dead?" If so, how, when and where?*

It was fortunate that I had not heard about the concentration camps in Europe and the murdering of millions of Jews by the Nazis. While in fact we had it much better than the Jews in Nazi Germany, if I had known of their plight, I might have gone over the edge. Fear of being shot or killed was never far from my consciousness. I felt compelled to stay close to Mama-san, Papa-san, and Yoneichi, and always to be on the same train.

The tension in the air heightened abruptly when the locomotive blew its whistle and slowed to a stop. We had been riding for about a day and a half.

I crossed my legs and tightened my arms about my body. *This must be it,* I whispered to myself.

A soldier suddenly appeared at the end of the car. "Okay, everybody off," he barked. People slowly got out of their seats, grabbed their luggage, and began filing out one by one. I followed those ahead of me to the doorway, then stopped as I glanced out the door. This camp was gigantic. I was overwhelmed. The soldier at the bottom of the stairway shouted at me, "Come on! Come on! Move ahead! Keep moving!" He rotated his forearm in continuous circles, as if that would force me to move faster.

What's going to happen to us here? I wondered. I felt sick to my stomach and my chest tightened as I looked at a blur of black barracks separated by huge bare spaces. Later I found out that the purpose of the wide, bare ground was to create firebreaks between the flimsy wooden barracks. The firebreaks divided the camp into seven wards. Most of the wards were made up of nine blocks; each block had fourteen barracks. There were sixty-four blocks altogether. With approximately 260 men, women, and children per block we had a population of over 18,000 people at this new internment camp. I had no idea there were so many Japanese people living in America.

We had arrived at Tule Lake Internment Camp, located twenty-six miles south of Klamath Falls, Oregon. Despite its name I never saw a lake anywhere near the internment camp. Like Pinedale Assembly Center, this camp was encircled with a high, chain-link fence topped by three rows of barbed wire, all slanted inward. Soldiers with machine guns watched us from tall watchtowers located strategically around the perimeter. These lookouts were equipped with large mounted searchlights that continuously swept 360 degrees at night. The vast expanse of dreary, regimented, black tar-papered barracks were like the ones we had just left, only this camp looked ten times bigger and I felt one hundred times smaller.

My head whirled as my eyes tried to take in the scene. A momentary wish flashed through my mind. *This is just a bad dream. I will wake up back home.* It took Mama-san's gentle nudge from behind and her soft voice saying, "Let's go find where we will be staying," to make me realize this was not a nightmare. I stepped down from the train. Just then three young Japanese men walked by, raised their right fists, and yelled, *"Tenno Heika Banzai*—Long live His Majesty the Emperor." In the midst of so much noise and tension, I barely noticed them nor had any inkling of what this signified for the future. People were milling all around us, shouting orders and flailing their arms as we piled up near the train. It was hot and dusty without any breeze to relieve the stifling confusion.

We were ordered to climb into waiting army trucks. A *Nisei* man drove us to our "space" which was 7404 C (block 74, barrack 4, apartment C) in the northwestern corner of the camp. The barracks here were similar to those at the Pinedale Assembly Center: 120 feet long, divided into varying sized "apartments," which were nothing more than rectangular rooms with openings above the seven-foot walls. These open spaces extended the full length of the barrack. Any sound made in any one of the living cubicles could be heard throughout the barrack.

When we got to our twenty foot by twenty foot space, I remarked to my family, "Look, the room is smaller but we don't have to share it with anyone else. That's good." Our parents silently nodded. Looking at the pot-bellied stove Yoneichi commented, "Must get cold here." That winter the doorknob would get so cold our fingers would stick to it. We would be plagued by the subfreezing temperatures, scarcely protected by the flimsy barrack walls.

The central part of the camp had already been occupied by Japanese-Americans who came first—mostly from Sacramento, California. Those of us from Washington and Oregon were sent either to the northwestern section of the camp or the southeastern part. This would become significant later. I would quickly realize that I felt more comfortable spending time in our own area with those from the Northwest and especially from Vashon.

Once again we fell quickly to the task of setting up "home." Papa-san and Yoneichi went to find ticking and straw for our mattresses. Mama-san and I looked around our living space, wondering what we could do to make it ours. There were the familiar army cots and blankets for each of us. Aside from the stove and the light bulb screwed into a ceramic socket on the end of a cord hanging from the ceiling, the room was bare. It was just a space waiting for whatever drama was to be played out.

Mama-san said as she pointed, "Let's line up the cots along this wall away from the window. In case the wind blows the dust in as it did in Pinedale, it won't be as bad when we're asleep."

"Okay. This time we can put our stuff wherever we want to." I was glad we didn't have to share our space with another family. It didn't take long to set up our few personal things out of our suitcases.

My initial shock at seeing the camp for the first time gave way to depression as reality set in. We were going to be here for awhile, perhaps forever for all I knew. The drab surroundings and familiar still air of the hot evening crushed whatever small hopes I may have had after leaving Pinedale.

There was a notice posted in our "apartment" that gave the name of the block manager of our barracks, what his duties would be, and his office location. The note asked us to come to his office to identify ourselves and to sign up for various jobs.

After we had taken time to look around the camp and had gone to the block manager's office, we came home to compare notes. The camp layout was similar to Pinedale. Yoneichi announced proudly, "Mr. Mayeda from Vashon is going to be the chief cook in our mess hall. I asked him if I could be his assistant and learn how to cook. He agreed so now I've got a job. I'll get paid sixteen dollars a month." He looked pleased to have a job.

Professional people like doctors, lawyers, dentists, and chief cooks were paid at the highest rate of nineteen dollars a month. Semi-skilled workers received sixteen dollars and unskilled laborers twelve dollars per month. Papa-san and Mama-san signed up as janitors for the school that was to be set up and they would each be paid twelve dollars a month. I signed up as a waitress at twelve dollars a month to serve breakfasts and dinners during the school year, and all meals during the summer. It looked like I couldn't qualify for anything else. Since I had only worked on the farm to help my family and did not receive an allowance, twelve dollars a month didn't sound too bad to me, especially given what everyone else was receiving.

While Papa-san waited to begin work as a janitor he signed up with the road crew and was active every day. Yoneichi was busy learning to cook, and Mama-san and I helped clean up in the mess hall after each meal. Each of us found ways to fill our time.

Because of the highly structured way of life in camp there was nothing specific for most people to do. Many drifted about aimlessly. If they were back at their homes they would have been working from dawn to dusk at their farms, greenhouses, hotels, or restaurants. In camp there were many tasks such as garbage collection, fire station watches, and block manager work, but all of these were quickly assigned. Later, the need for adult education classes, arts and crafts, and other creative outlets would become obvious. For now, the overwhelming social problem was simply that there was nothing to do.

The *Isseis* in particular had a powerful work ethic that made them successful in their careers back home. Many had not taken a proper vacation in years or even in decades. The initial weeks at the internment camp with the idle hours were a welcome relief. But before long they discovered that time had to be filled with what used to be considered trivial or unimportant, such as sitting around and talking, doing needlework for hours, going to the laundry room or mess hall, or just standing around complaining.

Some of the people found time to enjoy conversations with those who came from the same location. I noticed Mrs. Kumamoto and Mrs. Shimada from Vashon often sat in the shade of their barrack knitting and talking together. Ardith's mother was quite a seamstress. She would do a variety of needlework while she conversed with her neighbors. However, many people suffered from boredom, bewilderment, and depression. Our stress came from not having enough to do.

Papa-san was an adaptable man. He met others in the block and before long he was part of an older men's group who played *go,* a Japanese board game. Two players alternately placed flat, round, black or white stones on the board. The strategy is to trap the other player within a given area by surrounding the opponent's stones with one's own. Whenever a game was going on, observers stood close to the players and watched in rapt silence. Papa-san played with other men from Vashon, such as Mr. Yamamoto and Mr. Watanabe, and anyone else willing to challenge him.

To fill my time after my daily waitress job, I got out the little radio I had brought from home and listened to a program called the "Voice of Prophecy." It was a conservative fundamentalist Christian program that I thought could help me find some answers to my desperate questions: *Where does it say that Jesus is the Savior? What do I have to do to be saved from this terrible place?* I needed comfort, direction, and hope but all I heard on the "Voice of Prophecy" were words. The words gave me no hope that this would all end soon, but I kept listening carefully, red-lining passages in my Bible that were particularly meaningful. *There must be some answers somewhere,* I told myself.

I knew my parents were deeply spiritual people. I wished I were too. I searched the Bible but I couldn't find the key to help me. *I will just have to keep looking,* I decided. My parents didn't object to my listening to the sermons but I think Mama-san saw my preoccupation with the Bible and my isolation from others as unhealthy. On more than one occasion she urged me, "Mary-san, let's go outside into the sunshine and go for a walk. I think it will be better for us to get out and see what is out there. We might find something interesting and meet people."

I longed for the sunny days of spring on Vashon when the fog disappeared in the warmth of the bright sunshine. I imagined the pink and white fragrant carnations along the sides of our farmhouse. Honeybees were hard at work, birds were busily flying around, twittering as they caught insects to bring to their hungry babies huddled in nests. I thought about the quiet evenings, so still I could hear an ambitious woodpecker hammering into a distant tree. I especially missed our green lawn where I could lie down after a day's work and watch fluffy white clouds float across the blue sky, resembling horses, flowers, buildings, or a palace. I missed my classmates at school and my friends in the church, too.

Tule Lake Internment Camp was plagued with unpredictable dust storms that came and went as if the desert were throwing a furious tantrum. Then just as suddenly they would stop, leaving us gasping for breath as we ran for shelter. Covering our faces with handkerchiefs or some clothing was essential. The slightest breeze would pick up the dirt and swirl it around the barracks, chasing us as we scrambled for cover.

❀

After we had been in Tule Lake for a few weeks, I learned that my dance instructor, Mrs. Nakamura, had been asked to present a program at an upcoming outdoor event. She was well known in Seattle as an instructor and player of the *shamisen*, a Japanese stringed instrument. These programs were the first attempts to relieve the monotony of internment by using the talents of the community. Mama-san was pleased that Ardith and I were selected to perform, and so was I, although I didn't say anything since Mama-san often advised me to be modest at all times. Dancing was something I knew how to do and I could do it with Ardith. It was a great honor, but I wasn't sure about dancing in front of a large and unfamiliar audience.

Ardith and I practiced together diligently. We followed Mrs. Nakamura's instructions precisely as she strummed on the *shamisen*. Listening and dancing to the rhythm of the music, I escaped from the dreariness and fear of the camp. I was carried back to our teacher's spacious living room on Vashon where Ardith and I had practiced together. The room provided an atmosphere of beauty and serenity.

As we danced to the music traditionally played in a minor key, I had a vision of a pensive person walking beside a gentle stream trickling over rocks. The water followed the bends in the river, finally flowing into a serene pool. The music and the movements took me to a peaceful place where the two cultures unified for a brief time. I felt whole—Japanese by heritage and American by birth.

Ardith and I moved our bodies slowly and gracefully making each step with the bend of the knees. Each head, arm, and hand movement, each turn of the body flowed together into the next position. We practiced until Mrs. Nakamura felt confident in our movements. I was delighted to have her approval.

The evening of our performance finally arrived. Several ladies helped us put on our beautiful *kimonos* that Mrs. Nakamura borrowed from some families who had brought them to camp. Ardith's had red, purple, and gold leaves on a beige background with a red *obi* interwoven with silver threads. Mine was a dark blue *kimono* with soft, simple patterns in gray. My *obi* was also red with silver threads.

Getting dressed in *kimonos* is a lengthy, complicated process. I was prepared to stand for quite awhile as the ladies helped me into each successive garment. As they tugged and pulled the sashes snugly around me, I noticed beads of perspiration on their foreheads and upper lips.

First came the short-sleeved undershirt tied at the waist, followed by the under robe, which is long and visible only at the neck like the collar of a shirt. Next we put on the *kimono*, which is heavy and long. It must be folded up and tied with a cord to hold it in place. This was followed by a wide long *obi*, which the women wound tightly around my waist several times making it impossible to take a deep breath or take long, bold steps. Then they tied the *obi* into a special knot on my back and held it in place with various cords and clasps. With white *tabi*—Japanese socks—and *geta*—wooden clogs on our feet, and red lipstick, we were ready. Mama-san gave me her last-minute advice, "This is an opportunity to represent the Vashon Japanese community, so do your very best."

We arrived at the outdoor platform where a crowd had gathered to watch our performance. It felt almost unbearably hot in my heavy *kimono* in the still air of the darkening desert skies. Mrs. Nakamura, dressed in her muted colored *kimono,* stepped onto the stage and seated herself on a chair. Holding her *shamisen* on her lap, she smiled and nodded at us confidently.

As I approached the platform in my beautiful *kimono* my stomach fluttered but I was full of energy as if I had shrugged off the oppression of the environment. Ardith and I took our positions in the center of the stage and waited to begin our dance. In that moment I knew we brought hope to the audience, representing the beauty and value of our culture.

Suddenly the revolving searchlight from a nearby watchtower flashed across my face, blinding me momentarily. I dropped my eyes and froze. My legs felt heavy, my arms like stone. I struggled to regain my composure. Vulnerability and fragility exposed my old confusion: *Am I Japanese or am I American in this barbed-wire camp, about to perform a Japanese dance?* I was chilled to the bone in the hot desert air and sick to my stomach. *Can I really do this?*

As I waited for the cue to begin I told myself, *Listen for the first stroke on the shamisen. Concentrate on each step. Remember what Mama-san said.* I glanced out over the crowd in the direction towards Mama-san. She looked at me, smiled, and nodded her head.

On the third strum of the music I slowly turned my head to the right and raised my right hand higher than my left in front of my body. My hands opened like the wings of a crane. Bending my knees slightly, I slowly slid my right foot slightly ahead of my left. *Forget everything else and move with the twang of the music,* I told myself. *I know the steps by heart.* As if suspended in time and space, I numbly and automatically made each movement, slowly, slowly, step by step. Gradually the movements of my body and the rhythm and tone of the *shamisen* took over until I realized that Ardith and I were dancing, and dancing well together. Relief, self-confidence, and even some self-importance finally crept back in as I gained a sense of the appreciative audience. *Now enjoy the dance.* And I did. I had finally found my own place in this barren camp.

We had only been dancing a couple of minutes when suddenly, a blast of hot wind whipped up the fine dust, swirling it everywhere between the barracks and across the open spaces, especially at us on the exposed, elevated platform. It felt like a thousand bees were stinging our hands and faces. We could taste the dirt and grit, barely able to breathe.

Mrs. Nakamura stopped playing. We covered our noses and mouths, and scrambled off the platform in our beautiful *kimonos.* Everyone scattered like leaves before a giant blower. Ardith and I took cover behind the closest barrack. By then Ardith's hair, *kimono,* and *obi* were coated with fine dust. It clung to the bangs on her forehead, to her eyelids and eyelashes, and stuck to her lipstick. Tears ran down her dusty cheeks. When she brushed the tears aside the dust left a smudge across her cheek. I must have looked like a dust ball myself. Then the storm died down as abruptly as it had started. We ran back to our own barracks.

When I got home, dust had penetrated through the cracks in the loose-fitting window, under the door, and up through the floorboards. Like thick smoke that streamed out of a smoldering fire, it seeped through everything in its path, finding and filling every nook and cranny. It seemed as if God was speaking through the dust storm, creating in me a crisis of identity. It was as though God Himself was saying, "No." I wasn't accepted in the white community, but when I tried to be Japanese, I felt annihilated. I threw myself on my cot and sobbed. Mama-san sat down beside me, lifted me into her arms and silently rocked me back and forth, back and forth until my crying subsided.

Later we cleaned our apartment, then stuffed paper into every crack we could find but it didn't help. There was always dust everywhere—the dark cloud that invaded every aspect of our life at the camp.

⊰◉⊱

This was the last time Ardith and I danced together. Before the year was over, we would be separated forever. My family would be sent to the Heart Mountain Relocation Center in Wyoming and Ardith's family would go to the Topaz Relocation Center in Utah. Ardith's ultimate goal was to travel to the East Coast to be with Hanako, her older sister. Our letters flew back and forth for months. Then they stopped.

Months after our dance in the dust storm a letter came from Hanako telling me that Ardith had died from an unknown disease. When I read that, I rushed outdoors, stumbling and looking at the barbed-wire fence in the foreground. I raised my clenched fists into the air and shouted "Ardith" in anguish. A strong wind swooped down, picking up the fine dirt and sent it surging through the air, blinding me. I took cover behind the closest barrack and crumpled to the ground, sobbing.

Eyes closed, I pictured Ardith's large beautiful eyes, her black shiny hair against her clear, creamy skin. *How beautiful and graceful she looked as she danced with me on the stage,* I thought. *I will never see her again.* Our dance in the searchlight was Ardith's last, and in that moment I decided it would be my last dance, too.

CHAPTER EIGHT

DIGNITY IN THE FACE OF HARDSHIP

Days of the week no longer mattered. The slow hours were broken up by the mess hall gong calling us to breakfast, then lunch, and finally dinner. I was tired all the time, so I slept a lot. Sleep felt like being awake and being awake felt like sleeping. When I was tired of lying on my cot, I would go outdoors and aimlessly wander around various blocks. I had little energy or interest in making friends or participating in any activity. My days simply came and went.

It was now August, three months since our evacuation from Vashon. One evening after dinner when I was feeling especially low and confused, I told Mama-san I wanted to talk to her in private. "Mama-san, when we get back to our apartment can we talk about the evacuation?"

Mama-san lowered her head and looked sideways into my eyes and said, "Of course." We walked briskly back to the empty apartment. Papa-san lingered at the mess hall visiting with friends from Vashon, and Yoneichi was busy cleaning up in the kitchen. Smoothing the skirt of her blue printed dress, Mama-san sat down on her cot and I plopped down opposite her on mine. Without a moment's hesitation I plunged into my dilemma.

"I thought I was being a good citizen and helping in the war efforts by going along with the evacuation process."

"Yes," Mama-san replied. "You were."

"But," I insisted, "instead of feeling good for having done my part and being rewarded, I feel double-crossed. I thought every American citizen was supposed to have life, liberty, and the pursuit of happiness. That's what we were told in school back home, but that isn't what we have here."

Mama-san listened thoughtfully as she usually did, then responded gently, "Mary-san, we are in the middle of something that is much bigger than any of us. America is at war in many parts of the world. Things are difficult for lots of people everywhere."

"I don't care! I don't like it here!" I choked up as I tried to make my point. "There's nothing to do here! I'm tired of the dust storms, these awful meals, no privacy! I don't like anything about this place! I thought we would be here for a short time, but now it's lasting forever!"

"I understand, but we are not the only ones suffering," Mama-san replied, still calm. "There is much misunderstanding and misery in all of the camps, I'm sure. This is the time for us to *gaman shimasho*—Be patient." Then she added, "*Shikata ga nai*—It cannot be helped. We must do our very best to do what seems right every day."

"But I don't want to wait," I snapped back. "I'm tired of waiting. I want to go home now. I want to get away from this awful place." Hot tears stung my eyes.

Mama-san dropped her eyes for a moment, then looked up. She took a deep breath and said, "Some day the war will end and we will be able to go home. Then we will understand more. In the meanwhile, *shinbo shimasho*—Let us be patient. I know this is very hard for you, but it will all work out all right eventually. Have faith."

I listened to Mama-san and saw the concern on her face. I wanted to believe she was right, but I couldn't see an end to the dismal situation we were in. *What am I to make of my future?* I worried. I wanted to believe it would all work out sooner or later, but I couldn't get past the feelings of dread and anger whenever I looked at the soldiers in full combat uniform holding their guns, scrutinizing us from the watchtowers. Mostly what I couldn't get over—and couldn't talk about—was my deep fear that someday when I least expected it, the soldiers would come and kill us all.

The cultural norm among the *Isseis* and *Niseis* was to obey authority. Quietly accepting the order to evacuate was a survival technique. Resistance didn't seem like an option. However, our compliance would become the focus of criticism from later generations regarding our seemingly placid acceptance of all that we experienced.

.:◉:.

On September 14, 1942, Tri-State High School and an elementary school were opened at Tule Lake Internment Camp, as required by California law. I was now a senior and I looked forward to finishing high school, worried about what it would be like. Classes were set up according to a quarter system. I signed up for Typing I, English IV, Latin II, Problems of Democracy, Physical Education, Chemistry, and Senior Problems.

When I went to my English IV class, I was startled to see a white male teacher in the room. I looked around for books, pencils, paper, and other supplies. I didn't see anything. Embarrassed, I sat on one of the benches in the second row and waited awkwardly until some other students came and sat down, too. I wondered, *How are we going to learn anything when we don't have anything to work with?* The only person with a book was the teacher.

Later I found out there were other white teachers who came from "the outside" to teach some of the classes. Other teachers were *Niseis* who had their teaching credentials before they came to camp. But for both of these groups of teachers, it was difficult. All classes were held in barracks, and students sat on hard benches or on the floor. Initially, there were no supplies, no typewriters for typing classes, no supplies for chemistry lab, no blackboards or supplies for teachers.

In my typing class the teacher had drawn the keyboard on a large piece of paper and placed it at the front of the class. She taught us by pointing to letters on the "keyboard" and said, "Let's all type together, beginning with your little finger on your left hand. Type 'a,s,d,f,g.' With your right hand, begin with your index finger and type 'h,j,k,l, semicolon.'" We learned by "typing" on our laps in what must have been the quietest typing class in history. The chemistry class ran without a Bunsen burner, test tubes, chemicals, or other essential parts of a laboratory. We had to imagine mixing certain chemicals to produce certain outcomes. It was a challenging situation for everyone.

I respected these teachers and their desire to teach us despite such terrible odds. Of course, respecting teachers is what we always did. It was part of Japanese culture and emphasized in our home. Since education was extremely important in our family, I tried hard to overlook the limitations and learn what I could. I memorized the keyboard for typing class and practiced faithfully on my lap, making no errors, of course. Years later when I bought my own typewriter, I was surprised to see how easily my fingers found the correct keys.

One of the hardest parts of going to school took place first thing every morning when I stood outdoors with other students in front of an American flag. We had to place our hands over our hearts and recite, "I pledge allegiance to the flag of the United States of America…one nation indivisible…" I stumbled over the words "with liberty and justice for all." How strange it felt to be saying the Pledge of Allegiance after a forced evacuation to a prison camp.

After classes were out on the first day of school, I went straight home to talk with Mama-san. She was wearing a freshly ironed blue-and-white striped dress and sitting on her cot reading the newspaper when I entered our apartment.

"Do you know what we had to do this morning?" I asked heatedly as I dropped down on the cot across from her. I didn't think about how loud my voice must have sounded throughout the whole barrack.

"No, I have no idea." Mama-san looked up at me with interest in her eyes.

"We had to pledge allegiance to the American flag," I fumed. "I could see the barbed-wire fence in the background. I don't think we should have to do that here, do you?" I asked bitterly. Of course, there had been hundreds of times that I enthusiastically repeated the pledge back home, but we all did it without giving a thought to what it meant.

Mama-san glanced down and was thoughtful for a minute. Finally she lifted her eyes and said, "I can see your point. It's difficult to pledge your allegiance to a country that treats us this way, isn't it? What do you think you should do about it?"

I gathered all my strength and did something I never would have considered doing before. We didn't use swear words in our family but I steeled myself and blurted out, "Well, I'd really like to tell them they're full of bullshit and not say the Pledge of Allegiance!"

Right away I knew I had gone too far. Mama-san's body stiffened, her lips parted in surprise. It was the first time I had ever approached her in what she might think was a tantrum. Swearing meant losing one's temper, but I wanted her to know how mad I felt. Her eyes widened as she searched my face. A heavy stillness descended on the room, each of us lost in our thoughts. I could see her searching for just the right words. Soon her face relaxed and her eyes softened as she said, "Yes, you could do that. And what would that do?"

"It would make me feel a whole lot better."

"Yes, I'm sure it would." She cocked her head to one side, glanced past me for a moment and grew very still. When she finally spoke she raised her eyebrow and said softly, "But would it change anything?"

Her question disoriented me. I hunched my shoulders and looked at the floor to think about that a minute before I finally looked up. It was my turn to choose the right words. "I don't know if anyone else feels the same way I do. And even if they did, I'm not sure they'd do anything about it right now anyway." In a much quieter tone I added, "I don't know, I suppose not."

"You're probably right. I don't think it would change a thing either," Mama-san agreed. "You know there are times to *gaman*—be patient and persevere. This is one of those times."

Pondering this for awhile with all the feelings whirling around inside of me, I finally said, "That's going to be awfully hard to do," and fell silent. I didn't want to make a big fuss over this with my mother. A part of me knew she was right. She was so wise, but in my heart I didn't want to *gaman*. I kept thinking, *This isn't right! They shouldn't make us do it!*

In her youth Mama-san had studied ancient Japanese history. Her familiarity with Japan's history gave her the ability to look beyond this war camp and to see the bigger picture. While everyone else was caught in the suffering of the moment, she knew that with time, these events would make a different kind of sense.

"Let me tell you a story, Mary-san," she said, taking my hand. "You remember our discussion a few years ago about a beautiful female sun goddess named *Amaterasu Omikami?* She is still an important deity in Japan and considered an ancestor of the Imperial Family. She had a beautiful garden in heaven. The birds sang happily and the flowers bloomed beautifully.

"One day her mischievous younger brother, *Susanoo,* the god of storm, came by and wreaked havoc in her garden. In her shock and disbelief, *Amaterasu* went into seclusion in a cave behind a heavy rock door, taking all the sunshine with her. Darkness descended upon the world; it became cold and depressed. People became ill; unhappiness was everywhere.

"Finally other gods decided that life could not go on this way. One of the goddesses decided to dance to bring cheer back into the world. She persuaded the musicians and drummers to join her. As she danced and the music became louder and louder, *Amaterasu* came to the doorway of her cave to see what was going on. One of the strongest gods grabbed her and pulled her from the cave bringing the sunshine back into the world with her. Joy and happiness and health returned. Everyone was happy again."

As Mama-san came to the conclusion of the tale, she gave my hand a little squeeze. I looked at her graying, wavy hair softly framing her face as she looked at me with the clearest and kindliest gaze I had ever seen. She nodded and with her gentle smile, a dimple in each cheek deepened and crinkle lines spread out from the corner of each eye. In that moment I felt enveloped in her love, and my doubts quieted. Mama-san and her story had lifted me out of this time and terror into a world beyond war, a calm and serene world—the world of her love and hope. I took a deep breath as my anger dissipated. *Some day I will be able to see things differently,* I told myself. *We will go on.*

My mother tried hard to understand my point of view before expressing hers. Rarely did I see her get upset about anything we did or lose her temper when she had to correct our behavior. Her conversations were full of appreciation: a cool breeze on a hot day, the fragrance of carnations in bloom, the taste of good vegetables and fruit fresh from our garden, the enjoyment of interesting conversation, the times for relaxation. She consistently chose to look at life from a positive point of view. With my mother's guidance, I knew I had to think this issue through until I could come to some objectivity that I did not have at the moment. For now I had to trust what Mama-san said, even though I couldn't see an end to our plight.

◦◦◦

Every day we were in our drab room with our four army cots and a potbellied stove in the middle of our space. Our suitcases served as bedside stands. Aside from a crude table that Papa-san had made with scrap lumber he found among some discarded wood, and some nails pounded into the wall by the door for our coats, our room was bleak and bare. To make it a little more cheerful, Mama-san had purchased some fabric from the cooperative canteen at the prison camp and hand-sewed some curtains with bright red and yellow flowers with green leaves on a white background. She also made a curtain for the front of a crate that we could use as a cupboard.

But every evening when I looked at the one light bulb screwed into a ceramic socket on the end of the long cord hanging from the ceiling, I felt jarred. *How little light there is in my life right now,* I lamented. For long stretches I just sat on my bed and stared at the bare bulb.

Looking at the light reminded me of home, of the beautiful table lamp with a *shoji* lampshade that Mama-san brought from Japan. Each evening when she turned the lamp on, I would look at the warm glow of the light and the moths that circled hypnotically. It was pleasant and peaceful; I was happy then.

My memories became my haven from the ugliness of the camp. A typical summer day on Vashon began at dawn with Mama-san starting up the wood stove and putting the coffeepot on. The fragrant aroma of coffee would float up the stairs to my bedroom. From my warm bed I would hear Mama-san's pleasant voice calling, "Yoneichi-san, Mary-san, it's time to get up." I'd hop out of bed, jump into my clothes, and eat a hearty breakfast of scrambled eggs, two pieces of toast with strawberry jam, and cocoa. As a teenager I began a summer day by picking strawberries until pickers from around the island arrived. Later, Yoneichi would drive his truck down to the ferry and pick up more hired help who came from Seattle. Most of them were young white people, but there were a few blacks, an occasional Native American family, and some older men and women.

As help arrived, I showed the pickers where to begin their work and then walk around the rows of berries to supervise. Occasionally, I would squat down beside them and help fill their boxes with berries while we carried on a conversation about their family or their animals. They loved it when I'd pick with them because they all knew I would help fill up their boxes quicker. Some of the pickers brought their children every year and I loved watching them grow.

The days were long and hard under the summer sun at home, but the companionship with the pickers was wonderful. Every morning around 10:00 Papa-san would distribute butterscotch candy, Tootsie Rolls, peppermints, and other kinds of candy to everyone for a mid-morning snack to break up the long day.

I was not the only one who thought often about Vashon. One night as I was lying on my hard cot, Yoneichi came to bed. "Still awake?" he whispered.

"Yeah."

"Whatcha thinking about?" he asked, as he flopped down on the cot next to mine.

"Home."

"Yeah, I figured," he said. "I think about it a lot, too. We'd be finishing up trimming and tying up the loganberry canes right about now, if we were back on the farm."

Talking with Yoneichi, I realized I even missed the fights. There were times when Yoneichi and I would get into an argument about some silly little thing. Sometimes I would get so mad I'd plow into him and pummel him good. There were times when we would end up on the ground with him on the bottom and me on top pounding away at him until he'd had enough. Then he would flip me over on my back, sit on my belly as he straddled me with his knees and pinned my upheld arms against the ground, saying, "That's enough." Then he'd let me up. He usually knew when it was time to stop.

Usually our parents let us work things out in our own way. They knew we cared about each other, but one time he went a bit too far. We had had the usual sibling quarrel earlier that hadn't been resolved completely. It had to do with my backing up the tractor. Yoneichi thought I didn't do it right. We had returned to the house and I was taking a drink at an outdoor water faucet. He couldn't resist giving me a shove from behind. My head shot forward and the bridge of my nose struck the galvanized pipe. I bled profusely, frightening both of us. Mama-san came running and held a cloth to my nose to stop the bleeding. She scolded Yoneichi for being so careless and rough. I don't think he ever forgot that.

Home. I couldn't stop thinking about it and the natural beauty of Vashon. I loved to look to the east in the morning and watch the changing hues of pink on Mount Rainier. In the evenings the setting sun painted the western sky with a scarlet brush that gradually turned reddish-blue, then blue and drifted into a deep purple before it finally faded away. As thousands of stars emerged, a peace descended upon the land at nightfall. Before I went to sleep, I would get into a tub of warm water and soak luxuriously for as long as I wished. Home was where I felt safe.

That whole world had dissolved like a mirage. Now, the only reason to get up in the morning was to go to classes and do the chores I had signed up for. I tried to shut out the sound of people walking and talking as they passed outside our barrack. In the depths of despair, I became preoccupied with the mundane. Each evening I listened to the harsh voice of the woman down in the end apartment yelling at her child to pick up his clothes or brush his teeth or go outside and play. And in our own living space there was always the endless job of cleaning up after wind storms.

I tried to study hard and stay up with my classes but time hung over me, empty and meaningless; there seemed no point in living. I didn't have the energy to think about the future, I just felt trapped. Imagining the time when I would get out seemed impossible. I often thought, *When will I begin a normal life again? Will I ever get to go to college? When will I have the freedom to come and go as I please?* It wouldn't be until years later that I would realize how deeply the events of this period scarred me. At the time I went through the motions of the routine without really knowing who I was.

As was common for the oldest son in the Japanese culture, Yoneichi had been encouraged to be assertive and initiate contact with others. As the daughter, I was more retiring and supportive. In our new environment Yoneichi continued to reach out. He would go off and find others with whom to play Ping-Pong, volleyball, baseball, or just talk. It was easy for him to make friends and move among the young and old. I envied him. For me, it seemed difficult to get hold of anything meaningful. Whenever I wasn't in school, I spent most of my time in our barrack sleeping or daydreaming, withdrawn from the world. It was a world I needed to escape. Mama-san became concerned.

One night I awakened and overheard my parents talking. Mama-san said softly, "I'm worried about Mary-san. She seems so miserable and quiet."

"Yes," Papa-san replied. "I've noticed it, too."

"This experience seems to be overwhelming her," Mama-san added.

I wondered, *Do they know I am awake listening to their conversation? Are they having this talk for my benefit or for themselves?* I wasn't sure. I held my breath as I listened, afraid they might judge me. Perhaps they might be disappointed in me and say, "I thought Mary-san would do better than this." Or, "Mary-san is not as strong as we thought." I was scared. *Am I good enough?*

Papa-san let out a long breath. "I wish we could ease it for her. This is Mary-san's first taste of *haiseki*—prejudice. It's a big dose to swallow all at once." He was silent for a moment, then added thoughtfully, "If she can just get through this, an experience like this could make her into a stronger person."

Suddenly it struck me that he had faced prejudice far worse than I had ever experienced. I was facing a test. I asked myself, *Will I do something to shame my family and myself? Will I fail them?*

"I hope she can learn from this. I'd like to see her develop strength so that she can face whatever will come in her life," Mama-san replied.

Papa-san sighed again. "You and I know we're not alone in this. We know that God is even here, but life brings different kinds of pain to everyone, and each of us has to find our own way to cope."

"That's true, but it's so sad to watch," admitted Mama-san. "She is suffering so much and it's because you and I are Japanese. Mary-san had no choice in the matter. I know it does no good to look at it that way, but still, it makes my heart ache." Her voice broke.

I, too, struggled with my own emotions of anger and grief. Hearing how they felt, how could I blame them? I just felt sorry for myself. And yet, scared. I wondered, *What will I become in this terrible place?*

"Yes, I know," Papa-san replied gently, "but that's the way it is. We have to go on from here. Mary-san has to get used to being with our people— right here, right now. It would be different if she had grown up in California where *haiseki*—prejudice by the *hakujin*—white people—is more obvious. The Japanese there got used to it and figured out how to band together for moral support to look out for their own interests. We thought we were so lucky living on Vashon where our kids were protected. If we had lived in California, this would not be such a shock to her."

As I listened to their conversation in Japanese I realized again how formally they were speaking to one another. Not all Japanese families spoke this way, but it was my parents' way of caring for their family as well as others. I was amazed at how they could be so optimistic and strong at a time when it was so easy to complain and criticize the government. At the time I thought they were just being patient, but looking back I see that their dignity and inner strength were bone-deep in their character. Dignity was what defined who they were. Each of them had made a decision to face hardship when they left their homeland, but it pained them to see me facing hardships I had never chosen.

"Yes, I know you're right," Mama-san said. "We had it so good on Vashon. Now we have to figure out how to help Mary-san gain strength and perspective. If we succeed, she'll be much better off now and later. We *must* show her that we understand her pain and care greatly for her."

Papa-san nodded, "I agree. This experience is agonizing for her. I know we can't shield her completely, but this is where our life is right now. She needs to develop some perspective. Living like this in camp won't last forever."

"Yes, this whole experience is so overwhelming, so much bigger than our family," added Mama-san. "We've got to help her learn to understand what's happening and why. The best we can do is to tolerate the pain and confusion and eventually to forgive those that caused this to happen. Let's look for ways to help her."

With that they said *"oyasumi nasai*—goodnight" to each other and settled in to sleep. In the quiet the tension in my chest subsided. My parents were keeping the world solid for me. I didn't feel so alone anymore. I told myself, *If they can handle it, I can handle it.* Tears flowed freely down my cheeks and onto my pillow. The knot in my stomach released. *How lucky I am to have them for my parents.* In a world so mixed up, they were very clear about who they were. Their faith that it would all work out was profound. Their love was stronger than my fear.

I finally drifted off into the first restful sleep since we left home. Years later as I reflected on this conversation between my parents, I realized what a gift they had given me. We were all in this together. Bathed in their unconditional love and respect, my fear and depression decreased. They had given me a future, a model for my life.

CHAPTER NINE

COLLECTING SEASHELLS AT TULE LAKE

The following Saturday morning Mama-san said, "Mary-san, I was talking to one of the ladies in the restroom. She told me there is a rich supply of shells about two blocks from here. There are shells everywhere and in such abundance. Let's go and see how many we can find, *neh?*—all right?"

Still in bed after missing breakfast, I looked up at her and was touched by the concerned look on her face. I didn't want to get out of bed, but I wanted to do something to reassure her I'd be okay. Thinking about my parents' conversation I had overheard two nights before, I agreed.

We started a daily, early morning ritual of shell collecting before the heat of the day. I was surprised to see many other women and girls searching, too. Perhaps we were all looking for beauty or something that spoke of other times and survival.

About 13,000 years ago Tule Lake was a freshwater lake, but now it was bone-dry sediment and silt with thousands of tiny seashells mixed in, ancient remnants of a diverse and rich geographic era. As we looked for shells, it was easy to move the dirt from side to side. A handful of lake sediment might contain as many as thirty shells. Most of them were spiral-shaped, white, and tiny, about one-sixteenth of an inch long. I later had them identified as a kind of pebblesnail or *Fluminicola*. There were also a few ram's horn snails, freshwater pea clam shells, and beige-colored pondsnail shells with much larger spirals.

One morning I absentmindedly scooped some dirt and uncovered a scorpion. I jumped up and shrieked, "Look, a scorpion!" People came running over.

"Let's see," different ones asked as they huddled around me.

Squatting down in front of the critter I touched him with a stick. "Look, he's raising his tail again," I said. "He's ready to sting me. We'd all better be careful after this."

Everyone nodded as we all silently continued to look at the creature. Soon they lost interest and drifted back to where they had been searching.

I continued to watch the scorpion and touched his tan-colored body with a stick. Once more his tail shot up. This time he turned his body so his stinger pointed at the stick. Eventually he retreated into the loose dirt lowering his tail to conceal where he had gone.

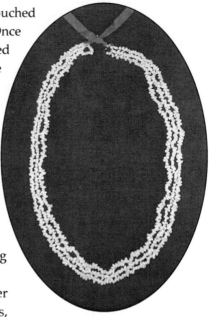

The sudden appearance of the scorpion became a metaphor for changes that would erupt in our internment and would create waves of uncertainty and danger. The first such jolt would burst upon us within the next three months and would be just as threatening as the scorpion's sting.

The *Tulean Dispatch,* the newspaper produced within the camp by internees, was an important resource for us. It was autumn of 1942 and we had been at Tule Lake for more than two months. It was reassuring to read that discussions were taking place to address the boredom

One of Mary's creations from Tule Lake shells, strung together with dental floss she bought at the camp's cooperative store.

that distressed us. The government did not provide funds for any recreational or adult education programs. So leaders in the community, including the block managers, came up with a plan that included sports, barrack gardens, various indoor activities such as art classes, and a variety of positive educational programs to stimulate us. The goal was to provide interesting, constructive activities for everyone and, in the process, avert juvenile delinquency, which was no small job for the nearly 19,000 internees.

All sorts of classes and activities were organized by volunteer internees. Because most of us had so little expendable cash, we pooled what we could contribute and a nonprofit cooperative store was established. Through this effort, we could buy needed supplies.

Almost any kind of class could be set up providing there was a need and a Japanese instructor available to teach it. Volunteers formed clubs to put on public dances in mess halls and develop community entertainment using local talent. Movies were brought in periodically. I paid ten cents each time to help pay for the rental of the films and to purchase projectors. *Hold Back the Dawn, The Count of Monte Cristo,* and *The Plainsman* are memorable for me.

For the athletically inclined, Japanese coaches established numerous tournaments for hardball, softball, tennis, track, Ping-Pong, judo, and sumo wrestling. There were teams for men and women, and there were always enthusiastic supporters.

Another important announcement made in the *Tulean Dispatch* was the establishment of church services for the internees. There were Buddhist Sunday school classes for the children and adult Sunday services. Although people came from all Protestant denominations, there was only one Tule Lake Union Church. It provided church services for adults, a high school fellowship, and Christian Youth Fellowship meetings. In addition to conducting multiple services for the large population, the ministers or priests provided critical counseling for both young and old related to the complexities of life in what was essentially a prison camp. It would be in this setting that I would later meet a woman who would significantly influence my life.

⚬⚙⚬

One bright Saturday morning as we were digging for shells, Mama-san said with great fondness, "I remember those times when my mother and I were doing things together, she would tell me old fairy tales. I'd like to share one of them with you now, Mary-san.

"This one is about a young man named Sentaro who lived a fairly comfortable life from the generous inheritance he had received from his father. But one day he became very fearful about dying; he could lose all he had. He wanted to live for at least two or three hundred years or more without any worries so he could really enjoy life. It became an obsession. He went to the local shrine every day and prayed to the gods to show him how to prevent death. On the seventh day the inner door of the shrine burst open and a voice spoke out of a brilliant cloud. It said, 'You are a foolish man. You don't know what you are asking. But to answer your prayer, I'll send you to the Land of Perpetual Life.'

"Sentaro got up on the back of a crane that magically appeared and they flew for days over land and water until they came to a remote island. Gazing around he noticed that people looked well off here; there was an abundance of everything. He found a place to stay and made himself comfortable. Gradually he noticed how different things were here. People had no fear of death. No one ever died. They had heard from priests who had come from India and China of a beautiful land of contentment called Paradise that could be reached only by dying. Many of them wanted to go there and did things that would, in another world, cause death, such as eating poisonous foods or drugs. But that did not release them from living in this Land of Perpetual Life. Sentaro thought it strange that the people here were tired of their lives and longed for something else. He knew he was happy to be here.

"Sentaro established a business and settled down to live the good life. Things went well for him. He worked hard, his business flourished, and time flew by for hundreds of years. He had good years and bad years, but overall, it was a very satisfactory life. Still, gradually it dawned on him that his life would always be the same. Then he understood what the people were talking about. Now it made sense to him.

"Remembering the god who had granted his first wish, he began to pray to him once more to be returned to his former home. The crane reappeared. Sentaro got on its back and they began their return journey. On the way a big storm arose and the bird and Sentaro plunged into the sea below. A big shark came and would have swallowed Sentaro, but he frantically prayed to the god to save him from immediate death.

"Abruptly Sentaro woke up screaming. He had fallen asleep in front of the shrine during his long prayers. He realized his wish for perpetual life meant everlasting boredom and recovery of his former life meant eventual death. How foolish, absurd, and unrealistic these wishes had been. This understanding freed him to live a good and useful life."

We were silent for the rest of the morning while we worked side by side. I knew there was a lesson in that story for me and I needed time to ponder what that might be. But whatever that message was, I could tell in the gentleness of her voice and the occasional glances she gave during the telling of the tale that Mama-san was keeping a steady, benevolent eye on me.

Thinking about Sentaro led me to take more interest in gathering shells and noticing others around us. As our supply of shells increased we saw information in the *Tulean Dispatch* of various craft classes being established in different places around camp. Amy Nagata, a girl from our ward, joined Mama-san and me and we began attending one of these classes.

A young woman named Chiyoko from California was one of our teachers. She seemed to have many ideas of what to do with the shells.

"One of the first things you must do is buy some bleach at the canteen and bleach the white ones. Leave the tan ones alone. We'll use those as is.

And while you're at the canteen, buy some dental floss and the thinnest needles you can get. Better get a thimble, too. You'll need it. When you've done that, come back and we'll get started making things."

At our first lesson, Chiyoko took one of the needles and threaded it with a long piece of dental floss. Putting a thimble on the middle finger of her right hand, "so I don't poke my finger," she added, she began to string each shell. I took over from there and made a long strand. I tied the ends of the floss together and was delighted to have made a single stranded necklace. By lining up several strands and twisting them together, I had made a multi-stranded necklace. I was very pleased with the results.

Over time some of the women would make stunning seashell necklaces, corsages, and other art pieces from their found shells. I made several necklaces and learned to make other things, too. I went back to the cooperative canteen and bought fingernail polish and other kinds of paint to brighten up the broaches and pins I made. With just a few pointers from Chiyoko I made flowers, bracelets, elaborate wall hangings, and many other original decorations. Mama-san, Amy, and I had fun working together making pretty things. In time I began to feel calmer, more content with myself. Most of my creations became gifts that I mailed to my former classmates and friends at the Vashon Methodist Church. Sending these along with letters was my way of staying connected with the outside world.

As I worked beside Mama-san during those quiet days, I reflected on what life had become. *Instead of being at home on Vashon working or making plans to finish high school and go on to college, here I am stringing these tiny shells one by one, and forming a necklace to hang around my neck.* It was as though I was piercing each experience, one by one, to form a necklace of memories. Years later the shells from Tule Lake would be one of only a few mementos from my time in internment camps.

ANSEL ADAMS

People line up in front of a mess hall at Manzanar Internment Camp.

SHARING STORIES

I n spite of the positive changes that had started to take place in my daily life, I still longed for my life on Vashon—free. It was always hardest at night when I was alone with my thoughts. Listening to the night sounds that had become so familiar, I often tossed in bed, unable to sleep, my stomach aching, and my feet cold. Shame and anger kept crowding in as we faced the daily indignities of being imprisoned. These thoughts and feelings threatened to overwhelm me. I was now convinced, *America will never accept me as a full-fledged American.*

Here I was in a self-contained community that didn't feel like a community at all. More and more I felt as if I were in prison. We had a hospital, post office, warehouse, offices, and schools, but it was all surrounded by a barbed-wire fence and guard towers. The only way out was through the guarded main entrance.

There was no place to be alone or to have a private conversation with anyone. Each block was set up according to an identical plan. A block had fourteen barracks, a mess hall, a recreation hall, laundry room, and separate bathrooms and shower rooms for men and women. There were approximately 260 people living in our block. Tule Lake Internment Camp's population peaked at 18,789 Japanese-Americans. The heat, the freezing cold, and the invasive dust storms told me that America had found a special hell for us. What had we done to deserve this treatment?

The injustice of it all haunted me: They had declared me guilty without giving me a chance to prove I had been a loyal and patriotic citizen—but loyalty to the government meant the betrayal of myself. In this new world I was sensitive to every nuance. I began to notice the differences between the life I had lived with white Americans and my life here in camp. The dissimilarities between the *Isseis* and the *Niseis* were becoming obvious. For the *Isseis*, group solidarity and maintaining meaningful parts of the Japanese culture had been essential for their survival. Most of the products and services used by the *Issei,* such as Japanese food, clothing, entertainment, language school, personal care, legal advice, and other services had been an established part of Japantown for many years. They did not exist in the same way here in camp.

Exposed to the norms of the white community back home, I began to feel disconnected in this environment. The differences were becoming more evident in the behaviors of other *Niseis* around me, too. For example, boys and girls were pairing off, something we never did back in our pre-war lives. Mealtimes were no longer time for the family to be together. I felt squeezed between two cultures. I had no guide to help me.

At times, I thought about Mama-san's story of Sentaro and my parents' discussion I had overheard that one night. I wondered, *What did she want me to learn from Sentaro's story?* The last chapter was yet to be written, and I could only speculate on how that chapter would read.

I often wondered how my parents viewed our situation. Whatever they felt, I never overheard them complain to each other or to anyone else. Wherever they walked they did so with erect postures, or they sat with others, listening sympathetically to their complaints. I never heard them contradict others' opinions or try to impose their own. The only thing I was certain about with my parents was their inner strength, their sensitivity to others' points of view, and their love for our family.

I suspected a great deal of their sensibility and detachment from our catastrophe came from the way they grew up in Wakayama-ken, near Osaka, Japan. I recalled Mama-san telling me that children are almost universally prized in Japan, just as the elderly are. Much attention is given to them as they grow up, and discipline is gently and carefully provided to help the youngsters become mature and productive people.

Mama-san lost both of her parents when she was young, so her brothers and sisters had great pity for their youngest sister and cared tenderly for her. Although girls were often confined to their homes, farms, or immediate neighborhood, they sent my mother to school in another geographic location far beyond where girls of that time normally went. Her education, especially in history, and her outside exposure set her apart from other girls in the early 1900s.

I wondered what Mama-san would have done with her life if she had remained in Japan. With the limited opportunities that women had in Japan at that time, I suppose her life would not have been that much different from life in America. She would have married and had children and made a living working the land. Powerful norms would have dictated how she lived her life, limiting her choices.

Instead, in America Mama-san faced a different set of obstacles, those of racism and the language barrier. She was drawn to this country by the promise of a better life for herself and her family and by her own sense of adventure. She accepted the long hours in the hot sun or on cold, rainy days as part of the experience.

Mama-san always demonstrated her ability to see the big picture in a very practical way. It was amazing to see her care for our family and fifteen boisterous Japanese-American teenage boys who lived in our barn temporarily converted into a dormitory. During the summer picking season my father recruited these boys from families whose parents taught in the Japanese language school in Seattle. The boys stayed on the farm from early June into August each year. With some assistance from me, Mama-san cooked hearty, tasty meals, full of fresh vegetables and fruits from the garden. She washed the kids' clothes and managed all the details in running a household during the hectic harvest time. On top of all that hard work she still graciously welcomed the kids' parents when they came for a brief visit every weekend.

I often wondered what Mama-san's life would have been like if she had had more opportunity or had been born at a time when women had more life choices. Perhaps she might have become a social activist on behalf of the poor or worked for women's rights or some other cause. She might have had her own business or become a prominent professor in an esteemed university. Perhaps my mother might have had her own car, her own apartment, and her own title in a major corporation. But she never spoke about those possibilities, and never once did I hear her complain about any of life's circumstances. She would view the harsh reality of our current life in an internment camp from the perspective of one who had a larger-than-life view—one that would benefit us in the present and in the years to come. Even in the darkest days, Mama-san always found something to be grateful for.

One day when Amy Nagata and I were out taking a walk, we started talking about the kids from California. "We may all be *Niseis*," I said, "but it's like they're from Timbuktu. They're rowdy and use a lot of slang. I'm not used to that."

Amy giggled. "Have you seen those zoot suits those guys wear? I can't believe they have the nerve to dress like that." She hesitated. "But it's kind of neat, don't you think?"

I laughed. "Maybe, but you'll never get me to dance the jitterbug to that loud music like they do." To me, the Californians seemed boisterous and overconfident. It may have been my imagination but I thought they looked darker and taller than us, too. I figured it was from all the sunshine California is noted for.

One Sunday I met a girl from California named Michi. We sat next to each other during one of the church services and started chatting as we left. As we compared notes, I was interested to learn we had similar childhoods, even though she was from California and I was from Washington.

"We got some neighbors to promise to take care of our farm. I'm hoping we can go back there when this is all over," Michi explained.

"That's just like what we did!" I said, fascinated. "We have a man staying in our house, but I'm concerned because the farm is really too much for one person to manage."

Michi became quite animated when she talked about her cousin. "I'm really worried about my cousin, Emi, and especially my Uncle George. He was a fisherman and lived on Terminal Island."

"Where is that?"

"It's just off the coast near Los Angeles," Michi explained. "Not far away is the Long Beach Naval Station and that's probably what got the government nervous about the Japanese living there."

"We had a similar situation with some Japanese living on Bainbridge Island in Puget Sound, which is near the Bremerton Naval Base," I explained. "They were the first group to be evacuated from the Puget Sound area. They had to leave on March 30."

Michi nodded. "The FBI picked up Uncle George right after Pearl Harbor because he had been a leader in the Japanese community for years. All the other *Issei* men with fishing licenses were picked up, too."

"All the other men, too? Wow, that sounds like a lot of men," I responded. "The only man from Vashon who was picked up was the president of our association. I was really scared they would come for my father because he was the secretary for so many years."

"Some families left Terminal Island and moved in with relatives in Los Angeles, thinking they would probably have to leave the Island sometime anyway," Michi continued. "It turns out they were the smart ones. Around mid-February, all the remaining families, including Emi's, were told they had to leave in only forty-eight hours. Forty-eight hours! And they were the first ones to evacuate, so they didn't even have time to buy suitcases or anything.

Can you just imagine the panic?" Michi looked directly at me for a moment. "Think about it," she added. "First they took away the fathers. Then the mothers with their children had just forty-eight hours to settle the families' work of a lifetime. How absolutely outrageous!" Frustration and anger clouded Michi's pretty face. I found it hard to find words to comfort her.

"Forty-eight hours?" I asked in disbelief, stopping in my tracks. "That's outrageous! We only had eight days, but at least we knew what was coming."

"That's right, it was crazy," Michi recalled. "There was no word about where they were supposed to go. They had to leave practically everything: their boats, their homes, everything they had gained over a lifetime." She shook her head. "They couldn't stay, they couldn't take what was theirs, they had no place to go, and they had forty-eight hours to leave! What a God damn mess!"

"That really is bad!" I exclaimed, shocked by her profanity.

"It was awful." She stopped and turned toward me, lowering her voice. "And it gets worse. In the midst of the crisis, some *hakujins*—white guys— show up with their trucks. They offered to buy furniture and stuff from these families for pennies! My aunt was so desperate, she sold these vultures her dining room set and all of her appliances for only forty dollars! Chairs, a table, refrigerator, stove, washing machine, all practically brand-new! Some people even sold their beautiful antiques from the old country." Her eyes flashed in anger. "I mean, what was she supposed to do? She didn't know what to prepare for, and she might have needed cash just to eat, for all she knew. Besides, if she left that stuff in the house, someone might just have taken it anyway. She had to sell for whatever they would give her. It was highway robbery!"

This conversation really opened my eyes. Now I understood why the Californians were so mad. I would be, too, if I had been treated that way.

I told Michi about some of our desperate efforts around that same time. When we realized we were going to be forced to evacuate, the Vashon Japanese-American Club sent a scout out to see if we could voluntarily relocate to an area in Idaho. However, our scout reported that the people there were unwilling to lease, rent, or sell any land to any Japanese. Even the local Japanese there didn't want us—and with good reason. The Idaho governor indicated that he was considering having the evacuation orders extended to include his state should any out-of-state Japanese try to make a home there. "It was another piece of disappointing news," I told Michi. "We were not welcomed on the coast and we were not welcomed inland."

Michi and I sat in silence for a long time. I stared at the rows of barracks and thought about the thousands of us struggling to find meaning in the things happening to us. Countless times I asked myself, *"Why?"* There were no answers. All I could say to Michi was, "Time will tell, won't it? We'll just have to wait and see. Thanks for telling me about what happened in California. This is all news to me."

⁓◉⁓

Eighty percent of the Japanese population on the West Coast lived in California. Most Japanese were highly productive, successful people in whatever work they pursued. As a result they became the brunt of some non-Japanese people's fears, envy, and prejudice. The war provided the excuse for removing the Japanese from the West Coast and to eliminate competition and literally take over whatever gains the Japanese had made. Realizing what extraordinary sacrifices the first-generation Japanese had gone through, this fact made me profoundly sad and angry. I scolded myself, *How protected and naïve you have been and how callous your judgment is of the Japanese you call "those Californians."*

Sharing conversations with other people at the camp helped me. Their experiences led me to realize that even though I was still in camp, I was better off than they were. I felt guilty. I decided, *I better snap out of it and quit feeling so sorry for myself.*

When I wasn't in classes or working in the mess hall, I began helping in a variety of places. I started in the physical education program for grade school children. I liked being with the little kids, cheering them on, giving tips on how to hold a bat or hit the ball. I also helped in classes for the kids with poor eyesight by reading to many of the students. This school was named for Helen Keller. Helping these children made me realize I still had many things to be thankful for, including my eyesight. The cumulative effect of all these events caused me to gradually come out of my shell and focus on the changes taking place around me.

One day before dinner I heard a neighbor talking to his sons, "Bobby and Hiroshi, I want you to come and eat with us."

"Oh, Papa," the twelve-year-old Hiroshi protested, "none of the other kids eat with their folks."

"I don't care what other people do. This family is very important to us. I insist you do as I say," the father demanded heatedly.

"Oh heck! That's old country stuff," Hiroshi insisted. "I'm not going todo that anymore. I'm going to eat with my friends." He started to move away.

"Me too," echoed Bobby, his ten-year-old brother. "It's more fun. We'll come home to sleep, though." He dashed off with his brother.

"Hiroshi! Bobby! Stay here!" But the boys ran off to the opposite side of the mess hall to be with their friends. The parents watched helplessly.

"I don't know what this generation is coming to," the father commented quietly as he shook his head and watched his boys run across the huge mess hall. The mother was obviously worried, too. Looking around, it was becoming obvious that some children's groups were replacing families where parents and children used to sit together. Talking loudly and laughing, children jostled for positions near their friends. This became common during meal times.

This led to other changes. Children began moving from block to block, eating their meals with their friends at different mess halls instead of with their own families or in their own mess halls. The strongest among them became leaders. There were visible effects of Americanization beginning to appear among the young. Some teenage boys and girls began walking through the camp openly holding hands with each other. There were girls who wore very short skirts and T-shirts, popular during World War II, much to the astonishment and dismay of some *Issei* women. Jitterbugging to loud music became a common occurrence in the recreation halls. Everyone was exposed to different ways of doing things. Established traditions were unraveling. Mama-san didn't say much, but I'm sure she observed these changes and was disturbed, too.

At age seventeen, I watched these changes from a distance. I was curious, but I was not ready to join in—not yet. One day as I was cleaning up in the mess hall, a man about twenty-five approached me and asked, "Do you know how to play card games?"

"No, I don't."

"Would you like to learn how?"

I thought a minute. Playing cards was one of the taboos in our family. It ranked with smoking, drinking, gambling, and dancing as behaviors we were supposed to stay away from. Remembering that, I said, "I'm not supposed to do that."

"What's wrong with playing a little card game?" the young man persisted.

"I don't know. I suppose my folks consider it the same as gambling."

"Well, there's no betting involved," he reassured me. "It's a lot of fun. It's just a game. Why don't you try?"

Boy, I could sure use a little fun right now, I thought. *Maybe it wouldn't hurt to try it a little bit.* "I guess I could try it," I responded hesitantly.

"Okay, I'll go home and get a deck of cards and bring it over to your place," the young man said. "Where do you live? My name's Richard, by the way."

I told him and then I had to go home and tell Mama-san what I had done. She lowered her head and looked at me hesitantly. I could tell that she was not pleased, but she didn't say anything.

Up until this time I had never had a date with a boy. On Vashon the Japanese teenagers didn't date or go to dances at all. They might have done that in the urban areas like Seattle, but in the country, dating came much later.

Richard came over a few times and we played different kinds of card games. My parents were polite, but didn't approve. I could tell by their cool manner toward him, but I decided I enjoyed playing cards. It was fun to be doing something different and with a man.

One night not long after we started playing cards, Richard said, "There's a jitterbug session at the mess hall next Saturday evening. Would you like to go with me?"

Although jitterbugging was the rage, I did not know how to do it. I watched the kids whirling and swinging and laughing like they were having a great time, but the adults complained about how loud the music was and how the kids "just jump all over the place." It looked like fun to me, but I was hesitant about going. I told Richard I didn't know how to jitterbug, but he said, "That's okay. I'll show you. It's great fun!"

I went to Mama-san and asked, "Mama-san, Richard asked me to go with him to the dance this evening. Can I go?"

Mama-san paused, looked at me sideways, and quietly said, "Mary-san, I wish you wouldn't."

"How come, Mama-san? I know you and Papa-san don't approve of card playing and dancing, but why are they wrong?"

"Card playing isn't good because it causes one to waste a lot of time and can lead to gambling and loss of money," Mama-san explained patiently. "Papa-san saw that happen to some of his friends, and he vowed that he would not get snared like that. Besides," she added, "we think dancing is not a good activity because the closeness of the bodies and excitement of the music can lead a couple to have sex when that should be reserved for after marriage. And didn't you mention that Richard was a divorced man?"

"Yes, he is, but what difference can that make to me?"

"A divorced person is one who couldn't maintain a successful relationship, and marriage is for life," Mama-san answered. "I'm concerned about his influence on you."

I didn't like what I heard. I could feel the resistance building inside of me. Even though I didn't want to disappoint her, I felt like I just had to break out of the mold I was in. "Mama-san, I know you don't want me to go, but I want to do things like other kids my age," I insisted. "I'm tired of having nothing fun to do." Speaking louder than I intended, I blurted out, "I want to go and I am going." Tossing my head and without looking back, I left the apartment.

I went with Richard to the recreation hall where quite a few young people had already gathered. The music was blaring, and everybody was talking and laughing. A few couples were already in the center of the dance floor gyrating. We sat down at a table. I had mixed feelings of excitement and reservation. After awhile a lot of couples got up and started dancing. Richard offered his hand and I took it, saying, "Remember, I don't know how to dance."

"That's okay, I'll show you." We bobbed around to the beat of the music, but I felt like I had two left feet. I kept looking at his as he twisted and turned and rocked back and forth. I tried to keep up. I thought, *Here I am at the rec hall, my body bouncing to the beat of the music, but I can't make my feet go the same way as Richard's.* I felt stiff as a board, my eyes felt cross-eyed as I tried to watch his feet and tried to make mine go in the same direction as his. I only succeeded in stepping forward when he wanted me to twirl around. I thought I was supposed to twirl around when he wanted me to step away from him. I felt like everybody in the room was looking and smirking at me.

When the music finally ended I was relieved. When Richard looked the other way, I fled back home feeling defeated and embarrassed. I crept back into the apartment and didn't look at Mama-san or say a word. I had to admit to myself, *I don't fit into that crowd, but where do I fit?* I never went to another dance throughout our internment camp days, but I always wished I could have learned to dance.

Days later as I was walking home from the mess hall, I overheard a heated conversation between a girl and her mother in one of the apartments. It made me wonder if someone may have heard my discussion with my mother through the thin walls in the barrack. I felt embarrassed. The mother was pleading with her daughter.

"Nobu, please don't go down to Kenji's place. He is not good for you."

"I'll be okay, Mom, he's not so bad."

But the mother spoke cautiously, "You know he has lots of girlfriends and he drinks and smokes too much. He may get you into trouble."

"Mom, don't worry so much. I'll be okay," the girl responded. "And I don't care what you think!" As she burst out of her apartment she hurled back, "Anyway, I'm going."

Another afternoon I saw a teenager storm out of her place muttering, "Why does Grandma always have to question everything I do and say? She makes me sick!"

The strong family structure was crumbling. The young were rebelling and there didn't seem to be much that could be done about it. Everything was changing and becoming more difficult for everyone, especially for the *Isseis*. I felt myself being tugged in so many directions. All of this was compounded by the bottom line reality that we were prisoners and our normal lives were in limbo.

In the midst of these conflicts going on about us, I thought about my mother's favorite concept of *on*—the Japanese sense of obligation to family, a debt of gratitude and respect for each member of the family. It had always been a part of our lives and here in camp it would be tested by the changes taking place all around us. I had to figure out how much tradition I wanted to keep in my life. *Where do I fit in? How do I feel about this?* As time went along, *on* would really be put to the test as additional pressures began to bear down on all of us.

The *Tulean Dispatch* was now a well-established part of camp life. My parents enjoyed reading the news in Japanese, and Yoneichi and I pored through the English section. I always read the sermon titles for the church services, and I attended church regularly.

At the close of church services on a warm October day, I met a surprise visitor, a Caucasian woman named Zola Lenz. She was forty-five years old, tall and heavy-set with graying brown hair and clear, hazel eyes. She wore a lightweight tweed suit and sensible shoes. Zola was from a Methodist church in Hicksville, Ohio.

She approached me like a tank in battle, hand outstretched. "Hello, I'm Zola Lenz. What's your name?" I shook her hand and told her my name.

"I'm a housewife," she began, "and I'm here for a few weeks on vacation. I heard about the internment camps and wanted to learn more. I met Reverend Yasui and he suggested I attend the service today. I'm looking for someone who can tell me about life here. Would you be willing to do that?"

"Sure, I'd be happy to," I responded. "Of course, you understand that we are all different and come from different parts of the western United States so our experiences are bound to be different."

"Yes, I understand."

We found a couple of chairs off to the side of the room where the service had been held. I told her where I was from and then asked, "What do you want to know?" I wondered how I had become so much more bold and worldly that I could sit and talk with a stranger without asking my parents' permission.

"Tell me about your family, what brought them to this country and how they made a living before being evacuated."

"Okay." I took a deep breath, thinking, *What can I say to make this white woman understand how deeply shaken my world has become?* I wanted her to know about our family—our dignity, our history, and our uniqueness. We were not spies for the Emperor, nor were we faceless, yellow-bellied soldiers as portrayed in newspapers and magazines.

"My father was born in Wakayama-ken, Japan, on September 11, 1877, the fourth of five sons in a farming family. Not being the first-born son he was free to venture out."

"If your father had been the first-born son, he would not have come to the United States?" she asked with great interest.

"That's right. It would have been his responsibility to carry on the family name, take over the family farm, and care for his parents in their old age. That's the tradition."

Zola smiled and nodded. I took courage and continued.

"I know nothing about his early years," I went on. "I think his first trip to the United States took place in 1898 when he was twenty-one. He came to this continent as many other single Oriental men did, and learned a lot as he went along. He went first to Hawaii and worked for several years on one of the sugar cane farms as an indentured laborer. After he had worked off his debts, he worked in the coal mines, first in the Klondike, Alaska, and then in Cle Elum, Washington. In Alaska he and his co-workers barely escaped a lynch mob because of a warning from a white worker."

Zola leaned forward and frowned as she asked, "What? Some people wanted to kill him? Why?"

"I don't know. I suppose they didn't like the Japanese. But this wasn't the only time things like this happened to him," I explained. "Like the Chinese who came to America before them, the Japanese were not allowed to become citizens or vote."

"They were barred from citizenship and the right to vote just because they were Asians?" she asked.

"Yes."

Shaking her head, Zola lamented. "It's not right that some people could become citizens and others couldn't just because of racial backgrounds. We're all from immigrant families. My ancestors came from Russia."

Hearing Zola's sympathy made me feel great. She was the first white person to hear my story since the evacuation and I felt affirmed and supported.

"Right, but that's the way it was," I continued. "Another big problem was that Japanese immigrants weren't allowed to own property because of the Alien Land Law that was passed in 1913."

"They were barred from becoming citizens with the right to vote, and then they were denied the right to own land?" Zola asked, incredulous. "This is absolutely absurd."

"There's more," I said, buoyed by her interest. "Eventually all immigration by the Japanese was barred through the Japanese Exclusion Act of 1924. My father brought my mother over in 1922."

"Well, that was fortunate," Zola responded.

"You bet. The *Isseis* did not speak English and were not familiar with the way things were done in this country. They were forced to work at menial jobs that paid little. They had to save a long time before they had enough money to send away for a bride from Japan."

Leaning forward and cocking her head to one side, she said, "It's amazing they stuck it out."

I felt so knowledgeable as I talked with Zola. "They had to. There was no turning back. At the time of the evacuation the average age of the *Issei* men was sixty. The women they married were often much younger. They had children, the *Niseis,* born in this country, quite late in life. There is a whole generation missing between the two generations."

"Wow! That doesn't seem right," noted Zola. "But hang on a minute. You've used the terms *Issei* and *Nisei.* What do they mean?"

"The *Isseis* are people like my parents who were born in Japan, came to this country and became the first generation of Japanese in America. Those of us born here, like my brother and me, are called *Niseis,* the second generation in America.

"Although *Isseis* have lived in this country for decades, they kept many of the values and customs of Japan," I continued. "The *Niseis,* like myself, were born and raised here and are thoroughly Americanized."

"Oh, yes, the typical immigrant experience," Zola nodded, understanding the situation. "So there could be a cultural gap within the family?"

"Yes," I replied. "There can be if parents and children don't talk and share with each other. That's happening in some families now."

"What a pity."

"Yes, I agree." I shifted in my seat. So did Zola. The folding metal chairs were hard and uncomfortable. She seemed interested, so I continued, although I thought, *Mama-san will be wondering where I am.* But this conversation was too important. Suddenly, at seventeen, I was an expert in something with ideas worth hearing.

"Around 1919 Papa-san went to live and work on a truck farm for another immigrant, Mr. Yoshio Umani near Tacoma, Washington," I continued. "Before long, Mr. Umani had earned enough money and it was time to get married. He selected a woman from a picture bride album."

"A picture album?" Zola looked at me in disbelief.

"In the early days only young ambitious men came looking for work," I explained. "One way to find a Japanese wife was to pick one from an album showing photos of women eligible for marriage. The other method was to spend a lot of money and go back to Japan to find a bride. Most of the men chose the picture bride method. But whichever way was used, they had to ask a *baishakunin,* a person who served as a go-between or a matchmaker, to do the negotiating for him. Mr. Umani decided on the picture bride method."

Cocking her head to one side, Zola said, "I would think that would be hard on both of them to have someone else pick their mate for them."

"You'd think so here, but that was the custom in Japan," I noted with authority. "The family was important. Many times it worked out all right."

"Amazing," Zola commented thoughtfully as she gazed into the distance.

Most of the people had already left the church as we continued talking. I wondered, *Is Zola married? Does she have a mother-in-law of her own?*

"Yes, but Mr. Umani's chosen lady accepted his proposal," I continued. "In due time a son was born. One day Mr. Umani said to my father, 'Heisuke, don't you think it's time for you to have a wife, too?'

"My father agreed. But instead of using the picture bride album, he went back to Wakayama-ken, Japan and made arrangements for the selection and marriage to my mother. He wanted his bride to know about America and be willing to make her permanent home here."

"Your father knew what he wanted in a wife, didn't he?"

"Yes, he did. He was already forty-four years old. My mother, Mitsuno Horiye, was almost thirty." Then I told her the story of my mother's childhood before returning to the story of their marriage.

"The thought of marrying this stranger and leaving Japan to live in a foreign country didn't frighten her?" Zola asked as she cocked her head to one side.

"I guess not," I responded. "Once she mentioned that she had had some dreams about life in America and really wanted to see for herself. They left Yokohama, Japan, in March, 1922, and arrived in Seattle, Washington a little over two weeks later. She and Papa-san lived in a little house next to the Umanis' home until after my brother was born in July 1923. Then they moved to Seattle to a truck farm with the family of Mama-san's cousin. I was born there on January 23, 1925.

"Not long after that we moved to Vashon Island, Washington, which is located between Seattle and Tacoma in Puget Sound. My father eventually bought ten acres in the name of Mr. Umani's older son, to be held in trust until my brother came of age."

"Hold on, I don't get it," interjected Zola. "Why did he do that?"

I liked this woman. She really wanted to understand. "Because my father was not allowed to become a citizen and, therefore, could not legally own property."

"That's preposterous," she exclaimed.

I smiled. *Maybe some white Americans would get it,* I thought hopefully, *if we could tell our stories.* "I agree but that's the way it was. My brother and I are U. S. citizens because we were born in the United States. Soon Yoneichi will be twenty-one and old enough so the property will be transferred into his name. But this whole evacuation process has been just awful. The attack on Pearl Harbor turned our world completely upside down. I couldn't believe this could happen to us, especially because we are citizens—but here we are."

"What bothers you most about living in this camp?" Zola asked with great interest.

"Well, there are a number of things, like the monotonous food, the dust storms, the heat and the cold in these flimsy barracks. A big one is the lack of space—so many of us crammed into such tight quarters there is no privacy." After a moment's reflection I added, "I think the biggest problem is the bitterness simmering among a lot of people in all the camps over being evacuated and our having to live in these kinds of places."

Zola brought both hands up to her mouth. Her eyes widened. "What will you and your family do? Is there anything I can do to help you?"

"Thank you so much, I'm not sure what that would be. Each evening the four of us come together and share what we saw or heard during the day. That helps me a lot. It's hard to know where all of this is going, but we will have to deal with it as it happens."

Zola looked at her watch. "Oh dear! I'm running late." She stood up, extended her hand and said, "Will you write and keep me informed? I want to stay in touch with you. I would also like to share your story with my friends back in Ohio. Would that be all right with you? Most of the people in the Midwest don't have any idea what's going on."

Taking her hand in both of mine I felt touched and honored by her interest and concern. I said, "Yes, I'd like to stay in touch. Of course you can tell friends about what you saw and heard here. Thanks for listening. This has helped me a lot, too."

She turned and waved as she left the church. *Not all white Americans hate us,* I thought. I watched her walk out until I could no longer see her tweed jacket, wishing we could have talked even longer. Then I hurried home.

A letter of appreciation from Zola arrived promptly, and we began exchanging letters regularly. Hers were always encouraging and she repeatedly expressed appreciation for all that I had shared with her. Zola came into my life at a pivotal point, a time when I felt isolated and rejected by my country, and confused about my identity. I desperately needed someone from the outside to hear, understand, accept my pain, and acknowledge that I had a right to my feelings. I was ready to tell my story to someone from the white community and she heard me. To listen to my story and commiserate with me was a priceless gift in the midst of my hell. Because of Zola I put Ohio on my secret list of states I wanted to relocate to once I was free to leave the internment camp. Emotionally, I felt my heart flowering and turning toward the sun.

ANSEL ADAMS

Winter storm at Manzanar Internment Camp.

THE GIFT OF FREEDOM

We read in the *Dispatch* that the War Relocation Authority (WRA) in the Office of Emergency Management was planning to oversee the internment camps, replacing the army as soon as the system was set up. Originally, Milton S. Eisenhower, younger brother of the famous General Dwight D. Eisenhower, was selected by President Roosevelt to oversee the evacuation. Although the U.S. Army was initially responsible for moving us from our homes to the assembly centers and then to relocation centers, in a matter of months the day-to-day operation was transferred to the WRA.

When the change finally happened around October 1942, the most dramatic difference was the removal of the guards from the watchtowers for a few months. With the big relocation effort completed, the military was no longer needed, and a civilian authority could take over to run the camps. That was a huge relief. After months of feeling watched by armed guards, it was almost a shock to see the gates open and unmonitored. It opened up the possibility of our leaving the camp to explore the surrounding areas if we wished without having to ask for permission.

One day I decided to go beyond the barbed-wire fence. I wanted to hike up to Castle Rock in the hilly range surrounding Tule Lake camp. Others were walking outside the fenced camp and climbing up the hillside in droves. I wanted to go, too.

I saw Amy Nagata at the mess hall and I asked her, "I've been wanting to go climb up Castle Rock, do you want to go?"

"Sure I'd like to," she responded eagerly. "When?"

"How about right after breakfast tomorrow before it gets too hot?"

"Okay, I'll meet you here."

The next morning we started out as planned. Anticipating the warmth of the day but probably some wind at higher elevations, we both wore T-shirts and tied long-sleeve sweaters around our waists.

As we stepped outside the barbed-wire fence, we stopped, looked at each other, and took a deep breath as we smiled broadly. Raising both arms up in the air we shouted, "We're free!" Compared to what we had been through, this really felt free—at least, for the moment.

After a couple hours climbing up a winding pathway around boulders, sagebrush, and dried grass, we came to a natural resting place. Leaning against some big boulders we looked back at the huge camp. From that altitude we could see everywhere. There was a light haze over the barracks below, but in the hills the air was pleasantly warm and clear.

Looking at the camp below, I thought about my conversation with Zola. The cloudless sky above opened my heart to an expansiveness that filled me with acceptance and hope. *This is the first time that someone on the "outside" heard and acknowledged what I had to say,* I thought. I sat up and took another deep breath. High above the camp I made an imaginary flight and circled the buildings sitting on the floor of what must have been a gigantic lake thousands of years ago. I floated around looking at the bluffs, which surrounded the camp on three sides, the southern one bigger and taller than the other two. The bluffs were sparsely covered with sagebrush and dried grass. To my right I could see the warehouses, the hospital, the administration area not too far from the military area, and fire towers located in various places. Straight ahead was my block, 74, and I could see my barrack, 7404. A high fence encased the entire camp with barbed-wire along the top. The one big difference was the empty guard towers along the fence and the stilled searchlights.

I am free! I am transformed! I imagined I flew away from the place that had kept me confined, and soared over the Rocky Mountains, Yellowstone National Park, Chicago, and Washington D.C. I veered towards the deep South, picturing a city like New Orleans, and then flew to the Grand Canyon in the West. Then I headed for home, flying along the coastline. Once I was back on my farm on Vashon I stuffed my mouth full of sweet, sun-ripened strawberries. I glided over the pond on our makeshift raft and flopped down on the lush green lawn to rest in the sunshine. I listened to the happy birds singing nearby and watched the clouds floating lazily across the blue sky. Finally I fell into a quiet, peaceful sleep in my own bed in our own home.

My reverie was interrupted when I heard a strange voice exclaim, "Well, this is more like it." A girl had come around the bend. She stood looking back at the camp. "A grand view of the ugliest place on Earth," she said without a trace of humor.

I sat up and shaded my eyes to get a better look at who was talking. She was tall, slender, and about our age. Bold, scarlet lipstick carefully outlined her lips, just like the actresses in the movies. She wore tight, black slacks and a short sleeve, black shirt opened down to the fourth button. Something inside of me recoiled at her appearance and the sullen look on her face.

"Who are you?" Amy asked.

"I'm Mary Otani from Sacramento. And you two?" I could hear arrogance in her voice.

"I'm Amy Nagata from Tacoma, Washington, and this is my friend, Mary Matsuda from Vashon Island near Seattle."

"Hi. It's a nice day for a hike, isn't it?" I commented, trying to sound polite.

"Yeah, but even one day here is one day too many," she said heatedly.

Amy replied, "I don't like it any better than you do, but I'm not sure what we can do about it now."

"At least we're outside the barbed-wire fence right now," I said and shrugged my shoulders. "Maybe this is the first of more freedom to come. We can hope so, don't you think?"

"Well, maybe," Mary replied bitterly, "but I'm not going to hold my breath. I'm sick of the government. They came and took away my dad right after Pearl Harbor, and we still don't know where he is. We've probably lost our farm by this time, too." Her voice faltered. She turned her head sadly and looked across with unseeing eyes at the camp below.

My heart sank. *She still doesn't know where her father is? No wonder she's so bitter.*

"I'm terribly sorry," I said softly.

"Yeah, well somebody's going to pay for it," she said, her eyes flashing. "My brother's friends think we should go on strike and protest all this bullshit! We can't just sit around and pretend like everything is okay, because it isn't. We have to do something to get the administration's attention."

"Yeah, I can understand your feelings about that," I responded automatically, but I felt caught in a lie. I was shocked. How could she say such words? I could sympathize, but I was frightened that anyone would actually consider protesting. It felt very un-Japanese-like.

Mary sat down beside us and told us about her family's experience after Pearl Harbor, her father's disappearance, the FBI raid on their home, the difficulty trying to save their farm, and the evacuation. Hers was only a slight variation on a story very familiar to us. All I could do was nod my head in agreement, but my heart cried out at her pain and bitterness—which was worse than mine.

After a time we realized it was getting fairly hot. We decided it was time to go back down to camp, get some lunch, and take cover from the heat. We walked single file down the path, each of us caught up in our own thoughts. At the entrance into camp I turned to Mary, put my hand on her shoulder and said softly, "I wish there were something I could do for you."

"No, there's nothing," she responded. "But thank you for listening and understanding."

"I hope your dad gets released and joins your family real soon," I added, before going my own way. I didn't know what else to say. If I had been in her shoes and my father had been taken away, I would have been devastated. There seemed to be nothing more I could do.

⋰◉⋱

Tension gradually began to increase around camp. Groups of boys, mostly from California, were restless and openly bitter about the evacuation and continued confinement. They began roaming menacingly around camp. The traditional discipline and the moral code of the Japanese family was eroding. Now angry, rebellious young men began to badger people confined at the camp.

One day when my brother and I came out of a church service, a group of boys from California made snide remarks about us people from "the North." Before Yoneichi and I headed for home, I saw one of them "accidentally" bump into a boy from Vashon and apologize profusely as if mocking the Japanese way. He and his friends took off laughing loudly about the importance of being "polite." After that interaction I was afraid to go to church alone. Yoneichi noticed the increased tension, too. We decided to get together with other young people from our end of the camp and go as a group to church services. Before we left, the boys put the girls in the middle, and we proceeded to the services held in the central part of camp. There we joined some people we knew from the southeastern part of camp, the area we called "Alaska" because they were physically separated from the rest of the camp by an irrigation ditch. They, too, were from the Pacific Northwest. We would meet outside of the barrack where the service was held, and we all walked in together.

Throughout this period of time, there were those who saw what was happening to all of us: Either the growing apathy toward or simmering resentment against the restrictive regulations of the camp administration, the increase in parent/child friction, and the erosion of family customs and values. Reverend Matsui, our Protestant minister was a bespectacled man who looked tall and slim in his long, black clerical garb. He could see the encroaching problems threatening family life at the internment camp. In his sermons he urged us to "get away from the cancer creeping into our lives." He urged the Japanese families to investigate the possibility of applying for permanent leave and moving out of the camp. Several things took place that made these opportunities possible.

Dillon S. Myer was appointed to the War Relocation Authority by President Franklin Delano Roosevelt on June 17, 1942 to succeed Milton Eisenhower. Shortly after Myer took over, a WRA top aide advised him that long-term confinement of the evacuees was unwise and that the people should be resettled as quickly as possible. Myer made an inspection tour himself and came to the same conclusion.

Temporary leave opportunities became available during the fall of the 1942 harvest season when labor shortages warranted the use of Japanese-American workers, even on some farms in the West. A small group of educators, plus YMCA/YWCA officials from the San Francisco Bay area, and even California Governor Olson expressed concern for the Japanese students whose college education had been disrupted by the evacuation. In May 1942, the National Student Relocation Council was organized in Chicago and by fall many students were cleared by the FBI to leave for the Midwest and the East to continue their education. Students could not return to schools on the West Coast.

At the time I didn't realize that the cancer was creeping even into my own life. I knew vaguely that something ominous was going on, but I was too preoccupied to know what it was. I was living in a strange dream world in which everything seemed so temporary and I blamed the government for my misery. I found it hard to make friends. Even though I heard of some who were allowed to leave the camp for the East Coast or the Midwest, I couldn't imagine the day I would get out and make my own way in the world, alone.

Camp administrators backed up Reverend Matsui's statement that those of us who had no criminal record or a reputation for disloyal acts could qualify to leave; however, no one could return home to any West Coast state. We could leave but we couldn't go home. *What choice is that?* I wondered. The reverend's open, self-confident manner conveyed a sense of strength and personal power to those who looked to him for direction, and evoked fear and anger from those who disagreed with him. Reverend

Matsui made numerous trips to various cities in the Midwest and the East Coast to evaluate how the *Niseis* who had moved to the "outside" were getting along. He provided us with valuable information on how to make successful transitions "out there" where the climate was more normal. This encouraged some Japanese to request permission to leave and to re-establish themselves and their families in parts of America far from our homes on the West Coast.

Additional encouragement came from the editor of the *Tri-State High School* paper. An editorial read: "Jobs after the war will be difficult to obtain and the average high school student will not be qualified for the positions that will be open. It will be those students who have had some college training that will be considered for the positions. This is all the more reason why you should relocate and relocate now!" The word "relocate" in this context meant to move out and away from camp. We had already been uprooted from our homes and brought to "relocation centers," but the implication here was positive.

I wondered, *Is there another reason why we are encouraged to leave camp? Can it be that by now we have become an economic burden on the country?* The war seemed to drag on and on. There was no end in sight as to how long the government would have to pay for what it had created, like the reservations in the 1800s for the Native Americans.

Realistically, there were a large number of obstacles that interfered with people leaving the internment camp. We could not return to our homes on the West Coast, which was still a military restricted area. We had to decide where we wanted to go and what we wanted to do after we got there. A sponsor was necessary who would take care of initial needs, especially housing, food, and employment once we arrived at our chosen location.

Few Americans were willing to sponsor Japanese settlers in a climate of the wartime hatred of Japan, but there were a few courageous groups such as the Quakers and some other churches. Editorials in the *Tulean Dispatch* advised those Japanese who were leaving not to assemble in large groups, whether in living quarters or in social situations. This advice referred to one of the criticisms of Japanese people who came from California, in particular, where large numbers of Japanese congregated and became more noticeable. This led to them becoming targets of prejudice.

Before we could get clearance to leave, camp officials had to approve our clearance by making criminal background checks and reviewing evidence of what the government described as "loyal citizenship." Those who left camp were reminded in the *Dispatch* that they would be regarded as role models by which future evacuees would be judged, so they had to be on their best behavior.

By and large, students whose college education had been interrupted by the war were the first ones who took advantage of the leave policy. Most had to transfer to different colleges, but at least they could continue studying. However, efforts by the churches and the government to get large numbers of evacuees to leave were unsuccessful. This fact did not go unnoticed by the WRA.

After six months of imprisonment I was slowly emerging from my depressed state. Life seemed to gallop ahead, while at the same time stand still. Many things were happening: I was developing different skills, gradually making some friends, observing changes in the administration of the camp, and experiencing a measure of freedom that those shifts brought. Finishing high school and learning to make do with what was available became high priorities. Changes were taking place in many family relationships, and I noticed how much stronger my own family was.

Some families at the internment camp considered relocating to Japan, but this did not become an option until much later. My parents never considered this option, nor did I. Before they left Japan they had made a commitment to make their home in the United States. They were not caught in the ambivalence that plagued so many Japanese-American families.

In retrospect, I could not see a clear direction for my life. There was a tug to leave the camp behind and venture into a new life on the outside after I graduated from high school. But I realized once I left camp, there would be no coming back. I often worried, *What would happen to my parents?* The powerful feeling of *on*, loyalty to family, caused me to pause and reflect, *What might be the best thing for all of us, not just for myself?*

Still shell-shocked from the sudden, bitter disruption of my life, I couldn't imagine building a life in a different part of the country where I would be a visible and possibly hated minority. I was not yet ready to venture out alone. However, events would soon take place that would influence me to change my mind.

World War II Japanese-American Internment Camps & Assembly Centers

★ ASSEMBLY CENTER & INTERNMENT CAMPS
  WHERE MATSUDA WAS INTERNED

○ OTHER ASSEMBLY CENTERS
▩ OTHER INTERNMENT CAMPS
△ ISOLATION CENTERS

No No or Yes Yes?

On the evening of December 7, 1942, exactly one year after Pearl Harbor, my parents and I had just returned to our living quarters after dinner. Yoneichi burst through the door with enough energy to cause the three of us to look up in alarm.

"Hey!" he said grimly, "the guys are saying there was a big riot at Manzanar yesterday. Somebody even got killed." The three of us gasped as one. Mama-san blanched, and we bombarded Yoneichi with questions.

Rumors spread like wildfire. Everywhere in camp people talked about the riot and what it meant. In the laundry room women spoke in hushed voices. Outside, groups of young men held loud debates on the possibility of more rioting, martial law, and what the government should do. Most people were visibly afraid, but a few seemed excited, even energized by having something to break the monotony. Many different people made comments like, "I just knew that sooner or later, something like this was going to happen!" I heard rumors of conflicts between groups of people, of shady deals that drove people to the point of explosive action, and of general distrust of the administration. Meanwhile, official communications from government representatives about the riot at Manzanar Internment Camp in Central California were matter-of-fact, soothing, and not informative. I spent many long hours poring over the reports in the *Dispatch*, then wondering what was left out of the stories.

"It sounds like people have lost all reason," Mama-san said, wringing her hands.

Papa-san responded, "It looks that way, but I think we're only getting bits and pieces of information."

"I agree," Yoneichi added with a frown on his face. "I'm sure there were all kinds of things that led up to the riot. But the important thing is, I bet it's not over yet." He lowered his voice ominously. "There could be trouble here, too. I think it's best for us to keep a low profile. We don't want to become targets."

We would later learn that the Manzanar riots were caused primarily by two converging forces. One force was the general social unrest that was the inevitable result of the brutal evacuation, forced confinement, poor conditions, lack of meaningful work, and other problems of camp life. Manzanar held all of the Japanese-Americans forced to evacuate from Terminal Island. Their evacuation was particularly ruthless, their bitterness understandable.

The other factor was the presence in Manzanar of some members of the pro-American Japanese-American Citizen League (JACL). Throughout the internment crisis, the JACL conducted controversial but well-intentioned and sometimes secret work on behalf of all Japanese-Americans, including meeting with government officials to provide information and make recommendations. At Manzanar, JACL members were rumored to be providing the administration with the names of so-called "troublemakers," making other internees angry and suspicious. All of the internment camps to some extent were polarized into pro-American groups versus those who were not, but this was most extreme at Manzanar.

The riot at Manzanar was precipitated by a Japanese man at the camp accusing a Caucasian camp administrator of stealing camp supplies and selling them on the black market. The accuser, an extremely popular spokesman of the Kitchen Workers Union, was later implicated and arrested in the beating of a JACL member who was seen by some internees as being a "government informer." Amid charges of an administration "frame-up," a large anti-JACL crowd formed and demanded the spokesman's release. As more violence appeared imminent, troops were summoned. The crowd got out of control, and troops opened fire, killing two internees and seriously wounding nine others. Mess hall gongs at Manzanar rang all night for the dead. Government authorities imposed martial law at Manzanar for two weeks.

The news of the Manzanar riot shocked me. Fear became my overriding emotion. *Something is terribly wrong,* I thought, *even beyond what I was already aware of. Could the violence spread to Tule Lake? What will the government do? What will happen to us?*

The news reminded me of how I felt the year before when we got disturbing news from far away about Pearl Harbor. I knew instinctively it was the beginning of something that would soon overtake my life, but I didn't know where it might lead, and it was beyond my control.

Besides Manzanar, there were strikes and protests at Minidoka, open revolts at Poston Internment Camp, and general unrest in all the camps. I had a vague feeling that something ominous was about to take place at Tule Lake camp. Perhaps there would be riots or something even worse. People seemed poised for trouble.

⌐:◉:⌐

Immediately after Pearl Harbor, nearly all *Nisei* were declared unfit for military service, including those who were already in the armed forces. This was an insult to those who had served honorably. In late 1942, the army began reconsidering the status of draft-age Japanese-Americans. In November 1942, a small group from the JACL met in secret in Salt Lake City to discuss the possibility of reversing the *Niseis'* draft classification. According to Bill Hosokawa in his book, *Nisei, the Quiet Americans,* the national secretary for the JACL, Mike Masaoka, made a compelling case that "the *Nisei* needed a record of having fought for their country to bulwark their postwar struggle to win full citizenship rights."

This would mean that men of military age whose classification had been changed from 1-A to 4-C (enemy alien) immediately after Pearl Harbor would be reclassified to 1-A again—fit for general active military service. The leaders of the JACL believed strongly that military service by the *Nisei* was the only reasonable path toward eventually achieving full citizenship rights for all Japanese-Americans. The JACL met with officials from the U.S. government to argue for the creation of an all-*Nisei* fighting force. In doing so, these leaders fully expected an angry backlash, but they were willing to risk even their own personal safety for their cause. Several of these leaders were later beaten by anti-JACL internees, some severely, when their work was suspected.

The Manzanar riots created a crisis for the WRA, which was already aware of the tensions building in the internment camps. The U.S. government decided it needed to find a way to separate those Japanese who were pro-America from Japanese who were not. The government reasoned that if this wasn't done, and done quickly, more violence would inevitably result. In Washington, D.C., plans were underway to accomplish this task.

The WRA was working on a plan for mass registration of all adults to determine who qualified for school or employment outside of camp. The current system was painfully slow due to red tape. The WRA wanted to return internees to a normal life as quickly as possible, but only those whom government officials decided could be "trusted." The government wanted a systematic, documentable way to determine who was safe outside of the confines of camp.

On January 28, 1943, Secretary of War Henry L. Stimson announced the formation of a combat team made up of Japanese-American men from the internment camps and the Hawaiian Islands. Stimson had received the approval of President Roosevelt as a step toward returning the evacuees to normal life. In order to accomplish this, the army needed to assemble information on young men of military age. One critical piece of information was to determine whether these men would be loyal to the United States.

When the WRA learned about the U.S. Army's plans, it decided to combine the two projects and accomplish both tasks with a questionnaire. The intentions may have been understandable, but the results were disastrous.

In January 1943, the combined teams from the army and the WRA received extensive training on how to administer this questionnaire. One of those teams arrived at the Tule Lake center on February 6, 1943. We knew to expect this because the *Dispatch* published a statement from the administration explaining the team's mission. We were hopeful that the questionnaire would help bring an end to the conflict.

Three days later our block manager made an announcement at breakfast that the head of each family should come to the manager's office to pick up questionnaires for each family member seventeen years and older. Authorities hoped the questionnaires would be completed and returned within ten days. As it turned out, it actually took much longer at Tule Lake.

Papa-san brought the questionnaires back for each of us and we sat down promptly to read and fill them out. The majority of the questions were simple. They covered topics such as education, previous employment, knowledge of the Japanese language, number of relatives in Japan, foreign investments and travel, religious and organizational affiliations, sports interests, hobbies, magazines and newspapers customarily read, and possession of dual citizenship. But there were two questions with two variations that were anything but simple. Yoneichi's form read like this:

1. STATEMENT OF UNITED STATES CITIZENSHIP OF
JAPANESE ANCESTRY (SELECTIVE SERVICE FORM 304 A).

From the War Department's Adjutant General's office for draft age men who are U.S. citizens:

Question 27.   Are you willing to serve in the armed forces of the United States on combat duty, wherever ordered?

Question 28. Will you swear unqualified allegiance to the United States of America and faithfully defend the United States from any or all attack by foreign or domestic forces, and forswear any form of allegiance or obedience to the Japanese emperor, to any other foreign government, power or organization?

My form, and those of my immigrant parents, read like this:

2. APPLICATION FOR LEAVE CLEARANCE
WRA FORM 126 REV.

For Isseis of both sexes and all female Nisei over seventeen years of age:

Question 27. If the opportunity presents itself and you are found qualified, would you be willing to volunteer for the Army Nurse Corps or WAAC?

Question 28. Will you swear unqualified allegiance to the United States of America and forswear any form of allegiance or obedience to the Japanese emperor, or any other foreign government, power or organization?

I thought they were going to ask me about my loyalty—I had already demonstrated that beyond a shadow of a doubt. Now, it seemed, they wanted to stake a claim on my future, too. As I read and reread the questions, the hair on the back of my neck rose, caught between outrage and fear.

Do I really want to go into the Army Nurse Corps or the WAAC? I asked myself. Is that what I really want to do? Worse, Yoneichi was being forced to choose between an unknown, presumably horrible penalty from the government or join the service with the possibility of death on foreign soil.

Question 28 seemed even more mysterious and sinister. I thought, *I am an American citizen. Why would I have any allegiance to the Japanese emperor? Why are they asking me that question?* It was baffling. I didn't get it. And what did these questions mean to Papa-san and Mama-san? There seemed to be something unspoken here. Are these trick questions? I began questioning the government's motives, and felt overwhelmed with dread and confusion.

The questionnaire seemed to throw everyone off balance. My family was unusually quiet for nearly two days. Around us, everyone seemed to be in a trance or some kind of suspended animation. We were all dumbfounded by the sudden demand to declare our intentions. We also wondered about the consequences of our choice. But soon indignation and conflict replaced shock. People had different interpretations of what the questions meant.

The noise level in the mess hall, in the bathroom, and in the laundry room rose as people debated the issues. Soon arguments broke out within families, between former friends, and between people from the north (Washington and Oregon) and south (California). I had trouble sleeping at night, hearing angry voices at all hours.

Some *Isseis* focused upon the title of their questionnaire: "Application for Leave Clearance." "If I fill this out," one woman asked, "does that mean I am applying to leave camp? Where would I go? I can't go back to the West Coast. I don't want to leave yet."

To others, question 28 sounded like a trick question. Answering "Yes" would imply an admission of allegiance to the Japanese emperor in the past.

When U.S. Army recruiters arrived at Tule Lake Internment Camp to get men to register for the military, Yoneichi went to find out what the recruiters had to say and how the other men at the camp would respond. He came back shaking his head.

"That was some kind of wild meeting," he said. "You should have seen those guys. I thought some of them were about to explode."

"What were they so mad about?" I asked, naïvely.

"Some of them were old military guys who got kicked out of the army after Pearl Harbor because they're Japanese, but for some reason they are now eligible for the draft again. Others were there just to taunt and harass the recruiters about the questionnaire."

"Did you find out anything useful?" asked Papa-san.

"Yeah, the recruiters said that questions 27 and 28 are a way to determine who has security clearance for military service," explained Yoneichi. "When you put it that way, it seems fairly straightforward, but some of the guys had really good points. One of them said that serving in a segregated unit could put us into the riskiest positions at the whim of military leadership. Another man asked, 'Why an all-Japanese unit? Aren't we good enough to fight with the white boys?' Another guy said he didn't want to serve in the United States military because he might possibly have to fight against his brother or cousin in Japan." Yoneichi paused, then added, "I hadn't thought about that."

Mama-san listened with a worried look on her face.

For elderly *Isseis*, question 27 was ridiculous. How could old men and women who weren't even citizens of the United States possibly qualify for the Women's Army Auxiliary Corps? Why would they even want to consider the possibility?

Question 28 unthinkingly asked the *Isseis* to swear unqualified allegiance to the United States, yet the United States had prevented them from becoming citizens, and now imprisoned them. They were being asked to renounce their loyalty to Japan and possibly fight against the very country with which they were still citizens. For the aliens to answer "Yes" would mean they would be without a country, neither a citizen of the United States nor Japan. And what if Japan won the war? They would be traitors if they voted "Yes." But to vote "No" could result in deportation. We all wondered, *What are we supposed to do?*

"These questions made everyone mad," Yoneichi said emphatically, "and some of the guys really had a point. The way the questions were written sounded stupid, but I wanted to hear what everybody said so I could think about all this."

"That's wise, Yoneichi-san," said Mama-san.

"Whoever came up with these questions didn't think through what they were asking," Yoneichi added. "Nor did they consider all the different circumstances people would find themselves in." He shook his head. "You should have seen that place. I've never seen so many angry people. The recruiters couldn't follow the script they had been given. They were embarrassed, speechless, and maybe even a little scared."

It was obvious that these questions were critically important to our future, but what were the "right" answers? What would happen to people who answered one or both questions "No?" Could a person answer "Yes" to one question and "No" to the other? What could happen to the person who chose not to answer either question? We had no way of knowing any of this.

There were no simple solutions for anybody. Even those who felt strongly one way or the other had doubts that could not be answered. Previously amicable relationships were disrupted by heated arguments, sometimes leading to verbal threats, shoving, and even violence. The block managers who were local representatives to serve as liaisons between the people and the camp administration were hopelessly overwhelmed with questions they could not answer.

By trying to combine the purposes of the WRA and the army into one questionnaire, the resulting document was confusing and terrifying, creating paranoia among the internees. The questions had to be answered with a "Yes" or "No." Attempts to have meetings with government officials to discuss the questions and get additional information were denied in our camp.

117

Gangs of angry young men began to roam the camp, especially in areas where the Northwest families lived. Because many of us from the Northwest had lived more integrated lives with our white neighbors and we had been treated more respectfully during our evacuation, we were more apt to vote "Yes Yes." Some of the Californians considered us "stool pigeons." These men posted handwritten signs in both English and Japanese in various public places, warning: "Do not sign 'Yes Yes'" or "Do not fill out the questionnaire." The warnings implied dire consequences and later gangs beat up people who advocated differently. People dared not hobnob with camp administrators for fear of being labeled *inu*—an informer or betrayer—and then being ostracized by the other internees. Meanwhile, the camp administration began working desperately to identify and arrest the instigators of the violence. Mass confusion, anger, and agitation followed.

I had never been so terrified in my life. Suddenly I was hated not just by my government but by other Japanese-Americans. *Why?* I thought. *Just being from Washington State makes them think my family and I are disloyal to our own kind. This is totally insane.*

Within a week the army and the WRA authorities realized their mistake, quickly made a revision, and postponed the deadline for turning in the questionnaires. The following question directed at the *Isseis* was substituted for question 28:

> Will you swear to abide by the laws of the United States and to take no action which would in any way interfere with the war effort of the United States?

The revision came too late. The damage had been done. Incensed and insulted by the way the demands had been laid out, many *Isseis* declared they would answer "No No" in protest to the way they had been treated, not as a testimony to their loyalty or disloyalty. This became an anti-administration revolt. Talks among internees about repatriation or refusing to register mushroomed.

The efforts by the army to recruit volunteers for the all-*Nisei* fighting force were largely unsuccessful, at least on the mainland. Ultimately, only fifty-one *Nisei* men volunteered to join the army from Tule Lake, the smallest number from any camp despite Tule Lake having the largest population. The goal for all ten camps was 3,000 recruits, but only 1,181 volunteered. By contrast, in Hawaii (where the Japanese were not sent to internment camps) nearly 10,000 eager *Nisei* volunteered to fill a quota of 1,500 recruits.

The young Japanese-American men who refused to go into the military were labeled "No No Boys." The most vocal did so out of protest, but there were other reasons. Some of them took their role as the oldest male in the family very seriously, responsible for their aging parents and their siblings. Their position was to remain in the internment camps with their families and fight the whole evacuation process.

In their haste to get the registration underway quickly, the WRA had thrust every interned family onto the horns of a terrible dilemma, one that would rip families apart, ruin close friendships, and polarize the entire Japanese-American community for a generation.

We would later learn this was clearly not the government's intention. WRA Director Myer wanted to use this registration process to expedite leave clearance for all eligible internees. He could see what was happening to families and he wanted the loyal Japanese-Americans to get away from the seething caldrons of the internment camps as soon as possible and begin a normal life outside of camp. The reason for the loyalty questionnaire was to determine who could be trusted out in the larger community and not sabotage the war effort. But if that purpose was explained at the time, I never heard it and, I suspect, neither did many others. The process turned out to be a tragic mistake from which some individuals never recovered. As one of my friends said years later, "In all my life, answering those two questions was the hardest thing I have ever done."

⁓◉⁓

By this time many of us no longer trusted the U.S. government. This questionnaire seemed like another one of its demands to probe into our psyches to further manipulate us. The original good intentions were turned on their heads and became a huge liability.

Tension continued to escalate as the deadline for the questionnaire approached. Whenever I left our apartment, I looked for threatening signals from everyone. When I saw people from Vashon, I felt fairly safe, but with people I didn't know, I was wary. I especially stayed clear of those who looked angry.

Nightmares became more common. Often I would be running from someone whose face I couldn't identify. I'd stumble and fall, certain I would be trampled or hurt in some way. Then I would wake up in a cold sweat, my heart pounding.

The separation of the loyals from the disloyals became even more essential to prevent further violence. One day I went for a walk, as I often did, to try to clear my mind. Preoccupied with many conflicting feelings, I walked toward the latrines. I wanted to be away from the many people walking aimlessly back and forth, but when I entered the bathroom the stench mixed with the humidity nauseated me. Two *Isseis* were talking in Japanese to each other in anxious voices. The younger of the two women asked, "What is your family going to do?"

"I don't know," the older woman responded, her face drawn with worry lines. "My husband has been very distressed ever since we were evacuated from our home. He wants our whole family to vote 'No No' so we can all stay together. But my son, on the other hand, is very pro-America. He says we have to prove our loyalty and we can't do that by voting 'No No.' I'm afraid to think what this will do to our family." She wrung her hands as she spoke, her eyes darting back and forth as though looking for some sign of relief from her anguish.

As they continued their spirited conversation, their voices bounced off the blank walls and pounded in my head. *This is no place for me to think,* I told myself. *I need a place to be alone.* I left.

Deep in thought, I didn't care about the cloudy sky overhead and the chill in the air. I was only aware of a threatening buzz in my head and a tightness in my chest. I stumbled along the walkway between the barracks and onto the dusty, gray, gravel road. I approached the barbed-wire fence, then stopped, making sure to abide by the camp regulation to remain twenty feet inside the fence. I looked beyond to the guard tower and shuddered as I saw a soldier holding a machine gun, watching me. After the Manzanar riot, the army had returned and we were once again under constant surveillance. Behind the soldier were several tanks with their 12-mm cannons facing the center of camp. New barracks were being added to house additional troops assigned to guard us. I thought of the Japanese-Americans who had been shot at Manzanar and I recoiled from the perimeter of the camp.

Beyond the fences and guard towers the purple shadows of Castle Rock Mountain stretched across the barren hillside dotted with scrubby, gnarled trees. I tried to force myself to focus on the serenity of the land-scape, but a nagging, troubled feeling persisted. Dread and fear tumbled in my gut, an endless cycle threatening to pull me downward.

Suddenly I realized the darkest truth of our situation: *We really are vulnerable, the threat to our lives is real.* Once again I went back over the past, searching for things our family might have done differently to avoid what happened to us. I concluded, *There is absolutely nothing we could have done differently that would have spared us this fate.*

Then I considered, *If I couldn't predict that a situation this bad could happen to us then, what other more awful things could happen to us now? Will there be violence within our own community?* I didn't want to think about it. I brushed my hands across my forehead, over my eyes and down my face to try to wipe these thoughts from my mind, but nothing helped. *I thought I did everything I was supposed to, and yet, here I am, a number just like the rest of my family.* I looked toward Castle Rock again and a darkening sky. *Where is God in all this? Doesn't He care and watch over us?*

≺ ◉ ≻

One night around midnight we were awakened by the sound of someone pounding urgently on our door. When Yoneichi leaped up to open it, Bobby, Yoneichi's former classmate from Vashon, burst in. "Ken Ishimoto got beat up." Yoneichi threw on some clothes and disappeared with Bobby into the darkness. We didn't sleep the rest of the night waiting for Yoneichi to return.

When he came back, Yoneichi told us what happened. "I ran with Bobby to Ken's place. He was unconscious on the ground behind his apartment. His mom was beside him, calling his name."

"Was he hurt badly?" Papa-san asked.

"There was blood running from his forehead down his face. His clothes were all messed up. Several of us got there about the same time. I lifted his head and spoke to him. He didn't answer."

"He must have been knocked out," I said.

"Yeah. We got a blanket under him and six of us took him to the hospital. We stuck around awhile to see if he was okay. About a half hour later Ken came to."

"Did he know any of the people who beat him up?" Mama-san asked.

"No. They're probably from Sacramento or are *Kibeis* like most of the 'No No' guys. I heard Ken talking about signing 'Yes Yes' and telling other guys to do the same. That's probably why he got beat up." Yoneichi gave a reassuring look to Mama-san. "I've been very careful not to tell others how to vote—that's their business. There will probably be more of these beatings."

Mama-san said anxiously, "Yoneichi-san, please be careful." I looked away, troubled. *Surely other men suspect Yoneichi is likely to be "Yes Yes," I* thought. *These "No No" men are violent and frightening.*

121

Both sides hoped for ultimate vindication in the slow-moving legal system of the United States. Unfortunately, at least one ruling by the Supreme Court in December 1944, *Korematsu v. United States,* failed to deliver the hoped-for protection. Fred Toyosaburo Korematsu was a Japanese-American who refused to evacuate from the San Francisco Bay area, not out of protest, but simply because he was in love with a Caucasian woman. He was arrested and convicted of remaining in a military zone from which persons of Japanese ancestry were excluded. His case was taken to the Supreme Court by Wayne Collins of the American Civil Liberties Union (ACLU). Shockingly, Korematsu lost.

In later years this decision would be described as one of the most suppressive opinions in the history of the Court. Author Michi Weglyn would later write, "The court essentially said that racial discrimination is constitutional in cases of 'national emergency.'" This judicial decision still holds some fifty years later and can be used even today by those who seek political gain in times of crisis. A government-declared emergency—any emergency—could place another group of people at risk for incarceration, based on the decision in *Korematsu v. United States.*

᠅ ⑥ ᠅

The Loyalty Oath plunged me back into depression. Outrage streamed through my thoughts daily. *Now we might be torn apart because those in power are afraid of the possibility of sabotage. How could anyone, especially an eighteen-year-old girl like me be a saboteur under this situation—behind barbed-wire fences, watched twenty-four hours of every day by armed soldiers in guard towers? This business of being loyal or disloyal, how dare they question my loyalty?*

One of my cultural norms was absolute obedience to authority. I was expected to be a model American citizen. Juvenile delinquency or antisocial behavior of any type was unacceptable in our family as well as among most *Isseis* and *Niseis.*

Often I walked alone on the too-familiar path around the perimeter of the camp, trying to see clear of the angst, outrage, and disillusionment with my America. Always, always there were many people around, at any hour of the day, even on these walks. Every few seconds I would meet others coming and going, in pairs, groups, or alone. We were all people with black hair, slanted eyes, and troubled thoughts. We all walked a path of endless questions.

How would the government distinguish who was loyal from who was not? What would they do with this information? Would we be tricked in some way to split up our family? Would my father be taken away as some men were right after Pearl Harbor? No matter what I might do, it seemed like a no-win situation.

At our school assemblies in the internment camp, I repeated the Pledge of Allegiance daily and sang "America" and "The Star Spangled Banner." "My country 'tis of thee, sweet land of liberty" I sang, but I wondered, *Liberty for whom?* I pledged, "...One nation, indivisible, with liberty and justice for all," and how I longed for that equal justice and freedom! How I longed for the quiet, tranquil days on the farm, and the simple tasks of preparing the fields to yield the biggest, sweetest berries. What pleasure it would be for the chance to see a smiling Mama-san standing among the berries in her baggy dusty pants, wearing a loose work shirt, a straw hat over her kerchiefed head, tied under her chin. How I wanted to sit at dusk on the small hill on our farm where I could gaze at Mount Rainier, situated like a great snowy temple beyond reproach.

My mind went back to a recent vivid dream. In the dream my family and I were among a throng of people gathered for some kind of town meeting to discuss a problem I wasn't clear about. Our family was standing on the fringe of the crowd along with several others I recognized from Vashon. People were milling, loudly advocating one position or another. Some people began shouting, their clenched fists raised in defiance. Others began shoving, pushing, and waving their arms about. I caught a glimpse of a young man standing to my left. The corners of his mouth curled downward as the lines around his nose and lips deepened. His eyes narrowed and darkened as cuss words and spit exploded from his lips. I jumped aside as he began flailing his arms. Scanning the row of helmeted soldiers nervously patrolling on the outskirts of the crowd, I noticed several whose faces were white with fear, or red with anger. I was afraid. I didn't want to be here.

In my dream there were sudden blasts from a machine gun. As I whirled in the direction of the shots I realized with horror that people, including my parents and brother, were starting to fall like a wave as bullets penetrated their bodies. Blood gushed everywhere. Mama-san slowly began to sink with blood spurting from her chest. As I lunged to catch her, I bolted up in bed dripping with sweat, my heart pounding, my throat so tight I could scarcely breathe. As the rotating searchlight swept across our room, I saw my parents and brother sleeping on their cots. I pulled the blanket tightly around me as I shivered from the ice-cold deep inside myself.

As I continued my walk around the perimeter of the camp I forced myself back from the memory of that nightmare. I wrapped my arms tightly across my chest, stopped walking and rocked my body back and forth. I told myself, as I had before, *It was just a nightmare.*

Out of the corner of my eye I noticed a familiar-looking figure squatting on the ground leaning against the side of a building, her head resting on her arms. It was the old lady I had seen earlier. I approached her quietly and inquired, *"Konnichi wa, oba-san, Ikaga desu ka?* Hello, auntie, how are you today?"

She looked up sadly. *"Arigato gozaimasu*—Thank you very much." She paused and I could see her struggling with her emotions. Suddenly she burst out, unable to restrain herself. "I'm so frightened! What I was afraid of has happened! My husband is determined to vote 'No No' because of the way we've been treated. We lost our nursery business in California. Now if we sign 'Yes Yes' he says they'll probably force us to leave camp and where will we go? He says it would be better to vote 'No No' and stay here."

I asked, "What about the rest of your family?"

"We have only one son, Yonetaro, who is equally stubborn about voting 'Yes Yes.' He says that's the only way we'll get our rights back. But that means he will go into the army. He probably will not return. What am I to do? He is the only child we have."

She burst into tears. I sat down beside her and she collapsed into my arms. In between her sobs she tried to tell me, "We can't be citizens. How can we manage if Yonetaro is gone? What if he's killed? What are we to do?"

How I ached for her. Sharing her grief, I sat silently and held her while she sobbed out her anguish. Neither of us had the answers. I said gently, *"Mazui desu neh?*—That's bad, isn't it?"

In time her sobs subsided. She wiped her eyes with both hands, straightened her hair, and rose. While averting her eyes from me, she said, *"Domo arigato gozaimashita*—Thank you very much." She bowed to me and went on her way. I could see that she was reluctant to burden me with her cares, a cultural norm among the Japanese.

I returned her bow as she slowly shuffled away. She looked so tiny and frail, but she seemed much calmer. As I stood there looking at her retreating figure and drying my own tears, I realized my anguish was shared across all generations in the camp. Her grief and confusion confirmed what I had been feeling. I could now imagine many versions of the same dilemma going on in every family in every one of the internment camps that held our people. Each adult member of a family had decisions to make without knowing the consequences.

We had lost our right to be in the privacy of our own home, the right to come and go as we pleased, the right to voice our opinions openly without fear of retaliation, the right to be involved in creative activities of our choosing. I was loyal to the country that guaranteed these rights—and that country no longer existed for me. The sudden loss of all these rights forced me to realize that this whole mass movement against the Japanese in America was the culmination of more than a half-century of anti-Asian prejudice. And no one, not even the highest court in the land, the Supreme Court, would defend us. The clear message to me was that we did not deserve to be in the world because we were different. And because we were different, we must also be bad.

I remembered the first time I knew I was different. A blonde girl in the third grade pointed a finger at me, curled her lips into a snarl and said, "You're a Jap." All my playmates stared at me and drifted away.

At the time Mama-san helped me put that incident aside by explaining, "There are times when some people need to say those kinds of things to make themselves feel all right about who they are. It says more about them than it does about you."

That helped, I could dismiss it. But it happened again eight years later. That blonde girl would be replaced by a far more powerful individual, President Franklin Delano Roosevelt who, through Executive Order 9066, made the decision that took away my world and the life that I had known and loved.

When I got back from my long walk around the perimeter of the camp I found my parents sitting on Papa-san's cot just as I had left them. It was silent in the room as they sipped their tea, the newspaper between them. The grave expression on their faces told me they had had a long talk in my absence. I sat down on the cot opposite them.

"Mama-san, Papa-san, while I was out by the barbed-wire fence thinking things over, I met an old woman who cried like her heart would break. She was really worried about how this loyalty oath could split up her family. I felt so sorry for her, but all I could do was hold her as she cried."

Mama-san replied, "Ah, ah, *kinodoku, neh*—How miserable and wretched. The questionnaire will break families apart, I'm afraid. It was good that you could provide some comfort for her."

"Mama-san, is the government going to separate the loyals from the disloyals?"

Troubled, she confirmed, "Yes, it sounds like that's what is being planned."

"I thought we showed our loyalty by going along with the evacuation," I responded. "Now when we protest, we're disloyal? But how can they tell who is loyal and who is not? I don't understand why all of this keeps happening to us."

Mama-san nodded as she replied, "Mary-san, I don't know how the government will determine who is loyal and who is not. That's going to be an enormous task. This is one of those times when we are caught in something much bigger than we are. It's not possible to understand why or how things will go."

Papa-san added, "Remember, Japan and the United States are at war with each other. This is a difficult time for everyone, but Mama-san and I have lived long enough to know that sooner or later, all of this will pass. We'll understand more when this whole thing is over."

"The important thing now," Mama-san added, "is to make the best of it while we are in the middle of it. Let us help each other by reminding ourselves what's important and make the best decisions we can at this time. That will help keep us from getting too discouraged."

In the face of all the threats around us, I admired and envied my parents' serenity. Yet I also resented them for it. *Why can't I be certain that it will all turn out all right?* I worried. *Where did they get that kind of faith, and why don't I feel that from searching the Bible?* I didn't like my feelings of torment and isolation, but my parents' example helped calm my anxiety for the time being.

A few days later I was lying on my cot when Yoneichi came home from work. He hung up his cook's apron on a nail in the wall, kicked off his shoes, and flopped on his cot. He looked at ease in his tan slacks and white T-shirt as he laced his fingers behind his head and stretched out. Papa-san mentioned we had been talking about the escalating unrest in the camps.

Yoneichi sat up, swung his legs over the side of the cot and faced us. "Another internee was shot and killed in Manzanar," he said. "The story is that he was gathering some scrap lumber near the fence to take home and make some furniture for his family. The guard reportedly ordered him to stop, but he didn't and started to run away. So the guard shot him. People say the man was shot from the *front,* not the back." Shaking his head he concluded, "Nobody knows exactly what happened and that's added more fuel to the fire. It's getting pretty crazy out there."

Papa-san added, "I heard that at Topaz apparently an old man was shot when he tried to prevent his puppy from escaping under the barbed-wire fence. The man couldn't have gone very far. Sounds like the sentries are getting trigger-happy. Things are getting out of hand." Looking at each of us he quietly advised, "Given the unstable environment, let's not draw any attention to ourselves."

"I hope there won't be big trouble here, too," Mama-san added as she pressed her lips together. Sitting numbly on my cot, I said nothing, but wondered, *How much more bad news can I take? I feel the world shutting down around me.* We had always been a peace-loving family, but now we were hearing about threats, killings, and violent behavior all around us. *Will that sweep over the four of us, too?* I worried. *How can my family be so calm in the midst of so much turmoil?* I got up and paced the twenty-foot length of our living space.

⤨⚜⤪

At last the deadline arrived for turning in our questionnaires. A process originally expected to take ten days took two months. It was now April 1943. Even though it was assumed we were a "Yes Yes" family, Papa-san said that we should privately and deliberately discuss how each of us planned to vote. Papa-san sat down on one cot and I sat down opposite him while Yoneichi went over and gently shut the door. Then he came and sat down beside me.

Mama-san said, "While we think about all of this, I'm going to fix us some tea." I watched her reach for the jar filled with green tea leaves. She sprinkled a pinch or two into the pot and poured hot water into it. Watching Mama-san do this simple ritual as she had done hundreds of times in the past helped to calm me as we were about to make our momentous decision.

The single light bulb overhead cast an ominous glare into the room. We were finally going to talk this through and make our decision together. This would be my first adult decision. My parents were treating me as an equal. The seriousness of the situation scared me, but we were all together. I took a deep breath.

After a few minutes Mama-san poured the fragrant beverage into four cups and served each of us before she sat down beside Papa-san. They sat close together just as Yoneichi and I did. We quietly and thoughtfully sipped our tea.

Finally we leaned toward each other, putting our heads close together to speak in hushed tones. We knew conversations could be heard by others in the entire barrack, and we did not want ours to be overheard by anyone.

Papa-san started by saying, "We're all familiar with the growing tension in our camp. This questionnaire has created much discussion and disagreement within our community, but nevertheless we must decide how we will respond. So our choice is to vote 'Yes Yes' or 'No No.'"

Yoneichi pointed out, "The *Kibeis* are sure making their anti-American position obvious. They're going around posting bulletins and notices that say, 'No one should register, sign or answer questions.' One guy came up to me and told me I should forfeit my American citizenship."

"What did you tell him, Yoneichi?" I asked.

"I said, 'I suppose I could do that.' I didn't want to irritate him any more than he already seemed to be. Our camp area and 'Alaska' are favorite targets for the 'No No' group."

"That was a good answer," Papa-san replied. "You don't want to stand out right now."

Yoneichi added, "But giving up my citizenship is going too far, I think. The most valuable thing we've got is our American citizenship."

Papa-san cocked his head to one side, cast a steady look at Yoneichi and said, "You're right. Your American citizenship is the most valuable thing you've got."

"Yes I know," Yoneichi said emphatically, nodding his head. "I know what it's cost you to have gone all these years without it. I hope someday that will change. There's a guy I work with who was born here in the United States but lived with his grandparents in Japan from the time he was four years old until he was fifteen. He's trying to get me to vote 'No No' and join him to go to Japan."

"You wouldn't do that, would you, Yoneichi?" I asked.

"No, but I didn't want to say that to him."

I asked, "What if some people answer 'Yes' to one question and 'No' to the other? Or suppose someone chooses not to answer at all? What will happen to them?" I looked from one face to the other.

Papa-san held his teacup in his left palm and turned his cup around and around with his other hand. He said softly, "I really don't know, Mary-san."

Papa-san continued. "I'm sure there will be many versions of what you've just said. There's much at stake in every family where feelings are bound to be strong for Japan or for the United States. I'd like to say again that Mama-san and I originally chose to come to this country to make this our home. We wanted to raise our family here and live here for the rest of our lives. I have faith that all of this will work out."

As Papa-san quietly shared his views with us, he looked at each of us with a steady gaze. His jaws were set, his face calm and determined. I looked at his gray hair and his kind eyes and thought, *How wise he always seems to me. His decisions are well thought-out and well-timed. He knows the answers to most of the important questions, yet he can say, "I don't know."*

Papa-san had been out in the world for a long time, knowing he was part of a race that was not entirely welcome in this country. He knew the Japanese were not alone with this problem. There had been and would continue to be other groups who would be on the fringe of American society. Being a citizen of Japan, he was probably not too surprised we would be identified with the enemy. He must have resigned himself to this fate and encouraged us to be obedient to the law as one way to show our loyalty and to avoid drawing any more attention to our already tenuous position in a hostile society.

Because this period had been such a difficult time for our family and as taxing as this whole loyalty process had become, it was especially important for me to hear Papa-san express his point of view. I listened intently as he continued, "In spite of everything, this is still a good country with all kinds of possibilities. I've heard each of you talk about learning in some of your classes that this country was established to ensure freedom for all her people. This time will pass. It is important for me to maintain faith that this will all work out eventually for the best." He paused and looked at each of us in turn. "I choose to vote 'Yes Yes.'"

As I listened to Papa-san's answer I marveled at his attitude as I recalled the things that had happened to him and other *Isseis* living in this country. In addition, he gave each of us the opportunity to make our own decision rather than unilaterally making one decision for the whole family as some traditional patriarchs were doing.

In giving us his answer to the questionnaire, Papa-san established his crucial role as head of our family and used it as an opportunity to declare his view of the future. His strength never showed through more than it did during that hushed conversation in that little twenty foot by twenty foot room in April 1943. Papa-san's natural state was to affirm life and have faith in the strength of each of us to face the unknown. Through his words and actions Papa-san taught us the truths he had discovered for his own life.

I looked at Mama-san's face; it was calm and stoic like Papa-san's. She, like so many of the *Issei* mothers, had long ago established a subordinate but significant role within the family. But in this situation, it was clear to me that Mama-san had made her own decision based upon her values and hopes for the future. I did not expect her to defy or disagree with Papa-san, but I knew she would bring a different perspective.

Her hands were steady as she took another sip of tea, then set the cup on the suitcase used as a bedside stand. Clasping her hands in her lap, she agreed with everything Papa-san said, then added, "I know there are many troubling things going on here at Tule Lake and in many of the other camps. It's hard to understand what the government will do next, but no matter what, it is very important to us that we talk about these things so we understand and help each other. It is vitally important to Papa-san and to me that we all stay together in whatever we decide to do." With a firm voice and a steady gaze at Yoneichi and me she stated, "I, too, vote 'Yes Yes.'"

Most mothers would use a steady gaze to tell their children how they must vote, but that is not what I perceived. Her glance showed her confidence that Yoneichi and I would make the right choice for ourselves.

There was a long silence. Outside, the wind picked up pushing dust into the cracks in the walls and the spaces between the barracks. Finally, Mama-san asked, "Yoneichi-san and Mary-san, how do you see it?"

I looked at Yoneichi, knowing how critical his decision would be. There was an important, unspoken cultural value that entered into this decision. It is called *oyakoko,* which means caring for one's parents beyond what is required. A major problem faced each family, especially where there was only one son upon whom his aging parents would depend to help them in their old age. Even if the whole family was in agreement, for the son to be loyal to the U.S. meant abandoning the parents. Loyalty to one's parents meant being "disloyal" to his country. For Japanese sons it was an agonizing decision. I could only imagine how torn a family could be where there were disagreements.

In our family *oyakoko* was a definite part of our decision. Yoneichi and I felt as strongly about our parents as they did about us. We needed to make sure they would be cared for in their old age. What was important to me was that our parents never lost sight of their faith in God and in themselves.

Usually whenever Yoneichi was nervous he would rub his lower teeth against the first joint of his right thumb. But now he looked relaxed as he held his teacup with both hands in his lap. He sat erect, held his head up, his shoulders down and back, and spoke without hesitation. I noticed the same steady gaze that I saw in my parents' eyes. He looked at each of us and agreed with Mama-san and Papa-san. "My 'Yes Yes' decision will mean that I must go into the army and fight in the war. I'm prepared to do that. That is the one thing I can do to prove our family's loyalty to the United States."

Traditionally, Japanese men went into war expecting to die. This was a part of Japanese culture that persisted among the American-born Japanese. Yoneichi was willing to fight and die if necessary.

When Yoneichi said, "Yes Yes," tears clouded my vision. He was going to war, and he could be killed fighting for the country that was doing this to us. My brother was my mentor, my trailblazer who gave me his advice about my behavior or appearance—which I didn't always appreciate. I had followed in his footsteps, forming friendships and participating in student government in high school back at Vashon and feeling like an American citizen. Now I looked at him and was afraid for him and for us. *What would I do without my brother?* I blinked away the image of him dead on a battlefield.

And now I had to make a decision. I felt trapped. Of course, I should be an obedient daughter and just follow my family's lead. But in my heart I wanted to go in opposition to them because what happened wasn't right. How much more would we have to give up before it would end? How could I be sure that voting "Yes Yes" would ensure anything good in the future, or that voting "No No" was the right thing to do? How could I be sure that my vote would be best for our family—for me? If I did choose to follow my own way and challenge the United States government by voting "No No," how would that affect me? They were so calm and certain but I was caught in my painful ambivalence.

Everyone's eyes turned to me. My shoulders hunched up as I leaned forward gripping the teacup in both hands. I looked down at my cup as I lowered my head. I agonized silently. *If I agree to vote "Yes Yes," I will be agreeing with the rest of the family that Yoneichi will have to go to war. If I vote "No No," I could be separated from my family.* I imagined what that would be like. When the time came, Mama-san, Papa-san, and Yoneichi would go with other "Yes Yes" people to another camp. From there Yoneichi would go into the army. Having lost me, my parents would have to deal with the potential loss of their son as well. This would break their hearts.

My private scenario went like this: When the time came for the "Yes Yes" people to board the train to leave Tule Lake, I pictured myself standing alone outside their railroad car. I could see my family through the window beside their seats. When the "All aboard!" rang out and the train slowly started to move, I wondered when or if I would see them again. With that thought clawing at my heart, the tears would well up in my eyes. I saw myself walking slowly, at first keeping pace with the moving car, my tears flowing, then striding more vigorously as the train picked up speed, until I could no longer keep up. With an overwhelming sense of loss and pain, I would stagger to a stop and watch the train leave the station, taking my family away from me. Crushed with grief I would realize for the first time what I had done. Then I would wonder, What in the world ever caused me to give up the one thing I valued above all else—my family?

As my family awaited my decision, still I hesitated. Although I knew "Yes Yes" was the right choice, it broke my heart. It felt like giving in to the bully in the schoolyard. I looked at Papa-san and Mama-san. They had faced discrimination in the past, and then the recent forced choice questionnaire tested their loyalty. They knew that Yoneichi, their hope of the future, might not survive if they voted in the affirmative. Yet based on what they felt would be best for all of us, they chose to place their faith in the United States.

Clenching my hands together, I took a deep breath. The air in our barren, boxlike room felt oppressive. Once more I considered Mama-san's words about the power of love, forgiveness, and hope being the hallmarks of inner strength for difficult times. The barbed-wire fences, the guard towers, the guns, the rotating searchlights, and the dust storms all receded into the background. They were replaced by a vision of home where there was peace and contentment in the simple things of life; where we took such delight in the beauty of a camellia blossom, the song of a bird, or the taste of fresh corn from the garden. Home is where we had satisfying friendships with neighbors, and especially, family meals together around the kitchen table—the four of us, together.

At last calmness settled over me. I looked up at my family, and I took another deep breath. The tension in my chest relaxed. Instead of loyalty to any illusion of country, my commitment was to the reality of the love within my own family. *They* were my country. Each one looked at me with kind eyes and with a slight bow of their heads, they each acknowledged me and my place as a full member of this family.

Leaning my head near my brother and parents, I looked at each of them. "Yes Yes," I said and fell silent.

It took me more than fifty years to understand and appreciate the sacrifices of those who chose "No No." The "No No" people fought for our rights in a very different way that many traditional Japanese families did not understand at the time. Even when they were threatened with violation of the Espionage Act, punishable by a $10,000 fine and up to twenty years imprisonment, the "No No" people stood their ground. We were in agreement that our people's civil rights had been violated and the order for the evacuation was unjust. The Loyalty Oath was intended to separate the loyals from the disloyals, but it ended up separating us for reasons that had nothing to do with loyalty.

Knowing what I know now, I weep for the people who were labeled by the government as disloyal and thrust into a punishing environment without fair legal counsel. The "No No" people were denied leave clearance and other privileges, and some were tried as criminals and convicted on flimsy evidence.

Most troubling of all to me is the way in which we Japanese-Americans condemned our own because the "No Nos" chose a different way in which to respond. Although it was not obvious to me at the time, the "No No" people were also victims of intimidation perpetuated by those who voted "Yes Yes." For decades after the war, the "No Nos" were ostracized within the Japanese-American community. I see now that it took tremendous courage for them to face rejection by American society and by their own people. My hope is that the position of the "No Nos" will be understood and accepted as worthy of the highest form of respect. Dissent is an essential expression of democracy.

Mary Matsuda Gruenewald Collection

Heart Mountain Internment Camp in Wyoming.

Remembering Twenty Years from Now

The morning after our family meeting, Papa-san took our completed questionnaires and officially turned them in. While I was worried about the future consequences of our choices, I was greatly relieved by our unanimous family decision. That evening Yoneichi reminded us, "We'll have to keep our decision to ourselves. We don't want the 'No No' guys to get wind of it."

The pace of threats and beatings continued. One night I bolted upright in bed to the sound of many feet pounding on the ground outside our barrack. My family heard it, too. After the footsteps died in the distance and all was quiet again, I flopped back on my cot. It took awhile before I could drop back to sleep.

The following day we heard there had been a serious altercation in the central part of our camp during the night. People were running amok, so the camp administration called in the army and imposed martial law. The soldiers were quick to respond, since they were already on the premises, and they immediately went from block to block, barrack to barrack, primarily in the central part of camp searching for the instigators of the violence. When the suspects were found and caught, they were locked up in the stockade—inside an already barbed-wire camp.

Seeing the soldiers with their rifles on a daily basis was the norm, but the increasing tension and sporadic uprisings made me more fearful. It was now eleven months since we were evacuated from our home and I had recently turned eighteen years old. As the days passed, I became increasingly preoccupied with the question, *What will happen to us if the war doesn't go well for the United States?* And I couldn't help but consider, *This uprising might be the excuse the army needs to kill us all.*

A couple of months after signing the Loyalty Oath, Yoneichi and a friend decided it was time to register for the draft. This required a hazardous journey past the central part of the internment camp and into the administration building—a place that only *inu* would go. The two friends decided Yoneichi would go in first, and if he saw any sign of danger, he would give a hand signal, and his friend would run away immediately. It was frightening for me to hear them making their plans. When they left I waited nervously for them to return. About an hour later they got back. Yoneichi seemed casual about the whole thing. "It was easy," he said. "I'm glad I got that out of the way."

On July 12, 1943, a few days before I graduated from Tri-State High School, an official announcement of the process for segregating the internees according to the way we voted was made in the *Tulean Dispatch*. All relocation centers would be affected. The program was scheduled to begin around September 1.

The Director of the WRA felt that the longer the two divergent groups lived in such close proximity, the greater the chances for rioting and bloodshed. However, the segregation process proved to be much more complex than originally envisioned prior to the registration process.

The WRA had plans to divide the internees into groups with different degrees of loyalty, ranging from "loyal to the United States" to "loyal to Japan." In August 1943 the WRA defined the categories in its pamphlet:

SEGREGATION of Persons of Japanese Ancestry in Tule Lake Relocation Center

All internees would be divided into four major groups based on how they completed the loyalty questionnaire:

GROUP I: Persons who will be segregated without further hearing. The people in this group requested repatriation or expatriation before July 1, 1943, and did not retract their requests.

GROUP II: Those persons who would appear to be loyal to Japan rather than to the United States. Several procedures were outlined to determine if that remains their choice.

GROUP III: Those persons who may have stated their loyalty to the United States, but whose loyalty is in doubt. Hearings were to be given to determine the true loyalty of each individual.

GROUP IV: Those eligible for leave.

Unfortunately, the real-life complexities of the internees did not fit so neatly into these four categories. There were many exceptions, each requiring time-consuming analysis by the WRA before a decision could be made. Sometimes family members disagreed with each other, creating exceptions upon exceptions. The bureaucratic process was a nightmare for many, and still no one really knew what segregation would bring, so all decisions had to be made with incomplete information.

Although the registration process was fraught with confusion, the segregation program had been carefully planned. The WRA learned from the disaster it created with the original questionnaire. This time the administration gave the evacuees the opportunity to clearly identify if they were loyal or sympathetic to Japan or to the United States. Based on their loyalties, this would determine which internment camp the WRA would send them to. If they were labeled "disloyals," they stayed at Tule Lake for the duration of the war. The WRA granted the "loyals" clearance and assistance to move to one of the other nine camps if desired. At that point they could obtain clearance to leave the camps permanently.

By this time my experience with the U.S. government had been so checkered that I didn't know what to believe. *Now what?* I thought. *Is this going to be better for us? Show me.* The future still seemed full of fearful unknowns.

On July 16, 1943, two months after I would have graduated from Vashon Island High School, I graduated with 397 seniors from Tri-State High School. My classmates and I dressed in caps and gowns and sat on benches lined up in front of the outdoor stage. If we had been living at home, we would have been looking forward to all kinds of exciting future possibilities: going off to college, getting jobs, working independently, getting married, or traveling to foreign countries, to mention a few. Despite the oppressive situation we chose our class theme: "Today We Follow…Tomorrow We Lead." At the graduation ceremony a group of students who called themselves the Harmonaires sang "Invictus," a song written by William Henley with Bruno Huhn, composer.

INVICTUS
Out of the night that covers me,
Black as the pit from pole to pole,
I thank whatever gods may be
For my unconquerable soul…

I am the master of my fate
I am the captain of my soul.

The words of the song did not match my feelings at all. I was unclear about my identity and could not imagine being the master of my fate or the captain of my soul. All during my grade school and high school years at Vashon I had been looking forward to the time when I would graduate from high school and my life would open. But now the freedoms of that world had disappeared. World events and national policies had swept away all the choices I had taken for granted as a child. A few of my classmates did leave camp to continue their education, but for most of us, there was nothing to look forward to. It was more of the same monotonous routine.

By August 1943, the WRA completed most of the segregation decision-making. Based on our "Yes Yes" vote, our family received orders and clearance to leave Tule Lake on September 13 and relocate to Heart Mountain in northwestern Wyoming. I was glad we would be leaving this frightening place, but this move was harder than the last. Over the past fourteen months I had developed close friendships with a number of people in our ward and in high school. Now we would be separated again. Later I learned more than six thousand of us left Tule Lake and dispersed to the other nine camps. When we left, 8,559 people labeled "disloyals" came from the other camps to Tule Lake. This made an already crowded camp even more crowded.

As I rode the train with my family from Tule Lake to Heart Mountain, I was hopeful that this camp would be much better. I looked forward to being free from the constant wrangling that had become such a part of our daily lives at Tule Lake. Three days later we arrived at another treeless camp with the familiar black, tarpapered barracks surrounded by barbed-wire fences and beyond that sagebrush-dotted countryside. My heart sank. It would be in this desolate place that we would face one of our hardest times as a family.

I didn't know there could be so many bleak and barren places in this country. I longed for the greens of my home on Puget Sound. Looking across to the hills beyond, I could see a rock formation shaped like a heart, which was the reason for the name of the camp. I wondered, *Could it be possible to hope that this camp might be safer and people would have more heart here?*

The truck stopped in front of block 12, barrack 8, and apartment C. When we got off, I looked at the barrack and stopped.

"Something's different here," I said.

The truck driver pointed out, "That's an outer doorway and there's a recessed alcove behind it that leads to apartments C and D. You'll be in apartment C on the left."

"Oh, there is one entryway to two apartments?" Yoneichi asked.

"Yes. Last winter it was so cold here, down in the twenties most of the time. These alcoves keep out much of the wind, dust, and cold whenever people go in and out of their apartments. You'll be glad it's made that way."

We thanked him as we entered our new home. I was curious about the people with whom we would be sharing the alcove. After we put our luggage inside, Papa-san and Yoneichi once again went looking for straw and ticking for mattresses. Since our room was the same size as the one we just left in Tule Lake, it didn't take much imagination for Mama-san and me to set it up. Then we went outdoors and looked around. The environment here was not unlike the one in Tule Lake, but as before, we had to get our bearings. All the barracks looked exactly alike, and we didn't want to end up in someone else's apartment by mistake.

We went next door to apartment D. Bowing to the older couple, Mama-san introduced us and greeted them, *"Yoroshiku onegai shimasu—*I'm glad to make your acquaintance."

The gentleman bowed and returned our greeting. "Hello, we are the Yamaguchis. Welcome." His wife looked at us and nodded her head. She appeared very frail and withdrawn. They were a quiet couple; there would never be any cause for concern from that side of the building.

We went to the room on the other side of ours, to apartment B, and responded to the invitation, "Come in." There were four young people lounging on their cots. When we introduced ourselves, the older girl sat up and said, "I'm Tomoko Ogata, and these are my brothers Juro and Ken over there, and my sister, Mariko. Dad is over at the post office right now. I'll tell him you moved in next door."

Tomoko and her brothers were very attractive young people, possibly in their twenties. I guessed Mariko to be around thirteen. I learned their mother had died. It didn't take long for us to discover that the Ogatas were very sociable. Young people were continually going in and out of their apartment most of the day and late into the evening. Like the barracks in Pinedale Assembly Center and Tule Lake, the triangular-shaped opening between the walls and the roof allowed noise to echo throughout the barracks. To our dismay the loud music, raucous chattering, laughing, arguments, and fighting next door at the Ogatas became a frequent source of disturbance.

Once again we were in the midst of other families in another big camp. Guards in the watchtowers had become such a common part of our daily lives that they could be ignored. Yet I was aware they could shoot if we made any move that could be interpreted as out of line. I was confused.

Is this how the "loyal" people are treated? Is this our reward for voting "Yes Yes?"
At night I lay awake. Restless, I tossed and turned on my lumpy mattress, trying to find a comfortable spot. Eventually I would fall into a fitful sleep.

With the passing weeks I tried to stay in touch with former classmates on Vashon. My good friend, Betty, wrote about a tragic accident. Apparently four young men, three of whom were her cousins and with whom I had shared classes in high school, had gone fishing over a weekend. A sudden squall came up and in the violent storm that followed, only one survived. All of them had been sons of fishermen and were good, strong swimmers, but for some unknown reason the three cousins drowned. They were all handsome and popular among the students. I liked one young man in particular, and always enjoyed talking with him in the classes we shared. But I had consciously restrained myself from getting too involved, knowing our cultural taboo against dating anyone, Japanese or Caucasian. I was devastated by this news, realizing I was not the only one dealing with senseless tragedy.

I had come to this new camp hopeful things would be much better, that I could go about my life feeling safer and freer. But my original optimism quickly faded away in the monotonous routine. All of my friends from Tule Lake were gone, and I had to make an effort to make new acquaintances. I had already graduated from high school so it was more difficult to make friends. The only thing familiar was my family and the endless days with nothing to do.

One day I overheard some people talking and got really scared. That evening I found Yoneichi alone and approached him with a lump in my throat. "You're not going to volunteer for the army, are you?" I asked, my voice quivering.

He looked at me with a surprised expression, then smiled reassuringly. "No, don't worry about that," he said. "I think it's important for me to go into the service, but I'm not in any hurry. After all, I have to think about the folks." He paused, then looked more serious. "A few guys were so gung-ho they have already left. I'm not sure that's the smartest thing to do. As for me, I'll just wait for my draft number to come up. That will happen soon enough." I realized immediately what he meant—the early volunteers were most likely not going to survive the war. I hoped his draft number wouldn't come up for a long time.

About this time, a major debate took place in the nation's capital between the War Department and General John L. DeWitt, commander of the Western Defense Command who carried out the evacuation. The War Department no longer believed that military necessity justified excluding loyal ethnic Japanese from the West Coast, but it was unwilling to reverse its orders. Government officials were probably afraid of a political firestorm, of being unable to face down strong political objections to returning *Issei* and *Nisei,* regardless of loyalty, to the West Coast.

After the evacuation of all Japanese-Americans from the West Coast following Pearl Harbor, a period of relative calm followed, and the racist propaganda subsided. However, it returned in full force during the first half of 1943. Having successfully removed all of us from the West Coast, various groups began lobbying to make the banishment permanent. They argued that the government must have had evidence of disloyalty to warrant the evacuation, and therefore all of the internees should be sent "back to Japan" forever. Organizations such as the Native Sons of the Golden West and the American Legion supported the permanent ban. Newspapers such as the *San Francisco Examiner,* the *Los Angeles Times,* the *Los Angeles Examiner,* and the *Denver Post* joined in the escalating attack on Japanese-Americans. So did politicians like Earl Warren, the Attorney General of California.

However, by mid-July 1943, the tide was beginning to turn. Considerable discussion took place between the Western Defense Command and the War Department. The Dies Committee on Un-American Activities held hearings in which both sides battled it out. In time a consensus developed in which half-truths and lies were eclipsed by a more humane and rational approach to the whole Japanese internment question.

As a result, General DeWitt, labeled the "military zealot" by the *Washington Post,* was relieved of his duties with the Western Defense Command in the fall of 1943. By year's end Attorney General Francis Biddle urged the return of the internees to their former residences and recommended the WRA continue to administer the internment camps by making it a part of the Interior Department. Harold Ickes, who was already a champion for the Japanese-Americans, became the spokesperson for this more enlightened policy. At the time we were unaware that all of this was going on.

The tide turned in the war in the South Pacific in the summer of 1943, which may have also helped ease anti-Japanese sentiment in the United States. The *Heart Mountain Sentinel* reported that the American forces were on the offense in the Solomon Islands.

A national crisis had occurred following the evacuation in 1942. With men serving in the military, and civilians, many of them women, working in munitions factories, shipyards, or other war industries, thousands of acres of crops deteriorated due to lack of a labor force. Japanese and Japanese-American farmers on the West Coast, who had produced much of the fruit and vegetables for the West, were no longer available to provide the necessary food supplies. Although we were initially seen as threats to American security and removed from our farms, now the government decided we were essential. Japanese labor was needed to save the nation's crops.

In April 1942 the U.S. government had asked the state governors from Utah, Arizona, Nevada, Montana, Idaho, New Mexico, Wyoming, Washington, and Oregon to allow Japanese-Americans to voluntarily relocate to their states. Most of the governors were adamant about not wanting any Japanese in their states, even in internment camps. Now in August 1943 these governors suddenly saw the benefit of having us come to salvage their crops in a crisis even bigger than the year before. Responding to this gigantic need, the WRA made temporary or seasonal leaves available and urged internees to apply for clearance in eastern Oregon, Washington, Idaho, Utah, Montana, and Wyoming. *Isseis* and *Niseis* could leave temporarily, if they received clearance from the FBI. This seasonal leave appealed especially to the restless, young *Nisei* men who were already chafing against the restraints of camp life.

We had been reading about this latest development in the *Sentinel* and found the change of events ironic. One evening my brother brought up the topic. "There are three of us who have been talking about getting out of camp and seeing what things are like outside. I'd like to go with them. What do you think?" Yoneichi asked.

Papa-san did not seem surprised. "I think it's a good idea," he said. "You'll have a chance to get out of camp for a few months. I read that your transportation, housing, and safety are assured by the farmers who need laborers to come and save their crops. I think it's okay to go." My mother and I agreed.

It was all right for Yoneichi to go, but I was not ready to leave. I had never been on my own before. I had not given any thought to living alone nor how I would make my own way in the world. The war in the Pacific was still raging, and I was still coping with feelings of self-doubt and shame. My greatest fear was facing more anti-Japanese prejudice. The evacuation process had devastated me, and I was too fearful of leaving my family.

Yoneichi became one of the ten thousand who left the internment camps on temporary leave to harvest crops in the fall of 1943. It was a difficult time as this was our first separation as a family. Yoneichi worked for about two months harvesting sugar beets in Idaho and Washington. We were so glad when he returned. He seemed more self-assured as he shared his stories, which were a mixture of positive experiences and difficult encounters when he went into nearby towns for various services. These were disturbing experiences of racial prejudice, but not surprising.

"We were treated well by some of the farmers when we first got there," he reported, "but when we got through harvesting the crops, we were no longer welcome. One time a couple of us decided to go and get haircuts. We noticed a sign outside one barbershop, 'No Japs Allowed.' Of course, we moved on until we found a better place and we got good haircuts there. In one place in Idaho, we were having trouble getting groceries because they wouldn't sell to us," Yoneichi continued. "So we had to leave the store empty handed. I was amazed when a white man brought a variety of groceries to us in his van, and we could buy from him."

Papa-san remarked, "He was a courageous man for doing that."

"Yes, we told him how much we appreciated what he did and that we were concerned because he could be labeled 'Jap lover.' But he didn't seem to be too worried about that."

I listened to one of Yoneichi's friends tell a similar story about his experiences topping sugar beets and gathering potatoes. "I went to help out with the harvest and made pretty good money doing it," the friend explained. "Our boss was glad to have us Japanese-Americans come and help with the harvest. But when it was over, we were Japs again. He didn't want us around. I didn't like it that we were welcomed only when we were needed."

Those who remained in camp instead of going outside to work responded to the continued internment in different ways. In our family, the three of us went about our daily routine with quiet acceptance. But we heard about disturbances and general unrest taking place elsewhere. It was fortunate that I didn't know about the continuing turmoil at Tule Lake, which only grew worse after our departure. I would have worried about my friends still there, without having any way of helping them. It would have only made me feel worse.

One day I was talking to Keiko, one of my friends, who told me about an incident that happened in her family. Her mother was usually a very sweet, gentle woman, but on this particular day Keiko made some innocent comment about something—she couldn't even remember what—and her mother suddenly burst into tears. Keiko was astonished. She hadn't realized how much stress her mother had been silently enduring. They sat down, talked, and cried together over the stress of facing anti-Japanese hostility every day.

≺◎≻

One day I overheard Papa-san say to Mama-san, "We haven't heard anything from Mack. I wonder how the strawberry harvest went this summer. I hope it went all right."

"Yes, we haven't heard, but if anyone could manage our farm it would be Mack," Mama-san replied. "Let's just wait and see."

I had never concerned myself with the business dealings of the farm; that was Papa-san and Yoneichi's responsibility. But suddenly I realized that something was not right. Yoneichi had a lawyer draw up a contract regarding the operation of the farm in our absence. In that document the deputy sheriff on Vashon Island and Yoneichi had agreed that all profits and expenses for our farm would be divided fifty-fifty. That evening, I was stunned to overhear Yoneichi and Papa-san discuss that some other farmers had heard updates on the status of their farms on Vashon, but we hadn't, despite letters of inquiry. I wondered why we hadn't heard from the deputy sheriff as agreed. I began to worry. *Is he stealing our money? Is he paying our bills? Could we lose our home so there will be nothing to go home to?* A nagging suspicion was growing that something was wrong, but there was nothing we could do about it. These fears plagued me and became one more reason why it was hard to sleep at night. I dreamed our farm, like our liberty, was stolen from us.

I had made the assumption that Heart Mountain was a camp for "loyals," and things would be much better in this camp. But before long I was astonished to learn that all resisters to the draft were not at Tule Lake Internment Camp. There were people at Heart Mountain who were just as vocal against the Loyalty Oath. The resisters called many meetings to discuss the issues. Eventually they formed the Fair Play Committee (FPC) in January 1944. Yoneichi attended one of the first meetings to learn what they stood for.

"There were a lot of guys there," Yoneichi reported. "Three of them who talked the most seemed real clear that they weren't anti-draft. They just wanted all of us to have our rights restored and losses compensated before we signed up for military duty."

Papa-san said, "They have a point, but you know politics. It would take a long, long time before that could happen."

"I know, but I think that could happen only *after* we fight in the war, " Yoneichi said. "I think we have to *prove* our loyalty and go fight before something like this could take place. Most of us just sat and listened, not saying much."

I listened in silence. I could see the FPC's position, but was it even possible to achieve those goals given how things stood now? *If the internees protest for the restoration of our rights first, we could look as if we are anti-American and not to be trusted,* I thought. Furthermore, since Yoneichi was going to war to "prove our family's loyalty," I didn't want to think about being a resister. I dismissed the FPC's whole point of view.

The FPC continued to hold many meetings and its ranks grew to more than sixty members who agitated openly for redress and restitution of their rights. But it seemed to me that the majority of the population remained silent and watched. During this time our family observed the activities around us, but made no public commitments. Eventually the outspoken resisters were arrested and taken away. I learned later they were sent to various U.S. Marshal's offices in Pueblo, New Mexico; Denver County jails in Colorado; and county jails in Cheyenne and Casper, Wyoming. The U.S. government accused the FPC members of draft evasion, counseling draft resistance, and advocating draft evasion.

Throughout this tumultuous period my fear and futility persisted. Our hopes of returning home, of greater freedom, and the restoration of our status as loyal citizens now seemed more remote than ever. With the battles in full force in Europe and the South Pacific, the resolution of internment camp conflicts and my own inner turmoil seemed a long way off. Everything outside of the barbed-wire fence was beyond my reach. Isolation and impending doom not only would not go away, but intensified as the time for Yoneichi's departure steadily approached.

The day came when Yoneichi received a letter from the draft board. Papa-san looked grave as he handed the envelope to Yoneichi, who paused before taking it. He opened the envelope deliberately and read it in silence. There was another long pause after he finished reading. Finally, he looked up at the three of us, who dreaded what he was about to say.

"I have been very fortunate," he said. "I had a good draft number, but now the time has come. I have three months to get ready. I leave for basic training at the end of June."

I couldn't deny the inevitable any longer. I ran from the apartment blindly, tears streaming down my face, oblivious to the stares of others. I collapsed into a pile behind our barrack and sobbed inconsolably. Soon I felt Mama-san's arms around me. I reached over to hold her, my face against hers, our tears mingled together before dropping onto the dusty ground. It was many long minutes before either of us could talk. "I don't want him to go!" I finally gasped. "I don't want him to go!" "Yes, I know," Mama-san whispered quietly into my ear. "I don't want him to go, either, but he must." We spent a long time holding each other, talking and comforting one other.

A few days later, Mama-san told me about an ancient Japanese tradition, a stitched talisman for Yoneichi to carry into battle. It was called a *senninbari*, a thousand-stitch belt.

Mama-san went to the canteen and bought a yard of white cotton fabric, black embroidery thread, some sewing needles of various sizes, a ruler, and embroidery hoop. Back in our room I sat near her as she took the ruler and marked out a twenty-inch square in the middle of the fabric. Along each side she marked off a hundred dots approximately three millimeters apart and filled in the rest of the spaces between until there were a thousand dots in tight, neat little rows. The embroidery hoop held the fabric taut, and made it much easier to handle. Cutting off approximately twelve inches of the embroidery thread, she threaded one end through the needle and made a knot in the other.

As Mama-san worked, she explained, "It is very important that Yoneichi-san have this *senninbari* to carry with him while he is away from us at war. This will give him courage and strength when he has this symbol of our love. According to tradition, this *senninbari* carries the care and support of the one thousand women and girls who will make their stitches for him. Only stitches made by these people praying for his safe return have the power to protect him from the bullets of the enemy."

As Mama-san was about to make the first French knot in the fabric, she took a deep breath, bowed her head, and closed her eyes. She remained still for a long minute, her face composed, as her lips moved silently in prayer. She raised her head, then began making the knot.

She brought the needle up from below the hoop through the first dot and pulled the thread through. Laying the needle on the fabric where the thread came through, she held it firmly on the material with her left thumb. With the right hand she wound the thread around the needle three times, then inserted the needle down near the point that the thread had been brought up, careful to keep the thread taut as it was pulled through to the bottom of the fabric. She turned, bowed slightly to me, and handed the *senninbari* to me to make the next stitch.

I bowed my head as tears came to my eyes and spilled over as I thought, *My only brother is going off to fight in the war to prove our family's loyalty. He is my trailblazer.*

When Yoneichi was a senior and I was a sophomore, I remember feeling so proud of him when he was elected Secretary of the Student Body. A school advisor later told me how much she admired his many abilities in scholarship, athletics, and friendly relationships with all the students in school. Although he was short, Yoneichi was fast and fearless and made the Vashon High School varsity football team. To help him improve his skills, I learned to pass spirals so he could practice catching the football on the run.

What if he never returns from the war? I wondered, crying. Now I couldn't see where the next dot was in the fabric. Mama-san put her hand on my arm and waited as I regained my composure.

"Yoneichi-san will appreciate having this made by you and me and all the others. This is the time for faith that it will help to keep him safe." I completed my stitch. Mama-san and I then began to make the rounds of our neighbors and friends, asking each woman and girl to make her mark on the *senninbari*. Mama-san kept adding lengths to the thread to insure that it was continuous. In a way, Mama-san was the continuous thread that had kept the tapestry of our family intact throughout these years.

We moved from barrack to barrack until we had covered the entire ward. Beyond that, we relied on the recommendations of our Vashon friends to help us find those who would be willing to contribute a stitch for Yoneichi.

Most of the women we asked understood our position and made their stitches enthusiastically. But one woman smugly said to Mama-san, "I don't agree that the *Niseis* should fight for America but I'll make this stitch just for him. I still think you folks are foolish for letting him go."

Mama-san merely nodded her head and expressed appreciation for her making her knot, but I was outraged! I hated her! How could she be so rude?

One afternoon as we stood outside of our living quarters, thinking back over the people we had asked, Mrs. Watanabe from Vashon came bustling up to us. We had missed her when we went by her apartment. As she always did back home, she started chattering away effusively about hearing that Yoneichi was going into the army. She exclaimed, "It's wonderful that you are making this *senninbari* for Yoneichi-san to carry, and I would like to make a stitch for him." As she carried on I moaned inwardly. *I've always disliked this crotchety old woman who is always babbling about something,* I thought. Mama-san turned to her and politely replied, "Would you be kind enough to make a stitch in this for him?"

"Why, of course," she said. "I would consider it a pleasure to do that." She swept the material out of Mama-san's hands, took the threaded needle and made a bold stab at the dot all the while jabbering about something else. Then she stopped. "Ack," she said as she stuck her thumb into her mouth. She had poked herself. *Thank goodness she didn't get any blood on the material,* I thought. Mama-san and I looked at each other, then looked away to keep from bursting out in laughter.

The stitch was finally completed. Mama-san had waited patiently. She retrieved the *senninbari,* bowed slowly as she politely thanked Mrs. Watanabe for doing her part, then turned. We went looking for others to add their stitches. Within days we had one thousand stitches.

A few evenings later at our room, Mama-san bowed slightly in front of Yoneichi and said, "Yoneichi-san, here is a *senninbari* that the ladies and girls in our neighborhood made for you to take with you into battle. For hundreds of years men have carried this symbol of protection before they left their loved ones. This belt has special powers to protect you from the enemy. Remember that there were one thousand of us who made this for you. All of us will *inoru*—pray to God—for your safe return to us."

Yoneichi received it with both hands, closed his eyes, and bowed his head as he raised the gift to his forehead. After a moment, he raised his head, and with tenderness in his eyes said, "*Arigato gozaimasu*—Thank you, Mama-san. I will keep it every day with the New Testament in my breast pocket, over my heart."

We bought a picture of a tiger for Yoneichi and hung it on the wall opposite the entryway, a place to catch our eye whenever we came into our apartment. The tiger is a symbol of strength and protection, and we wanted that for Yoneichi.

∢ ◉ ∾

One evening when the four of us returned from dinner, I felt especially despondent. I sat lost in memories of our evenings on Vashon. I had been so comfortable in the certainty of my life in those first sixteen years. Then my sweet memories slipped into despair and this strange world I had been catapulted into. *I've been caught in the reach of the sweeping searchlight; caught* with yellow skin, slant eyes, black straight hair with buckteeth. I am like the "yellow-bellied" soldiers on the front page of Time magazine clutching helpless women and children as they trample the burning cities of America! I could not shake the feeling that I was bad and not to be trusted. That was why I was in prison here, and there was nothing I could do about any of this.

All the things they had used to divert my attention in the camps hadn't changed a thing for me. They can have their sports, their evening variety shows, the movies, and the dances! I thought. They can have it all! I'm still in prison and isolated! Then I thought about the deputy sheriff on Vashon. We can't trust him. He's going to take our home and farm away from us! Then my worries quickly jumped to Yoneichi. He is going into the army and will be sent off to war in Europe to be killed and when he's gone, they'll come after the rest of us. And no one can save me! Within minutes I was emotionally sunk.

I looked over at Yoneichi who had his back to me. In a few weeks, I might never see him again. A churning feeling rose in my gut and spilled over, out of control. I bobbed my head and slapped my thighs with my hands as I burst out, "I can't stand it any more! Yoneichi is going to die! We're going to lose our home and farm forever! Why? We haven't done anything wrong! We're still prisoners! God has abandoned us! There's nothing that can save us! Not even you, Mama-san!" I lamented, sobbing.

The sound of people walking by our barrack was in the background. No one moved or uttered a sound in our apartment. My family sat stunned for a long time, all of us looking down at the floor. I was as horrified as the others, unable to take back what a moment before I had been unable to contain.

In the shocked silence, a look of calm determination came over Mama-san. She recognized the anguish in my words and realized that I was— that we were—at a crossroads. The truth had been told, and there was no turning back.

She looked up and quietly said, "You are not alone in your feelings, Mary-san, because I have them too."

I let out a sobbing breath, astonished. "You do?"

As I looked at her through my tears, her face came into focus. It was warm, sad, and old. Why had I never seen her despair? I asked myself. I knew the sad stories of her parents' deaths.

Several years before Mama-san had told me about her parents while we washed dishes on the farm. "I don't remember much about my father because he died when I was two years old," Mama-san explained. With a faraway look on her face she continued, "But I was six when my mother died. My mother must have been very ill because she stayed in bed for days. That was not like her at all. Whenever I went in to see her and asked her why she was still in bed, she'd apologize for being so lazy and put me off with some excuse.

"One day a lot of people came to our home. Some came to help clean the house, others to cook extra food. It was all very confusing. My oldest sister, Chizuko, took me aside and tearfully told me that our mother had died, but I didn't understand what that meant. I kept opening the *shoji* panel door to the room where my mother slept, but she was not there. I looked among the futon comforters piled in the storage cupboard hoping to find her, but she wasn't there either. Weeks later I finally realized that my mother would not be with us any more. I went looking for Chizuko-san to ask her. She took me in her arms and rocked me back and forth, back and forth. I cried and cried and even now, when I think about it, I feel sad for that little girl so long ago, longing for her mother."

I looked at Mama-san sitting on her cot across from me, the stress of so much loss clouding her eyes. I thought with total amazement, *Here is a woman who not only lost both of her parents during her early years, but also left her home, her family, and everything of her native country. She faced racism, saw her children imprisoned beside her, and now at age fifty-two faces the possibility of losing everything she has worked for all these years, including her only son. How could I not have known that she has heartaches of her own?*

In the harsh light of the barrack, Mama-san reached across and took my hands in both of her warm ones. She held my hands for a moment, then got up and sat down beside me. Placing her face against mine and wiping my tears with her handkerchief, she put her arms around my shoulders and rocked me gently back and forth, back and forth. Papa-san and Yoneichi gathered around us in silent support as my sobbing quieted.

Then she said softly and slowly, "There are times when things happen to us that we can't explain. We have no control. We are here because of forces outside of our family. We had no part in creating any of this, but we cannot expect to live in a world in which there is no pain or fear, where everything goes along without disturbing events. Our situation could be unbearable, unless..." and after a long pause and a faraway, serene, upward look on her face, she added quietly, "unless we reconsider how we will face it."

At first I didn't understand. I relaxed a little, but still I felt we were trapped.

"Let's imagine," she said after a thoughtful silence, "that we are now twenty years into the future, looking back on our situation as it is right now." She looked at Yoneichi, then glanced briefly at Papa-san. "Some of us *may* survive this time. Twenty years from now, we may have nothing more than the memories of how we conducted ourselves with dignity and courage during this difficult time." She paused. "What kind of memories do we want to have *then* of how we faced these difficulties *now?*"

She looked at me and nodded. Her tender smile deepened the dimples in her cheeks and the laughing lines at her eyes. She dropped her arms from my shoulders and took my hands again.

I felt disoriented, dazed, breathlessly bewildered. Suddenly, reality didn't matter. It was as if I was released from my body, from camp, from suffering. I felt like I was floating in space with no boundaries to control me—just a profound feeling of freedom.

What kind of memories do we want to have then of how we faced these difficulties now? I asked myself.

What a startling suggestion! It felt like the pressure of a massive balloon in my chest suddenly deflated. I could breathe. Mama-san had taken this wretched situation and transformed it into one filled with hope and possibility. My heart opened up to what I had just heard. The darkness of my depression began to lift and for the first time I knew in my core I could choose freedom and a different attitude. *They can trap my body,* I told myself, *but not my spirit and not my future.*

Papa-san and Yoneichi's bodies and facial expressions relaxed, too. Their breathing was deeper and slower just like mine. The tension in our shoulders eased. A long pause followed as we each considered the question. A cool breeze gently stirred the curtains of our window, bringing relief from the afternoon heat.

Yoneichi was the first to speak. "I'd like to remember that we agreed as a family to do whatever it took to prove our loyalty to our homeland, America. I want us all to be proud of our family." We all nodded thoughtfully.

Papa-san looked around at each of us and spoke with obvious pride. "I'd like to remember that we listened to each other, but decided things as a family and acted as one, with courage and honor." We each thought about Papa-san's comment and nodded in agreement.

Then Mama-san said, "I'd like to remember that during this time we never lost our love for each other and developed hope and faith that we would come out of this time stronger and with a greater appreciation for each other." Each of us nodded and smiled at each other.

Outside, the sky had grown darker with the approach of night, leaving our four faces illuminated by the single light bulb suspended over our heads. What was so clear to me was the power of Mama-san's love and faith and hope in me and in our family. Just as her arms surrounded me, I felt enveloped in her love. I was no longer alone, even in my despair. Our family could continue to face together whatever was ahead.

Listening to everyone else, I realized it was time for me to lay aside my bitterness, self-pity, and feelings of inferiority. I blushed with embarrassment, but everyone nodded at me, waiting. Taking a deep breath I said in a shaky voice, "I'd like to look back and remember that, in the middle of this crisis, I was able to see my family take everything that was happening and use it all to help me grow up." In that moment, with their patience and love, I became an adult.

·:◉:·

That evening, as had been our custom, we had our snack before bed. On Vashon our snack might have been a piece of watermelon, cantaloupe, persimmon, or pear. Or it could have been a slice of delicious peach pie with a flaky crust or chocolate cake with white, seven-minute frosting. But here at camp, we each had a soda cracker. Mama-san suggested we imagine what kind of bedtime snack we were having that evening. The others kept changing their dessert selection, but mine was always the same—the most luscious banana split ever created.

That night as Mama-san gave me the soda cracker to eat I received it in my open palms, bowed my head, and closed my eyes. I placed the cracker into my mouth, and the dry saltiness slowly dissolved, just as it had every evening since our arrival at Heart Mountain. But this time the sweet richness of the ice cream positively exploded in my mouth, the strawberry seeds crunching delicately between my teeth, the thick caramel slowly enveloping my tongue. The banana was a perfect state of ripeness and the chocolate perfumed and heady. Even the nuts and cherry combined for a sweet crunch. I swallowed, raised my head, opened my eyes, and smiled with the sweetness.

CHAPTER FOURTEEN

GOODBYES

Days flew by. Yoneichi's dreaded departure day was rapidly approaching. I worried that his preparations for leaving would make it obvious to resisters in the camp that he was loyal to the United States. Maybe he would become a target for groups of young men opposed to the Loyalty Oath who continued to agitate against the government. As more young men left the internment camp for the service, there was a palpable tension in the air.

One evening as we gathered for our evening snack, Yoneichi started to act silly like he used to do back home. Sitting at his usual place on his cot, he said, "Look at this." He pulled his lower eyelids down with the thumb and middle fingers of one hand revealing the whites of his eyes. Taking the index finger of the other hand and pushing his nose upwards, his features looked all squished together. When he rolled his eyes around in circles, he looked so ridiculous we couldn't keep from laughing. His comic behavior broke the tension. It felt wonderful to focus on something different, especially something funny.

Then he said, "Watch this." He pulled down the outer corners of his eyes with his index fingers and pulled up on the corners of his mouth with his thumbs. His eyes and white teeth popped out. When he added a wagging tongue to all this, we laughed so hard we had to hold our stomachs, completely overcome.

Mama-san was not to be outdone. She said, "Here's Mrs. Watanabe and Mrs. Yamamoto trying to be polite and urging the other to take the first cup of tea." First she'd bow as one woman and then quickly turn to bow as the other like two mechanical dolls with incessant bobbing heads.

As Mrs. Watanabe, she repeatedly bowed as she said with an exaggerated voice accent, *"Purreesu, Yamamoto-san, habu somu cukisu*—Please, Yamamoto-san, have some cookies. They are inferior to your wonderful delicacies, but I ask you to do me the honor of having some."

I clapped my hands and laughingly said, "I can just hear her saying that."

Then she turned her body around to portray Mrs. Yamamoto in a falsetto voice with a different regional dialect, all the while repeatedly bobbing her entire upper body in an exaggerated deep bow. We laughed until tears rolled down our cheeks. Even Papa-san, who is usually quiet and dignified, opened his mouth and laughed out loud. When she stopped she looked at us with a mischievous innocent look on her face, obviously pleased with her successful imitation. That got us laughing even more.

I suppose our neighbors thought we were crazy to be laughing so hard when everybody else was having such a tough time. Conversation and laughter were always a part of our family life—even when anxiety was under the laughter.

ᴥ ⑥ ᴥ

The June days got longer and hotter. Every few days the wind would abruptly kick up sand and dust, sending us running for cover. Yoneichi's impending departure grew closer. There was no way for us to take cover, dodge, or overlook this fact. Finally that morning arrived. We all ate breakfast in the mess hall and sat closer together than usual. The scrambled eggs didn't taste good, the toast was cold and dry, and the coffee was bitter. I wasn't hungry.

When we got back to our room, Yoneichi slowly looked around the apartment. It was as though he was trying to imprint the setting in his memory. We sat down on two cots and faced each other as we had each evening before each family discussion time. Mama-san quietly made a final pot of tea. We were silent with our individual thoughts as we sipped our fragrant beverage. Papa-san held his cup in his left palm as he slowly turned it round and round with his right hand. His hand trembled a bit as he brought it up to his lips to take a sip.

Finally Mama-san began to speak softly. "We have a wonderful family. Yoneichi-san and Mary-san, I am so proud of both of you. And now, Yoneichi-san, it has come time for you to leave us. Let us remember the good times we have shared. That will help us all as you leave us." Her eyes became moist.

Yoneichi looked tenderly at her and replied, "I will. Yes, ours is a wonderful family. It will help me to think about all of us together."

Papa-san looked at Yoneichi and with a steady, strong voice said, *"Shikkari shite kudasai, neh*—Be strong for all of us, all right? There may be many difficult times ahead for you but whatever hardships come, be strong and bring honor to our family."

"I will, Papa-san," Yoneichi replied firmly as he nodded his head.

Mama-san added softly, "You will be in our thoughts every day. Would you like us to pray together now?"

"Yes, Mama-san. That will help me."

Mama-san was a devout Methodist, and prayer was a part of her daily life. Mama-san looked upward as she spoke clearly and slowly.

Sunset at the internment camp.

"*Kamisama*—God, this is a very difficult time for all of us." After a moment she continued, "We know Yoneichi-san carries the burden for our family and for all other Japanese families to fight with courage and bring honor to our community. Guide and protect him. May his battles be fought with a pure heart. We know You will be with him wherever he goes. Thank you for your constant presence with him and with each of us giving us strength and hope and love. In the name of *Kamisama*, amen."

She bowed her head and closed her eyes. All of us were silent. When we raised our heads, Mama-san looked at Yoneichi with such tenderness in her eyes. He said, "Mama-san, thank you. I will carry that prayer and the *senninbari* with me wherever I go."

Then he turned to me and said gently, "This will be a difficult time for our folks. Take good care of them for me, okay? Doing that will help me the most."

"I promise," I whispered, trying to control the tremor in my voice. Sadness and dread threatened to overcome me, but I managed to control my tears.

Yoneichi looked at each of us and with a steady voice said, "We've had a good life together on the farm, and I'm grateful for this time of remembering all the good things that have been a part of our family. That will help me a lot while I have to be away."

Then he stood up beside his cot, and gazed at each of us. "I'm proud to be going on behalf of all of us. You know my good friend, Sinch, will be going at the same time. We're both going to Fort Blanding in Florida, so we may be together quite a bit of the time. Try not to worry. I'll be careful."

Then he picked up his bag, and we accompanied him silently to the front gate where a bus waited for the men who were leaving. Like us, members of other families were there to see their sons leave, but everyone was quiet. It was hard to engage in small talk while we waited. Never had I felt so close to my brother, and I braced myself against the time of parting. We had all dreaded this moment. Despite the hot sun, my hands felt like ice.

My brother turned to me and I wrapped my arms around him. I didn't want to let go of him. All I could say was, "Be careful. I'll be praying for you every day."

As he looked deep into my eyes, he said, "Take good care of the folks. You know how important that is to me. It's up to you now, you know."

I nodded in acknowledgment. Just before he stepped into the bus he turned, lifted his hand in a motionless goodbye and said, "Thank you for everything. Take good care of each other and try not to worry."

He turned away and boarded the bus. We watched to see where he would sit, and we huddled close together in front of the window where we could see him just as other families were doing with their departing sons. As the bus started up and eased away, we saw him return our wave and smile bravely. Having been raised with an older, protective brother, I felt lost, empty, and especially fearful as I watched the bus move towards the horizon. I could not control my tears. Even Papa-san's eyes were teary, but being the stoic head of our household, he struggled to contain himself.

We stood a long while looking in the direction the bus had gone. We all knew without saying—this might be the last time we saw him.

Finally I turned to Mama-san. "I hope he comes back to us alive." And Mama-san whispered through her tears, "Let us pray he does."

When we returned to our apartment, I looked at his tidy, empty cot next to mine. All three of us sat looking at his cot, each of us deep in thought and prayer for our beloved Yoneichi. I went through the activities of the day mechanically, almost in a trance. That night I struggled to sleep. I kept staring at his cot and then at the ceiling as the rotating searchlight swept through our apartment. My parents moved restlessly on their cots, sleepless.

During those first long days and nights without Yoneichi I grappled anew with my own confusion. How could I make sense out of the fact that we were confined and controlled by the government that my brother was now going off to defend? I also thought about the memories, back to the times when Yoneichi would stay up until 3:00 in the morning working on his calculus problems. Or the playful bantering we had about my love for classical music and his teasing questions of why I was listening to Beethoven and Bach. All I had now were memories, and I couldn't keep from crying. Repeatedly I thought, *My only brother has gone off to fight a war for a country that is keeping us imprisoned like criminals.* I cried until I fell into a fitful sleep, waking up in the morning more tired than when I went to bed.

The peaceful days on Vashon now seemed like a dream from the past. *Did we really live such an idyllic life?* I wondered. It all seemed so crazy now.

Years later I would tell my grandson, Matthew, how his grand uncle, like the brave Momotaro in the classic Japanese fairy story, went off to war to fight the giants that were raising havoc in the world. This is the way Momotaro's elderly parents must have felt as he left them to go fight the monsters who were plundering the countryside.

During the following days, Mama-san looked sad, preoccupied, and resigned. From time to time she would brush away a tear and heave a big sigh. The three of us sat closer together in the following evenings. We didn't talk much; we were with our thoughts and silent prayers for Yoneichi's safety and courage. From time to time Mama-san whispered, *"Sabishi desu neh?—*It is lonely, isn't it?" as she quietly tried to adjust to life without Yoneichi. She looked forward to his letters, which came regularly during basic training at Fort Blanding. They were always written in Japanese and that pleased my parents. He occasionally wrote a separate letter to me in English, but I received most of my information about his thoughts and his activities through his letters to our parents.

Days stretched into weeks, but each day and each week was the same as before—depressing and directionless. In one of those aimless, dreary days, I came to the realization that I was focusing only on what *wasn't* in my life. *What if this way becomes permanent?* I thought about it some more, then I asked myself, *Is this the way to live, always in the shadow of what used to be and might not be any more? What if someday I wake up and realize that I could have gone places but didn't, that I missed opportunities I could have taken advantage of, that there were people I could have met and perhaps loved?* I was troubled by this thought. I was nineteen years old now—I'd better do something!

The next day I decided to go to the employment office in the camp's administration building. There was an opening as a nurse's aide in the camp hospital. This job title triggered a memory of a conversation Mama-san and I had when I was in the eighth grade.

"Mama-san, what should I do when I grow up?"

She looked at me with interest, and paused for a moment. "There are several things you could do. If you became a secretary, you would sit at a typewriter and write letters and reports for a boss. That would be a very practical kind of work. If you became a teacher you would be in a very worthy profession. You would help children to learn important things to help them make their way in the world. If you became a nurse, you would help people recover from operations or sicknesses and that would be a very good profession. But any kind of work has its good points and not such wonderful parts."

With all the wisdom of a thirteen-year-old, I considered all three options for awhile and finally said, "If I became a nurse what would that be like?"

"When you were about one and a half years old," Mama-san began, "I was in the hospital a long time recovering from a ruptured appendix. The nurses were so wonderful to me. They bathed me, fed me, took care of my personal needs, and made me as comfortable as they could. I had a great deal of drainage that kept oozing from my wound, but they never backed away from taking care of me."

"Ooo, that's awful!" I interjected, scrunching my face.

"Yes, it was, but they took good care of me and made sure that I was always comfortable," Mama-san continued. "They always found ways to entice my appetite. They did all of those things and never seemed to mind doing whatever needed to be done to help me recover. Nursing is more than putting your cool hand on the patient's feverish forehead. It includes all the things the nurses did for me at the hospital and much more."

Reflecting on that conversation helped me decide I should explore what this position as a nurse's aide might offer. I requested an application form and took it home to tell my folks what I planned to do. They were pleased.

The following morning I submitted my application. I was asked to wait while someone reviewed it in the inner office. An administrator quickly approved my application and he asked me to report to the hospital the following morning. Apparently they were very short of aides.

My first day on the job I received my nurse's aide uniform, a general orientation to the hospital, and an assignment on Wards 5 and 6, the medical and communicable disease wings. The head nurse gave me a thorough orientation on the care of these special patients. I had to wear a mask and an extra gown over my uniform. I learned about a special hand washing technique to protect myself and not carry any contaminants to other patients. Then I was introduced to the ward and given simple tasks such as passing out fresh water and reading materials to the patients.

Going to work each day and meeting people in the hospital gave me a whole new way of looking at my life. I was absorbed with learning how to take temperatures and blood pressures, how to give baths, make beds, and various other nursing tasks. I enjoyed my interactions with the hospital staff and patients.

One day on the communicable disease ward while I was taking fresh water around to the patients, I stopped and talked with a patient named John. He was a young man, perhaps twenty-five years old. He was thin, his skin almost translucent, and he had dark circles under his eyes. I asked him how he was doing. He replied, "When you have tuberculosis the main thing you have to do is rest. I read or listen to my radio, but other than that and talking with others on the ward and those of you who come to take care of us, there's really nothing else to do. It gets pretty boring. You get to go home after work and be with your family, but I can't even do that. This is my family here," he said as he moved his arm around indicating the other patients in the ward.

The young man had been in a sanitarium in Seattle for three years before the government transferred him to the internment camp. I wondered, *How could they think of this patient as a threat to the country's security?*

When I asked John how long he had to be in the hospital, he responded, "That's the heck of it. I don't have any idea when I'll be well enough to get out of bed. In a way I have no future. I can't set any goals for my life."

"Oh," I said, "I'm sorry. I didn't even think about that."

As I went about my work that day my thoughts returned time and again to John. His future looked bleak. John's dismal predicament helped me appreciate what I did have. This job and the new people and experiences shifted my perspective and I began to find my life and work meaningful despite the internment camp. My folks were pleased with my changes.

At the hospital the Caucasian nursing supervisor, Miss Crosman, observed my interest and aptitude and suggested I become a registered nurse (R.N.). To encourage me, she gave me a pair of bandage scissors, which I later had engraved with the initials "M M" for Mary Matsuda. Whenever I used them I thought about Miss Crosman. Those scissors would stay with me in my purse throughout my fifty-year career as an R.N.

As I continued to gain more experience, I often thought about Yoneichi and the *Nisei* men fighting overseas who needed medical attention. I wanted to talk it over with my folks, but I was nervous. I mulled the idea over for several days before I broached the subject. One evening while we were having our snack and tea, I said to my parents, "I wonder who is taking care of the *Niseis* injured in the war over in Europe."

Mama-san replied, "I've wondered about that too. I hope they are taking good care of them."

I hesitated, then added, "I've been thinking that if I became a registered nurse, I'd like to go over to Europe to take care of them. What do you think about that?"

They both fell silent and looked thoughtful. Papa-san picked up his teacup, took a sip, then turned it round and round as he pondered this question.

Finally Mama-san answered, "It would be very hard for us to have you go to war, too. But I know that if Yoneichi-san were wounded, I would want you there to do everything you could for him. I would be proud of you for doing that kind of work in that kind of setting for our boys."

Papa-san nodded in agreement and added, "You may be in a war zone. Things could be very primitive, and you would have to be resourceful, but you can do that. We would miss you, but it would be a comfort to us knowing you would be taking care of the wounded."

I was both relieved and pleased with their reaction. It would mean another sacrifice for them, but they were willing to let me go. Once again, their wisdom and love touched my heart.

Letters had been coming fairly regularly from my friend, Zola Lenz in Hicksville, Ohio. One came about the time I had this discussion with my folks. I had written to Zola about my job as a nurse's aide in the hospital and how much I enjoyed the work. This time I included my thoughts about becoming a registered nurse and possibly going overseas to care for soldiers like my brother.

A reply came back immediately. Zola mentioned a new federal program that trained nurses for the war effort. She suggested talking to my nursing supervisor to find out if information was available in camp. If not, she would send it to me.

The next day the nursing supervisor took me to the bulletin board where information about the United States Cadet Nurse Corps was posted. She suggested I consider applying. I read over the information and sent off an application form. A reply arrived promptly. I was delighted to learn the Corps would cover the cost of the training in a certified school of nursing anywhere in the country. Since Japanese-Americans could not return to the West Coast yet, I applied to nursing schools associated with universities in the Midwest or the East Coast. I thought I would like to live in Ohio because Zola lived there, or possibly New York or Minnesota. But I learned the government had established a quota for *Niseis* to prevent too many Japanese from living in concentrated numbers in any one state. Either the government was concerned about higher incidences of prejudice in areas with larger concentrations of Japanese, or maybe they were afraid we would make trouble.

Although the quota for the three states of my choice had already been filled, I learned that Iowa still had openings. Jane Lamb Memorial Hospital in Clinton, Iowa was listed as a possibility. I was hopeful. As I filled out the application form, I was mindful of the agreement:

> In consideration of the training, payments and other benefits which will be provided me if I am accepted as a member of the U.S. Cadet Nurse Corps, I agree that if accepted, I will be available for military or other Federal governmental or essential civilian services for the duration of the present war.

I sent in my application in July 1944. If accepted, my training would last until 1947. It seemed a long way away, but I thought, *The war can't possibly last that long, can it?*

At the same time I also filled out the necessary papers to get released from camp. I promptly received clearance to leave Heart Mountain Internment Camp, and an acceptance letter from the Director of Nursing at Jane Lamb Memorial Hospital arrived a short time later. In her letter the director noted, "You might be interested to know that Jane Sasaki from Oregon has already been accepted in the current class. Her twin sister, Janet, and you will be in the next class beginning in September."

This was terrific news. I knew the Sasaki sisters because we were recent graduates from Tri-State High School at the Tule Lake camp. Now we would all be together in the same hospital. I could not have anticipated anything so wonderful, but something was troubling me. As excited as I was about my own plans, I felt increasingly guilty about abandoning my parents. We needed to talk about their future.

"Mama-san, Papa-san, now that I am going to Iowa, I want to know what you want to do. Do you want to stay here?"

The two of them exchanged knowing glances. "Papa-san and I have been discussing this," Mama-san said. "It will be lonely here without both of you. We heard from the Umanis just last week. They have left camp to be with their son who is living on a farm in Nampa, Idaho. They have urged us to move to Minidoka, which is not too far away. Personally, I would like to be closer to the Umanis."

The Umanis could live outside of an internment camp because they had a son who had a successful farm outside of the evacuation zone. The majority of Japanese had no such resources available. With Yoneichi now in the service, living outside of camp was not a practical option for my parents, but they could move to a camp closer to their dear friends.

Papa-san nodded in agreement with Mama-san's explanation. "Yes, I'd like that, too. In addition, I think camp life would be a little calmer in Minidoka where there are more people from Washington State. I suspect there would be less agitation over the Loyalty Oath."

The Umanis had been their closest friends since their earliest years in the United States. We had been at Heart Mountain for nearly a year, but we certainly didn't have any attachment to the place. At least Minidoka Internment Camp seemed like it might be calmer. I submitted an application to transfer all three of us to the Minidoka camp near Twin Falls, Idaho. Clearance arrived without much delay.

It was time to move to our fourth internment camp, only this time it was by choice. I had mixed feelings of regret, anticipation, and some anxiety about leaving a known situation for an unknown challenge. But I knew this was the right thing and the right time for me to do it.

My parents and I packed our meager belongings and walked to the main gate of the camp. It was exciting to hand over our pass that permitted us to walk right through the gate without anyone stopping us. We boarded a Greyhound bus at the administration area of Heart Mountain and headed for Minidoka.

The bus was crowded with servicemen and all kinds of folks traveling during wartime and gas rationing. During that twelve-hour trip, interrupted only by brief rest stops, the three of us had to stand along with several others in the crowded bus. We gripped the straps that hung from the ceiling or the seat-backs as the bus negotiated turns and bumps in the road. Mama-san, now fifty-two, and Papa-san, sixty-seven, looked as tired as I felt, but no one offered them a seat. I suspected it was because we were Japanese. None of us complained.

Finally, the bus stopped at Pocatello, Idaho for a layover before the last leg of the trip. We had a little time to see the town, so everyone went for a walk, eager to stretch their legs. We walked along the main street lined with stores, restaurants, and apartments. All of the other passengers had drifted ahead, including my parents, but I wanted to window shop a little longer. What a treat to look at the colorful displays and all the wonderful merchandise so beautifully displayed. It had been two years since I had seen anything like this. I looked longingly at the slim mannequins with their glamorous dresses and stylish shoes, the sparkly jewelry in gold and silver, and the handsome living room and bedroom furniture. I longed for some of that beauty for myself.

As I strolled along I noticed a barbershop nearby with the traditional revolving red, white and blue barber pole. There was a sign in the window that declared, "No Japs Allowed!" I glanced at a man whom I assumed to be the barber in his white smock. He leaned against the doorframe, scowling. His jaws clenched and his lips pressed tighter together as he watched the bus passengers walk past his shop. As I walked past him, a little ways behind the group, he bolted toward me. He grabbed me around the neck and pulled my head back against his chest with his left arm while pressing what I thought was a straight-edged razor against my throat with his right hand. The spittle flew from his lips as he hissed in my ear, "I oughta slit your throat from ear to ear you goddamn Jap!"

I froze. Blood pounded in my ears. My mind raced. *I am going to die.* I imagined blood spurting from my slit throat. A split second later I felt a clear, impenetrable crystal ball totally encase me. It was as if I were inside of it, yet not inside of it. I didn't know where it came from or how it happened. All I knew was I could hear and see what was happening, feeling terrified and yet strangely calm. The man's thick muscular arm around my neck cut off my breath. I felt cold and faint but stood perfectly still, waiting for his next move. Just as abruptly he released me with a grunt and a jarring shove as he growled under his breath, disgusted, "Get outta here, you goddamn Jap." A man's voice somewhere in the distance yelled, "Hey, Ken, knock it off," followed by loud laughter.

I felt myself falling, but I stretched out my arms, took several giant, staggering steps and regained my balance. *I mustn't fall*, I told myself, my legs like soft rubber. I took several more lurching steps, vigorously rubbing my neck and taking long, deep breaths. I stumbled away as quickly as I could

Finally I caught up with my folks just as Mama-san looked around to see if I was following. My breathing was slower by this time. My racing heart had slowed down. I was glad they had been far enough ahead and so engrossed with the sights and conversation that they did not see what had happened to me. I walked with them back to the bus stop without revealing my terror and I *never* mentioned the incident.

Something deep inside of me resisted sharing that horrifying experience with my parents. I was beginning to feel more like an adult, and I wanted to act like one. I could deal with racism and protect them from one more assault, just as they had shielded me for many years. *My folks have had enough of their own heartaches,* I thought. *I want to protect them from further pain.*

Two hours later we arrived at the Minidoka Relocation Center, which was similar to all the other internment camps. My parents were assigned to one of the small living spaces for two people on the end of one of the barracks: 24-5-A. It was about twenty feet by twelve feet. I was relieved to see several people from Vashon near them and was particularly pleased knowing the Umani family was only a few hours away.

I stayed at Minidoka for about a month, just long enough to be sure they were settled. My departure was nothing like it was for Yoneichi. We all knew where I was going and we all knew I could come "home" during school breaks.

The night before I left, I had trouble sleeping. I had never been away from my family, and I was going a long distance. I tried to imagine what it would be like living among strangers with demands on my time and intelligence. The unknown worried me. *Will I measure up?* I wondered. *What if I don't? What if I get sick? And what if other white men grab me by the throat and put a razor to me?* I shuddered at the memory of the Idaho incident. *Mama-san won't be there to take care of me. What will I do?* I began counting questions like sheep and finally dropped off to a troubled sleep.

After breakfast in the mess hall, Mama-san and Papa-san accompanied me to the gate where a bus waited to take me to the train. Before I got on, Mama-san said, "Study hard and be mindful of your health." I put my arms across her shoulders and gave her a squeeze. Then I shook Papa-san's hand as he said, "We're counting on you to become a very good nurse." I tried to smile and present a cheerful face, but the tears won out. "I promise I'll write," I said tearfully, then boarded the bus. After two years and three months confined to internment camps, I was finally leaving.

I left Minidoka in late August 1944, and traveled by train to Clinton, Iowa. It was a long and lonely trip. Mama-san made sure I had enough food with me so I wouldn't have to go to the diner. For three days I ate peanut butter and jelly sandwiches, carrot sticks, and cookies, and drank water from the camp kitchen. For hours I stared out the window, eating, thinking, and dreaming.

Life on the "outside" seemed both scary and exciting. At last I was moving on with my life. Already I missed my parents and Yoneichi, but I was also intrigued with my dream of becoming a nurse.

As the train carried me farther and farther away from the horrors of internment camp life, I felt myself lulled into a dream state. Everything was a feast to my eyes. I was mesmerized by the changing landscape—rolling hills, green grass, flowers and trees, people in cars driving along winding roads, and rivers meandering beside the railroad tracks. *I am going as a free person,* I thought. I looked around at the other passengers and noted with a start, *These are all white people.* Everyone seemed preoccupied with their own issues and paid no attention to me. I reassured myself, *I can dismiss any fears about another experience like the one with the barber.*

But even as I enjoyed the scenery my thoughts continually returned to my parents. Hopefully they could make a satisfactory transition to their new environment even though Yoneichi and I were gone.

When I arrived in Clinton, Janet Sasaki was at the train station to greet me. I was relieved to see her familiar face. We caught the city transit bus and rode to the Jane Lamb Memorial Hospital. It was a one-hundred bed, four-story hospital and nurses' home. The large, red brick building was situated on a slight bluff with an imposing entryway. We walked to the nurses' home, a white, three-story, box-like building not far from the hospital. A covered walkway connected the nurses' home to the hospital. During my three-year training there would be many times that I would run through that walkway in the middle of the night to assist with emergency surgery or the delivery of a baby.

The large, sedate sitting room in the nurses' home had a high ceiling and big windows that overlooked a sloping front lawn. The housemother, Mrs. Morrison, took us upstairs to the third floor and showed me my room. After she left, I said to Janet, "Wow! A whole room to myself! After what we've been through, this looks like a palace." I didn't know what to expect, but this was a wonderful beginning as I started my nurses' training in the Midwest.

❖

In the days that followed my departure, my parents went through the monotonous routine of camp life, going for meals at the mess hall, doing chores, engaging in idle chit-chat with others. But in between those activities, Mama-san was preoccupied and struggled to fill her days meaningfully. Later, in a letter Papa-san told me about an incident that prompted her to make a big change.

One day when Mama-san was in the laundry room, Mrs. Ohashi, a friend from Vashon came to do her wash at the same time. She said to Mama-san, "I heard that Yoneichi-san has gone into the service. Have you heard from him?"

"Oh, yes," Mama-san replied with quiet pride. "We got a letter from him last week telling us about his training."

"I'm surprised you let him go," Mrs. Ohashi said smugly. "My three sons are going to college in the Midwest."

Mama-san stiffened slightly. "We felt it was important to show our loyalty," she said defensively. "Yoneichi felt it was the right thing to do." She turned her head and looked at the other woman warily.

"But he's your only son. He could be killed. Then what would you do?" She shook her head with mock exasperation. "And now your daughter could end up going, too. How could you let both of them go? I would never let my children risk their lives for a country that's doing this to us."

Mama-san stared at her, astonished. She quickly finished her laundry and returned to her room. She put away the clothes angrily, then sat down on her cot to think about what this "friend" had said to her. When Papa-san returned soon thereafter, he noticed that she seemed especially quiet and troubled.

Mama-san explained what had happened. Then she stood up and began pacing the floor, wringing her hands. As she paced back and forth repeatedly, Papa-san saw how agitated and disturbed she was. He led her back to the cot and sat down opposite her. "That was a terrible thing for her to say to you!" he said. "What would you like for me to do about it?"

After a moment, Mama-san said, "Papa-san, did we do the right thing?"

Papa-san was firm. "Of course we did. You remember our family discussion about this matter. Mrs. Ohashi was wrong to say those things to you, but you and I know that our children have done the right thing."

Still, Mama-san remained troubled. With her two children gone, she suddenly found herself without a meaningful role. Everything she had done since her arrival in this country was as our mother and protector. For the first time since our evacuation, the pressures of camp life had become too much for my mother.

My parents discussed the possibilities. Mama-san wondered about leaving camp for some temporary work outside, and decided that it would be good to get away, even for a short period of time. They went to the administration building and learned that openings were available at a vegetable canning factory in Ogden, Utah. Mama-san shared the idea with Ochiyo-san, a distant relative who also lived in Minidoka, and asked her if she would like to go with her. Ochiyo-san thought the idea was a good one. Both of them applied for leave and received it promptly.

Papa-san fully understood Mama-san's need, but they decided that he needed to remain in camp to serve as a focal point for all of us. He was immune to mean-spirited comments, so staying in camp was no special hardship. He felt strongly that Mama-san should take a break away from the stress that threatened to overwhelm her and do something that would be renewing for her.

Papa-san wrote several letters explaining Mama-san's plans. I understood and was glad that Mama-san would be getting out of camp for a while.

In a brief letter dated September 3, 1944, Mama-san wrote in Japanese:

> Mary-san. I arrived in Ogden at 3:30. Please be relieved. After many, many miles of sagebrush, we finally arrived in Ogden. From the beginning to the end of our journey, it was sagebrush. It's beyond talking about—all this sagebrush along straight roads. It felt wonderful. I wish we could have been together, you and I. The cannery doesn't seem to be very big but it seems good. We will begin working from Monday morning. Four of us women are in the same room. Ochiyo-san and Ohide-san will go to another place in two evenings from now. Mrs. Yamaguchi-san and I will stay here. She is a very fine person. There aren't enough workers yet. The cannery is beside some woods near a mountain. It is very quiet and it feels very good to be here. Please be sure and take care of your body. Mama.

This was the first time, to my knowledge, that Mama-san had done something away from the family for her own well being. It told me a lot about how much stress she had been hiding from us. She obviously enjoyed the long journey on the bus where she could go miles and miles of straight highway away from camp. To be with other fine women in a quiet, peaceful environment near trees and mountains must have felt like heaven after two years of the congested, noisy, dusty camps. I imagined her looking frequently at her gold wedding band on her ring finger and stroking it as she thought about Papa-san giving her the opportunity to get away from the oppressive environment. In this quiet, peaceful place Mama-san could live each day thoroughly appreciating the gift of freedom, productive work, and an unusually understanding husband. I was relieved and grateful to Papa-san for allowing this.

In a letter written in mid-September, Mama-san wrote:

> Mrs. Yamaguchi and I have become very good friends and work happily together every day. I don't want to go back to camp. If there is work to do, I'd like to stay here and work as long as possible. When I work I forget about everything else. I don't even worry about Yoneichi-san. I don't know how it is but I can work with a happy heart here. I think it comes from God. Mama.

Mama-san's desire to remain in Ogden was understandable. I was deeply grateful that this could be so. During this critical time, Papa-san provided the stability we all needed. He made it possible for us to connect with each other as we individually faced our own challenges. Papa-san clearly understood Mama-san's fragility at this time and willingly gave her the space she needed in which to regain the strength that had become so frayed. I saw this as the most powerful evidence of his love for her. In spite of the traditional subservient role that many Japanese women followed, Papa-san honored her need to seek change.

I was often too exhausted to write letters on a regular basis to my parents, but my letters were very important to them. Mama-san wrote in her letter of November 15, 1944:

> It is reassuring to read that you are well and studying hard. Do you realize how much your letters mean to me? When I get one of your letters, I forget all about being tired....Now that you have traveled away, you can feel the warmth of our family, can't you? I am in the same place too. Both you and Yoneichi-san are bearing up and experiencing stress. I am doing the same. Bear the stress and become an outstanding person. Both you and I will endure the stress and become great people. I will watch you become a great nurse. That is all I ask. Through your letters I have been reassured about your thoughts. Don't change your heart. Don't allow your body to become too tired. Mama.

Another letter written on the same day from Mama-san:

> This afternoon when I opened your letter, your picture dropped out. It was such a wonderful picture showing how you are getting along so fine with your white friends. I was very pleased to see it. Even among

the best of people, there will be those with whom you may not fit. Getting along with them may be hard. But to be among strangers is the hardest of all. If you turn a sour face toward someone or gossip about someone, it will all come back to you. I trust that you understand this. But sometimes when you are with friends, things can get out of hand. Please be careful. When you are alone in Iowa and homesick, be mindful of your heart. As for me, I, too, am careful about not saying anything negative about anyone. I am paying attention only to my own things. Thank you for the pictures. My mind is joyful and I feel like you and I are living together for looking at them. Mama.

In his letter to me on November 23, 1944, from Minidoka camp, Papa-san wrote:

I had not heard from you in awhile and was worried about you. I understand now that you have been busy with your studies. With Yoneichi gone as a soldier and you studying and each of you persevering with patience, it is hard for me at home to just be playing. I think our Mama-san with her acquaintance with suffering is the greatest person. Mary-san, you must be very thankful for her. Write her about that. Mama-san will be very pleased about that. Even though they may be short, please write one letter per week to your Mama-san. I repeat myself. Even if it's short, please be sure to write to Mama-san every week. I ask you to do that for her. Papa.

I could tell from this letter that Papa-san was very aware of Mama-san's struggle. I promptly wrote to thank and commend him for his support of Mama-san.

To occupy his time, Papa-san engaged other old men in his favorite board game, *Go*. This game requires great concentration, similar to chess, and Papa-san could play for hours, completely lost in the game. No matter what mean things people said, Papa-san could ignore them all. He was totally involved in a military game in the internment camp while countries were embroiled in a real war around the globe.

By the time Mama-san wrote to me from Utah, she sounded like her own self again. Her letters written in Japanese were filled with her concerns for my health as well as other matters. In her letter of November 24, 1944, she wrote:

Mary-san. It has gotten cold these days, hasn't it? Are you well? I am well and working hard. Be reassured. You must have received a picture from Yoneichi-san. It is beautiful, isn't it? With a picture from Yoneichi-san and you, I am very happy. With this kind of splendid soldier, it would be nice to live in America. I imagine you feel that way too. Please take good care of your *body* [word emphasized]. Become the very best nurse.

Did the *sembe* [Japanese crackers] arrive? It may not be much but may be handy when you want something so I am sending it. If you can buy it, get some eggs and eat it. I think it will be good for you. When you have to work so hard, you must pay attention to your body. Mama.

Mama-san often reminded me to pay attention to my body. In one letter she mentioned that if I neglect my body and skimp on nourishing food, the body could get worn down and I would not be able to study hard and care for the patients in the hospital.

In the fall of 1944, each of us faced ongoing internal challenges while the world outside seemed turbulent, frightful, and unresolved. Yoneichi was in basic training at Camp Blanding, Florida. Mama-san was sorting peas in a vegetable canning factory in Ogden, Utah. Papa-san was the center for all of us at "home" in Minidoka, Idaho. And I was engrossed in my studies in Clinton, Iowa.

Mama-san regained her perspective on her family and the world. Her letters were full of encouragement and faith that all of this would pass and we would come back together once again. We felt connected to each other, informed, and loved in spite of the distances and issues that pressed upon each of us. We would all need to gather our strength for the trials that lay ahead.

ON MY OWN

Yoneichi departed for basic training about two weeks after D-Day, the Allied Forces' invasion of Normandy on June 6, 1944. Newspapers were filled with reports of terrible fighting, some wins, and heavy losses. I didn't want to keep imagining Yoneichi dead in Europe, but I couldn't help it.

He spent six months in basic training, then came "home" to Minidoka for a short farewell visit with our family before going overseas. I also got a short leave from nursing school, and boarded the train from Iowa to Idaho with ambivalent feelings. I was elated because we would be together again, but heavyhearted knowing this might be the last time we would see each other. Mama-san returned to Minidoka from Ogden, Utah a couple days before our arrival.

Yoneichi visited Vashon to check on our farm for a few hours before leaving for Minidoka, arriving on December 23, 1944. This was a risky thing for him to do since Japanese were still officially restricted from the West Coast, but he felt compelled to go. Yoneichi reported that on the surface the farm seemed run down but otherwise okay. Mack was nowhere to be found, which was not surprising, considering it was the Christmas season.

On his way to Minidoka Yoneichi stopped in Nampa, Idaho to pick up legal documents drawn up by a notary public. It was complicated because our family's property was still in Daiichi Umani's name. Following Japanese tradition, the property needed to be transferred to Yoneichi's name as the eldest son now that he was twenty-one. But since he would be overseas, Yoneichi would temporarily delegate the farm ownership to me. Daiichi Umani and his wife had already gone to this notary public and had the documents created, ready for Yoneichi to pick up. With papers in hand, Yoneichi arrived at Minidoka to spend a few days with us before leaving for Europe.

I was feeling a bit self-conscious about visiting the internment camp in my nurse's uniform—a soft gray suit and topcoat, both with red epaulets, and a beret as a member of the United States Cadet Nurse Corps. When I arrived,

Mary and Yoneichi in uniform at Minidoka before Yoneichi left for combat, 1944.

the internment camp no longer seemed as threatening and confining with its guardhouse and armed soldiers. When I first saw Yoneichi I thought, *He sure looks handsome in that khaki uniform of the United States Army.* But I also realized with a sharp attack of panic, *That uniform could kill him.*

When we went to the mess hall for dinner that December evening, people stared at us. I whispered to Mama-san, "Aren't these people used to seeing young people in uniform by now?"

She smiled and replied, "They're used to seeing more and more men in uniform, but I think you are the first woman."

I shrugged my shoulders and smiled. *Yes,* I thought, *I suppose seeing a woman in uniform is an unusual sight. I wonder what they think about my becoming a nurse as opposed to joining the WAAC?* It was an interesting thought, but fleeting. What mattered most was being with family again. We caught up on the news of one another's lives, talked about new and old friends, and reminisced about the years on our farm.

"Do you remember the time when you were about seven years old you dug up all those bulbs at Morrison's yard?" I asked Yoneichi. "Why did you do that?"

Breaking out in a big grin, he replied, "I wanted to see what the gardener was doing. He took so much time placing all those things in the ground and they weren't put in rows like I saw Mama-san plant things. I just wanted to see what they were."

"When Mrs. Morrison told me about it later, I was mortified," Papa-san said with a chuckle. "I thought, 'Oh no! What a terrible thing Yoneichi did.

I must make sure he doesn't forget that doing that kind of thing brings *haji*—shame on our family. He must never do that kind of thing again.'"

"That was the first time I ever saw you spank him, Papa-san," I added.

"That's right," Papa-san said. "Then there was that other time when you told me Bobo threw your mittens in the Sound. Remember?"

"Yeah, I was afraid I was going to get heck for losing them so I thought an easy way out was to put the blame on him," Yoneichi admitted. "He was sort of a bad boy anyway."

"And that was another session in the woodshed, huh, Yoneichi?" I added.

"Yeah, I seemed to get into a lot of trouble," Yoneichi replied, laughing.

Our precious days together slipped away like ice cream on a hot day. Before we knew it and before we were ready, it was time to leave. This time it seemed harder for Mama-san to watch us approach the bus; but seeing us together seemed to give her some comfort. I shook Papa-san's hand and held it longer than I would have normally. I gave Mama-san a big, long, bear hug, something I did spontaneously. We never hugged or kissed in our family, it was not customary among the Japanese. Bowing was the custom, but this was no ordinary leave-taking.

"Try not to worry, Mama-san. We must trust God to help us through this," I said as much to myself as to her.

She nodded. "I know. It will not be easy."

Traditionally, a Japanese soldier goes off to war because of a deep sense of loyalty to his family, community, or nation. This loyalty rises above and beyond the value of his own life. When Japanese mothers send their sons to war, they send them away to die. Knowing that, hot tears stung my eyes for Mama-san as well as for myself.

Yoneichi took Mama-san into his arms too, and held her for a long time. This was the first time I had seen him do that. "I'll be careful. Try not to worry, Mama-san," Yoneichi said, holding her as if he might not see her again.

She nodded through her tears as she said, *"Ochitsuite yo*—Be calm, be self-possessed."

Yoneichi nodded and reluctantly released her. He then gave Papa-san a firm handshake. Both of their eyes were moist, too. Then it was time to go. We both boarded the bus and waved to our parents as they watched with brave smiles on their stricken faces.

We caught the train in Pocatello, Idaho, and rode together heading east, saying little during the first hour or so. This was one of the few times when the two of us were alone together. I wondered, *Will this be our last time together?* Finally I said, "You said to our folks that you didn't see the deputy sheriff when you went to Vashon and that you hadn't heard from him either. Don't you think we should have heard from him by now?"

"I don't know what's going on with him," Yoneichi responded. "Why don't you write and ask him to send the statements for the past three years to you instead of to me. He should have them by this time."

"And if he doesn't?" I asked.

Yoneichi thought a bit, then replied, "There isn't a lot we can do from where we are. You could write to the administration office at Minidoka and see if they have people there who could help. But at this point, just wait a little while and see what happens."

Before I got off the train at Clinton, I gave my brother a big hug and said, "I'll be thinking of you every day. Bye, and be careful." As the train pulled away from the station, I stood, waving a long time until the train disappeared. An emptiness settled into my chest as I raised a silent prayer on his behalf.

Yoneichi traveled to the East Coast to join the rest of his group who, by then, were at Fort George Meade in Maryland. He learned to use different weapons for the next two to three weeks. Then he and the other men gathered at the assembly center at Camp Killmer, New Jersey and boarded a freighter for a nineteen-day journey across the Atlantic. They landed at Marseilles in southern France and were assigned to the 442nd Regimental Combat Team.

While the United States was fully involved in fierce battles in Europe and in the South Pacific, I heard from a former classmate, Angie on Vashon:

> We are all participating in blackouts and civil defense drills now. Consumer goods like refrigerators are harder to buy because factories have converted to war production. All kinds of supplies are now rationed, including gasoline, tires, coffee, sugar, meat and shoes. We received ration cards for these items and we can use them only for a given period of time and only if the local store has the product. There was a call for skilled workers to work in defense jobs. I am planning to apply for some kind of work at Boeing.

Many women left their homes for the first time and stepped into the work force, taking factory jobs vacated by men who went overseas to fight. "Rosie the Riveter" became a common phrase, a symbol of hard-working women in factories during the war.

It was hard for me to feel at home in Iowa, especially because I stood out as one of the first Asians in Clinton. One day when I was returning on the bus to the nurses' home, I noticed a couple of women sitting across the aisle on a seat facing me. They were whispering to each other and glancing at me. I looked away, but whenever I glanced back, they were still talking and staring at me. Finally I thought to myself, *That's enough. I can stare too.* I frowned and stared back. They quickly averted their eyes and before long got off the bus.

Another time, Ellen Evans, one of my classmates invited me for an overnight. She and I had become close and I had visited her home on a number of occasions. I felt included and loved like another daughter in Ellen's family. On this particular day, Ellen and I were walking back to her home when we met her "Uncle B.," the chief of police. His real name was Byron but he preferred to be called "Uncle B." He was talking to a man sitting in a car. As we passed, we waved, greeted him, and went on our way. Later that evening at the dinner table, Uncle B. told us about the conversation that took place after we passed them. "Mr. Jones said to me, 'That's a nice looking Chinese girl there with Ellen.'"

"I responded, 'That's not a Chinese girl. She's Japanese-American.' Mr. Jones got this weird look on his face, and he says, 'Gosh, she looks almost human.'" We all burst out laughing.

When I heard Uncle B. say that, I understood immediately what Mr. Jones could have meant. He had probably seen only caricatures of Japanese soldiers in the newspapers and magazines and probably thought all Japanese people looked nonhuman, more like monkeys or some bizarre creature. I felt a pang of pain and embarrassment for a moment but when they all burst out laughing I felt reaffirmed. It meant so much to me to be included and loved by this family that an incident of this kind didn't make any difference to them. It would be a little while later that Ellen would again provide significant support for me.

In her letter dated February 21 Mama-san wrote:

> Letters do not come from Yoneichi-san. It is really, really lonely. And you are so far away. I think about you and Yoneichi-san every day. No matter how much I think about it or feel about it, and know that it is *shikata ga nai*—it can't be helped, I can't keep from thinking about him. I think he must be somewhere overseas. I had a vivid dream about him last night. I find that disturbing, especially since I have not heard from him in quite awhile. I heard from Mrs. Ota that one of the Japanese homes on Vashon had burned last week around midnight.

Mama-san's letter was chilling. I hadn't heard from Yoneichi either. That night I stayed on my knees beside my bed a long time lifting prayer after prayer to God for strength and comfort for all who suffered because of this terrible war.

And what about the house burning on Vashon? Did someone deliberately set that fire? I later learned three Japanese families had stored all of their personal belongings in that house before they were evacuated. Now they would have nothing from their former lives. In the midst of my sleepless night it suddenly occurred to me that the same thing could happen to our house on Vashon.

On March 6, 1945 Mama-san wrote:

> Mrs. Umani wrote us a long letter saying how well things were going for her in Nampa. She has invited us to go join her there. We may go in August or September, but once we leave camp, we would not be permitted to return. I will let you know what we decide.

> It is wonderful that you are making such good friends. Be kind to those who come after you (underclassmen). You have had a head start and you are familiar with everything. To show a superior face to them is unacceptable, but you know about that so I needn't say more. Mama.

While Yoneichi was never far from my thoughts, I had to devote my full attention to learning the art and science of nursing. There were few registered nurses in civilian hospitals in 1944, since many were in the military. We students filled in the gaps. There were periods when I put in fourteen-hour days, working double shifts to cover patient needs. Often I was on call for twenty-four hours at a time for emergencies.

One of my favorite classes was dietetics, studying nutrition and learning about special dietary needs of patients hospitalized with specific types of disease. Our teacher was a young, vivacious woman named Mrs. Heidinger.

One day my classmate Janet Sasaki and I were in the nurses' home talking about the class and Janet said, "I'm going to ask Mrs. Humdinger to explain the diabetic diet again."

"Janet!" I exclaimed, shocked. "Don't say her name like that. You wouldn't want to do that in class."

Sure enough, the very next time when we were in our dietetics class, Janet raised her hand and asked, "Mrs. Humdinger, would you explain the…" and her voice faltered. She suddenly realized what she had done. Her face turned scarlet, she put her hand up to her mouth and stammered, "Oh, I'm sorry, Mrs. Heidinger. Please excuse me."

The rest of us looked at her in astonishment, then down at our desks, smiling and inwardly chuckling. Mrs. Heidinger smiled, too, and said, "That's okay, Janet," and let it pass. Janet never did that again.

We didn't know that when our course work in dietetics was over, Mrs. Heidinger would be leaving. One day I was called to the Director of Nurses office. Mrs. Heidinger was there, too.

Miss Rinehart, the director, said, "Mrs. Heidinger is returning to her home in Illinois, and we are unable to find another dietitian to replace her at the moment. She tells me you have done very well in the class and seem to have grasped the intricacies of special diets. Would you be willing to make up the menus and prepare the trays for patients who need special diets? We'll have you do that for the period of time until we can locate a replacement for her."

Mrs. Heidinger added, "What you would need to do is to make up diet sheets for each of the special diets for two weeks in advance and send them to me to review. After I've checked them over and sent them back to you, you can go ahead and use them."

I was surprised they chose me for this responsible position. I thought, *They are willing to have me take on this huge responsibility. They must have faith in me. I'd better give it my very best effort.* My self-respect and my faith in America began to be restored.

"Yes," I said enthusiastically, amazed with this offer, "I'll do it. It's a bit scary, especially when I think about the responsibility. If you will give me close supervision, I think I can do it."

"I'm sure you can, Miss Matsuda," the director said. "That's why we're asking you. Of course, you'll be free from other nursing duties on the floors during this time, so you can devote all your time to making these trays both attractive and nutritious."

I plunged into my new work. I reviewed all the books available on various diets including those for diabetes, ulcers, and gall bladder difficulties. Many of the patients' diets required great care—fat, protein, carbohydrates, and other dietary requirements were calculated precisely for each patient. There were other kinds of diets I wanted to know about, too. I especially paid attention to the way the trays were made up so they looked appetizing. It was one of my most satisfying times as a student.

In mid-March 1945, Mama-san wrote that letters were arriving from creditors requesting payments for fertilizer, plants, labor, and other costs associated with running the farm. I was stunned. Based on the contract that Yoneichi and the deputy sheriff had signed prior to our evacuation, the deputy sheriff was supposed to handle all of these details. It was clear to us that this was not happening. The deputy sheriff had apparently pocketed the profits, and failed to pay the expenses. I had no money to pay those bills, Yoneichi was overseas, and my parents were aliens with no civil rights.

Mama-san wrote about something else in her March letter:

> We heard that camps will close on January 1, 1946, or so. Once we leave camp, we cannot return. Therefore, we have to think this through carefully before we leave.

Now the internees faced a new problem. The people still in the ten internment camps began to worry about the dilemma that now engulfed them. I thought about all the ones who had lost their homes and their farms, like Mary Otani from Sacramento, whom I had met while hiking up Castle Rock above Tule Lake. Or what about all those families who had lived on Terminal Island in California where the fathers had been arrested and the fishing boats had been seized? What about the farmers and the entrepreneurs throughout the western states whose previous livelihoods had to be left behind? How would they support themselves with no assets? If they had sons in the service and they were killed, what would happen to their foreign-born parents?

Whatever the circumstances, the news caused alarm and severe agitation among all the internees. They had become accustomed to enforced idleness and dependent upon the government for their food and shelter. Now they faced the reality that all of this would evaporate in the near future. Although most of the Japanese-Americans wanted to return to the West Coast where they had lived and worked since their arrival in the United States, the memory of severe prejudice that forced them out still lingered. I wondered, *How will they be received?* After all, the war against Japan was still going on.

In her letter on April 1, 1945, Mama-san explained their dilemma:

> Papa-san is not a citizen and without you around and without a legal authorization from you, he cannot sell the produce nor pay the people who work for us. This is true for California, Oregon and Washington only, I think. That is because of this complicated law. If you [Mary] were with us, then Papa-san could do the work and there wouldn't be any trouble. Until Yoneichi-san returns you are the boss and the boss isn't here with the land document. We can't do a thing. Therefore, you have to ask a lawyer to make this letter of authority so you can entrust Papa-san to do the work for you. The WRA showed us how this is to be done. When you have completed the document, please send it to us. The WRA placed a collection notice on Deputy Sheriff Hopkins, but we haven't heard a thing yet. Thank you for taking care of this for us. Mama.

Sitting at my desk in my room, I was shocked to read this letter. *I can't do all this on top of everything else I have to do in nurses' training,* I thought. *Where would I begin?*

Mama-san and Papa-san were reasonably sure they had the farm to return to, but at the time of the evacuation they didn't realize that Yoneichi and I would not be going back with them. Before they left for Vashon, it was imperative that they have this legal document.

While we were trying to solve this problem, many dozens of frantic letters flew back and forth between my parents and me trying to figure out how to get this done. Telephones were not available in camp, making communication much slower. Mama-san always wrote in Japanese and there were times when I had difficulty translating certain characters. It was agonizing to read and write in Japanese when my thoughts were in English. I had to understand what they were saying, think about an appropriate response, translate it into Japanese, and identify the correct character to use before writing it. To compound the problem, my parents wanted me to do things, but they didn't always know specifically what it was they needed me to do.

Because I was twenty years old and inexperienced with no college education and no training in law or finances, I felt terribly frustrated. But I knew I had to help my parents. The problem got even more complicated and perplexing. First, I wrote a letter to the deputy sheriff and requested reports for the years since our departure. His response was slow to arrive; then he wrote that he had sent them to Yoneichi. Without Yoneichi to ask, we wondered where (or whether) the deputy sheriff really sent them. We finally began to doubt that the deputy sheriff had sent any of the reports for 1942, 1943, or 1944. We wondered if he had kept any records at all. We suspected he kept all the checks for the strawberries and paid only minimal expenses, leaving major debts for us to deal with later. At least, this was the way it appeared to us.

Another thing bothered me. *Why didn't we hear from Mack, the man whom we entrusted to actually work on the property?* Could he give us any clues about what was going on back home? But I could imagine that he might have been too exhausted to write at the end of each long day. Or, he just might not have known how to write. I would never know.

While handling all these problems on the farm, I also worked extended hours at the hospital. Often I lay awake at night wondering what to do. One day my classmates and I were in a classroom listening to a lecture on a common medical problem. It was in the afternoon after lunch, and I was sitting at the side of the room beside the open windows. The hot summer sun poured in on me as I listened to the white-haired Miss Schlapper drone on about the proper technique required in the care of elderly patients. The last thing I remember her saying was, "Man thou art fearfully and wondrously made." The next thing I knew I heard her very loud voice barking:

"Miss Matsuda, you are falling asleep in class."

I jerked my head back and glanced up to see her staring at me with a severe frown on her wrinkled face. It was dead silent in the room. The blackboard behind her with an outline of the subject for the afternoon lecture was illuminated by the blazing sunlight. I had brought *haji,* a sense of great shame, on myself, and there was no place to hide. I took off my glasses, put them on the desk in front of me, rubbed my face, and responded truthfully, "I'm sorry. I didn't sleep well last night." I kept my eyes diverted—I didn't dare look at my classmates. I was afraid of being disciplined. Other classmates had received severe reprimands for smaller infractions because Miss Schlapper normally was very strict.

Miss Schlapper and the Director of Nursing were good friends and always ate their meals together in the same dining room where we students ate ours. Perhaps they both were aware of the extra demands on my time and energy from my parents in the camps and a brother in the service. The class proceeded with no further comment. At the time, I was relieved for not being punished further in front of my classmates, but thought it was amazing that nothing came of this incident.

On April 10, 1945 Papa-san wrote:

> I am sorry I have not written to you in awhile. The last letter you sent was about Yoneichi-san's land ownership papers, right? There may have been some confusion in our letters but I am reassured when I received your last letter that you fully understand what must be done. I know you are very, very busy studying but it is your responsibility to help us in Yoneichi's absence. And it is *shikata ga nai*—it can't be helped. Papa.

One day during my off-duty hours, I worked up my courage and went to a lawyer in Clinton. Tense and nervous, I explained our situation and then asked for his assistance.

The lawyer paused for quite a while as he shuffled papers back and forth on his desk as he thought about my request. Finally he looked up, frowned and responded, "You're asking me to take on a deputy sheriff and the United States government in a dispute happening two thousand miles away." He looked at me darkly. "Good luck, but frankly, I can't help you." He turned away in his chair. It was obvious this was the end of the conversation.

While I had braced myself for this kind of response, I still felt my face flush and my muscles tighten. *Okay,* I said to myself, *I guess this man isn't going to be any help to me whatsoever.* Maybe he was reluctant to deal with a huge federal bureaucracy, or maybe he just didn't want to get involved with a Jap. The trouble was, he was the only lawyer in town.

After I got back to the nurses' home, I paced in my room, clenching and unclenching my fists as tears of frustration and anger rushed through me. Finally I sat down to write a disappointing letter to my parents. As I stared out the window with my arms across my chest, pen in hand, I felt overwhelmed and resentful. Suddenly, Yoneichi's face appeared before me and I heard his words: *"Take good care of the folks. You know how important that is to me. It's up to you now, you know."* I stopped frowning and realized this was something I *must* do. It was my responsibility and my privilege to do it for Yoneichi, for our parents, and for me. This was *on,* a sense of loyalty, respect, and gratitude toward one's parents.

CHAPTER SIXTEEN

NISEI SOLDIERS

Yoneichi never talked about his wartime experiences with any of us. Many soldiers did not talk in detail about their involvement in the war except among themselves. But the *Nisei* soldiers seemed especially reluctant to discuss those times during the war and even decades later. Periodically I asked Yoneichi about some of his experiences, but he would always look away and say, "I'll tell you about it some other time." Unfortunately, that time never came.

In searching for my brother's story, I had to go to his friends with whom he fought in the war. There was one friend in particular who had been a classmate of Yoneichi's in high school and who fought in Italy at the same time. Years later I met with this man many times and he shared his memories, books, and various papers to give me more specific information. Using these resources along with books from the library I learned about the courageous stories of the Japanese-American soldiers of the 100th/442nd Regimental Combat Team.

Initially the 100th Battalion was made up of all Japanese-American volunteers from Hawaii. After the attack on Pearl Harbor when the draft status of the *Nisei* men was changed from 1-A (fit for general active military service) to 4-C (enemy alien) and back again to 1-A, an overwhelming number of Japanese-American men volunteered for the military from Hawaii. They became the 100th Battalion. Their outstanding success in campaigns in North Africa and Italy confirmed to military leadership how valuable the Japanese-American soldiers could be.

By the time the first large group of *Niseis* from the mainland arrived in Europe in early 1945, the men of the 100th Battalion had distinguished themselves through months of rugged fighting. The embattled survivors retained their special identification as the 100th Battalion in recognition of their combat record. With replacements from newly arrived Japanese-American soldiers to fill the ranks, they joined the 442nd. Together with the

2nd and 3rd Battalions, they made up the 442nd Regimental Combat Team. When Yoneichi arrived in early 1945, he was assigned to Company G of the 2nd Battalion.

By that time, the heroics of the *Nisei* were already legendary. In *Honor by Fire: Japanese-Americans at War in Europe and the Pacific*, Lyn Crost wrote:

> The 100th/442nd Regimental Combat Team had rescued the Texas Division's Lost Battalion after five days of continuous night-and-day battles. It suffered more than 800 casualties to rescue 211 Texans—all that were left of the 275 originally entrapped.... The men of the Lost Battalion later presented a plaque to the 100th/442nd, thanking it "for the gallant fight to effect our rescue after we had been isolated seven days."

The reputation of the *Nisei* fighting spirit was both a blessing and a curse. It was a blessing in that it proved their loyalty beyond a shadow of a doubt, but it was a curse because they got the deadliest assignments and paid dearly with their lives. The fear among Japanese-American families was that our men would be expendable and could be sent on the most dangerous missions.

In a book by Masayo Umezawa Duus, *Unlikely Liberators, the Men of the 100th and 442nd*, there is an account by a 442nd chaplain that describes the struggles of the *Nisei* soldiers as they fought to rescue the Lost Battalion. On October 30, 1944, Reverend Masao Yamada wrote a long letter to his friend Colonel Sherwood Dixon, who had trained the *Nisei* soldiers of the 3rd Battalion at Camp Shelby.

> The cost has been high. I admire the courage and the discipline of our loyal men. They take their orders in stride without complaint and go into the volley of fire, with one spirit and one mind. Actually, those that saw the charge (our men call it the "banzai" charge) came home with a vivid and stirring account of our men unflinchingly charging on the double, falling under machine gun fire, yet moving on as the ceaseless waves beating on a sea shore.
>
> I am spiritually low for once. My heart weeps with our men, especially with those who gave all. Never had combat affected me so deeply as has this emergency mission. I am probably getting soft, but to me the price is too costly for our men.

In *Honor by Fire*, Lyn Crost adds this from Reverend Yamada's letter:

> I feel this way more because the burden is laid on the combat team when the rest of the 141st [Battalion, 36th Division] is not forced to take the same responsibility.

Years after the war I wept as I read these words. Here was the evidence that I feared—the Japanese-American soldiers were dedicated to giving their all, knowing they could be considered dispensable. *Was this the bias that Yoneichi could never speak of?* I wondered. I would never know for certain.

I knew *Nisei* men like Yoneichi were determined to fight hard to prove their loyalty to the United States. I suspected their determination would put them in harm's way, but I found it hard to believe. There was racism in World War II that justified putting the *Nisei* soldiers on the frontline, often facing impossible odds. War correspondent Lyn Crost wrote about this:

> October 29, 1944 at 0830 General Dahlquist was on the phone, ordering officers at 442nd headquarters: "Keep them [the Nisei] going and don't let them stop. There's a battalion [the Lost Battalion] about to die up there and we've got to reach them."
>
> Sixteen minutes later the general was on the phone again: "Let's keep them going. Even against opposition."
>
> Captain Pershing Nakada, commander of the 232nd Engineer Company, was up front supervising the removal of a roadblock when he heard that order. Nakada...later recalled that nobody in the 442nd respected Dahlquist. "He didn't give a damn how many people we killed, as long as we just got up there."

Once Yoneichi went overseas, he wrote infrequently, but when he did, my parents always promptly relayed his updates to me in Iowa. He wrote only in generalities, such as, "I am *genki*—in high spirit, vigorous. How are you? I hope all is well with all of you."

He chose his words carefully. They did not reflect the horrors of the war he was fighting in France and in Italy. In those days of censorship and war secrets, Yoneichi would not have been allowed to tell us much even if he had wanted to.

In *I Can Never Forget*, Thelma Chang wrote:

> [A soldier who fought in the 100th] remembered Italy and a young German soldier, about 18 years of age, who was badly wounded. "We cut away his trousers and tried to stop the blood flow, but we soon realized he was going to die. We were too far from the aid station, and there was no way to save his life. He tried to tell us something in German, but we couldn't understand. By arm and hand motion, we gathered he wanted us to take out his wallet, which we did. And then he wanted us to take out some pictures. By his facial expressions, by his tears, we knew somehow that he wanted us to tell his mother about his last moments on this earth. And that, I think, hit us very deeply. We

realized very very vividly that he was another human being—young, innocent, who meant no real harm to us, other than he was in the same bind we were.... War is as close to hell on earth as man can create, and why people fight them, if you've ever been in one, you never understand.

In March 1945, General Mark Clark asked General Dwight Eisenhower, commander of Allied Forces in Europe, for the return of the 442nd/100th Battalion to his command with the 5th Army. He knew the fighting capability of the *Niseis,* and wanted them to regain control of the "Gothic Line" in

Yoneichi in 1944.

northern Italy. The Gothic Line was a two-hundred-mile line of more than two thousand fortified dugouts along the Apennine Mountains. The Germans considered their defense impregnable, and it was the last major German stronghold in Italy. General Eisenhower granted this request, and Yoneichi became a part of this unit and participated in the major battle that was to follow.

On April 5 under cover of darkness, the men of the 3rd Battalion of the 442nd scaled the treacherous, sheer cliffs of the slopes of Mount Folgorito for a surprise attack that became legendary. The soldiers were sworn to keep silent when scaling the cliffs, which they did, even when some of them fell off the slopes and lay injured. At 6:00 a.m. after an extremely difficult eight-hour climb in full battle equipment, the soldiers reached the enemy position and attacked, taking the Germans by complete surprise. This assault was the beginning of the end for the Germans in Italy.

It was during the ensuing battles that a classmate of Yoneichi's from Vashon High School witnessed the heroic action of Private First Class Sadao S. Munemori. Under heavy fire, Munemori single-handedly destroyed a pair of entrenched machinegun nests, clearing the way for his company to advance, then saved the lives of two of his men by diving on a live grenade and smothering the blast with his own body. He was posthumously awarded the Medal of Honor, our country's highest honor.

At the same time, Yoneichi and the men of the 2nd Battalion waged similar campaigns on the nearby peaks of Mount Belvedere and Mount

Pizzacuto. In successive bloody battles Yoneichi and his comrades fought until the Germans were routed. In spite of heavy loss of life, the determined Allied forces broke through the massive defenses on April 18, 1945.

It is estimated that World War II (1939-1945) killed more people, destroyed more property, disrupted more lives, and probably had more far-reaching consequences than any other war in history. Exactly how many soldiers died is unknown, but historians estimate military deaths probably totaled about seventeen million. Civilian deaths were even greater due to the devastation of this war because of starvation, bombing raids, the mass murders of millions of Jews, massacres, epidemics, and other war-related causes. Few areas of the world were left unscathed by World War II.

For years I could only imagine how bad it was for my brother, but Yoneichi never told us. Only once in a letter to Mama-san did Yoneichi mention any of the fierce fighting. Mama-san then reported to me that he wrote, "Some of the bullets came pretty close."

After the backbone of the German army had been broken, Yoneichi's letters began arriving weekly. He still kept the news general in nature, and gave few indications of the suffering he must have gone through. But it was wonderful to hear from him and know he was alive.

Years later I read about an incident that has become part of the 100th Battalion's folklore. Lyn Crost wrote in *Honor by Fire:*

> On July 18 (1944), Livorno fell, and the 100th Battalion moved in to protect key installations. Most of the unit was placed where the main highway entered the city, because General Mark Clark wanted to prevent looting. An incident occurred here that has become part of the 100th Battalion's folklore; no story about that battalion would be complete without it.
>
> A private, just topping five feet tall, was standing guard at his post when a long line of army trucks stopped in front of him and a colonel stepped out. This is the conversation that followed, starting with the colonel:
>
> "We are from the Engineer Corps. We are here to secure the port and make it ready for the ships to come in with the supplies. Let us through."
>
> "May I see your orders, sir?"
>
> "I don't have orders. I must get through."
>
> "Colonel, nobody gets through without orders."
>
> "I can kill you right here and take my convoy through."
>
> The private drew a line with his foot and said: "Colonel, you cross this line, you *ma-ke!*"

"Ma-ke? What is *ma-ke?"* the colonel demanded.

"Ma-ke means you're dead."

"We can take you; you are only one," the colonel threatened.

"You think me stupid? I am a combat soldier. You are now covered by many machine guns. Cross the line and you *ma-ke!"*

The colonel and his convoy withdrew.

The story went all the way to the top of the Fifth Army—to Gen. Mark Clark—and he came to Livorno with a bevy of newsmen and staff.

"Bring this private to me," he demanded. "I want to meet him."

As the five-foot private stood beside the six-foot four-inch general, Clark put his arm around him and turned to the press corps. "I commend this soldier to you," he said. "I personally selected the 100th to guard Leghorn because I knew my order would be obeyed and carried out. I can depend on the 100th to successfully carry out any mission. I have absolute faith in every soldier in the 100th. This private is an example of my trust."

Another group of *Niseis* fought in the South Pacific in the Military Intelligence Service. In all, there were about five thousand Japanese-American men who completed intensive training in language education. They trained for counter-intelligence to interrogate Japanese prisoners of war and interpret Japanese documents. Over the duration of the war, these soldiers were under tight security wraps since they were subject to both enemy fire and friendly fire because they looked like the enemy. Little was publicly known—before or immediately after the war—about these brave soldiers.

According to General Charles Willoughby, G-2 intelligence chief, these Japanese-American linguists secretly saved countless Allied lives and shortened the war by two years. More than fifty years after World War II, in April 2000 the Military Intelligence Service received the Presidential Unit Citation for their contributions during the war.

The records show that the "Go For Broke" Regiment, as the combined 100th and the 442nd Regimental Combat Team was called, suffered 700 men killed in action, 67 missing in action, and nearly 10,000 wounded. For their size, they were the most highly decorated units in the history of the United States Armed Forces. Over the course of the war, about 18,500 soldiers served in the 100th/442nd. The unit earned more than 18,000 individual decorations, including 9,486 Purple Hearts, 12 French Croix de Guerre, 560 Silver Stars, and 4,000 Bronze Stars. The soldiers' actions also earned seven Presidential Unit Citations, the nation's top award for combat units.

On July 15, 1945, part of the 442ⁿᵈ Regimental Combat Team marched down Constitution Avenue in Washington, D.C. On the White House lawn, President Harry Truman presented them with the seventh presidential citation. "You fought for the free nations of the world.... You fought not only the enemy, you fought prejudice, and you have won," President Truman said. "Keep up that fight, and continue to win—to make this great Republic stand for just what the Constitution says it stands for: 'the welfare of all the people, all the time.' Bring forward the colors." He pinned the citation on the regimental banner. It was noted they were the only military unit returning from overseas battlefields to have the honor of being reviewed by the president. When I heard about the honors received by our fighting men, I was very proud. It was not until decades later that most people would learn of the heroism and sacrifice of the *Nisei* soldiers.

Whatever Yoneichi endured during the war, I know he felt it was worth it. Sixty years after Yoneichi fought in World War II, I learned that he had received the Bronze Star for "distinguishing himself by heroic or meritorious achievement...in connection with military operations against an armed enemy on or about 20 April 1945." None of us will ever know what he did to earn that medal; he never mentioned it. I learned about it from his widow, who found it among his wartime memorabilia after his death.

Although I am not surprised that Yoneichi did not talk about his Bronze Star, how I wish I had known about it. I would have acknowledged the award, and expressed my deep gratitude and pride in Yoneichi's unselfish service to our people and the United States. Like most of the *Nisei* men who went to war, Yoneichi did not want to take credit for what he had done. It is part of our Japanese culture to always be modest, and never brag about our successes. "I was one of many" was a statement commonly made by the Japanese-American men who fought in the war. Yoneichi felt the same way.

I am certain Yoneichi suffered a great deal of anguish about the war, no different from any other GI who lost his best friends in combat. Yoneichi was a religious person, and the idea of killing others, even in a "just" war, was philosophically unacceptable to him. But he had to go and fight, while daily facing the possibility of his own death.

◁ ◉ ▷

After months of seeming slow progress, the war turned rapidly. In a matter of days stunning news heralded the end of the war in Europe with the execution of Mussolini and his mistress in Italy on April 28, 1945, followed by Hitler's suicide on April 30, 1945 in his Berlin bunker.

The evening I read about this incredible news, I was in the nurses' lounge, relaxing. Immediately a dam of emotions broke inside of me as I thought, *The war is finally over!* I rushed upstairs to my room, fell on my knees by my bed, and tearfully thanked God. *At last I can release all the tension I have held back,* I told myself, sobbing. *Our family will be together again.* Repeatedly I reassured myself, *Yoneichi will be safe, alive, uninjured.* My hope was that Yoneichi could soon rest out of harm's way and eat decent food again. Then he could come home and help us with the farm and relieve our parents who had lived with anxiety for so long.

Things were improving in other ways, too. As Mama-san and Papa-san requested, I had written letters to the War Relocation Authority offices in Chicago, Illinois; Des Moines, Iowa; and Tacoma, Washington. I appealed for help with the matter of ownership of the farm. I knew we were not the only ones needing assistance.

In the meantime, my parents finally found a lawyer in the social service department at Minidoka camp willing to help untangle our situation. The lawyer sent a letter to several creditors requesting a postponement of debt payments until we could get our legal issues straightened out or until Yoneichi returned from the war. Replies came back saying this would be acceptable.

The same lawyer created the power of attorney we needed and sent it for my signature. Now Papa-san would have the authority to do whatever he needed until Yoneichi's return. This was a gigantic burden off my shoulders. After VE Day (Victory in Europe) on May 8, 1945, we felt quite certain Yoneichi would return home soon, and all our problems would be resolved.

In many of her letters, Mama-san expressed concern for my health. One time she wrote, "White people are bigger than Japanese people so it will require more effort to take care of them." I was only 5′ 3″, so it was hard for me to lift some of the larger patients. She knew my work and study in a distant place away from my family would be difficult, but she was also concerned about the stress that accompanied the tasks she and Papa-san were asking me to accomplish for them.

The battles in the Pacific continued. On July 17, 1945, seventy scientists signed a petition and gave it to President Truman stating, "The liberation of atomic power, which has been achieved, places atomic bombs in the hands of the Army. It places in your hands, as Commander-in-Chief, the fateful decision whether or not to sanction the use of such bombs in the present phase of the war against Japan."

On the afternoon of August 7, after a full day at the hospital's diet kitchen, I returned to my room to rest and prepare for classes the next day. In the downstairs lounge I picked up the local newspaper and saw the headlines:

"First Atomic Bomb Dropped on Japan; Missile is Equal to 20,000 Tons of TNT; Truman Warns Foe of a 'Rain of Ruin.'"

An aerial photograph taken shortly after the bombing showed a huge mushroom cloud above the devastated Hiroshima. The United States had used its atomic power on August 6. *Oh, no!* I panicked. *An atom bomb has been dropped on Hiroshima!* It was the first time the public had ever heard of a weapon of mass destruction, and our country had used it.

When the pictures appeared on the front page, they showed the total devastation of what was once a bustling city. The few remaining buildings in various stages of collapse stood out in sharp contrast to the dark, thick clouds of dust, smoke, and debris billowing into the sky. The ground was littered with twisted, naked bodies, many burned and charred. Photos showed dazed people running or walking with scorched hair and skin hanging from their arms and legs. *The people in this picture are Japanese, just like me,* I thought as I stared at the photographs.

I had hated the Japanese government for its role in starting this war and thrusting me into a situation that resulted in my imprisonment. It wasn't until after the war that I gained perspective about the evils of Japan's aggressive militarism in Asia. I am sure Mama-san, who was a student of history, knew at the time about those terrible events in China and elsewhere, but she never mentioned them to me.

Japan's attack on Pearl Harbor became the impetus for corralling all of us of Japanese descent into internment camps, but when I saw the pictures of Japanese people burned and charred by the atomic blast, I was heartbroken for them. I was an American by birth, but at that moment, I was Japanese. The full impact of that event instantly seared upon my heart.

When I looked at the pictures, I felt nauseated and dizzy, as if I had been hit in the head and stomach. So many innocent lives wiped out. I knew instantly that the United States had won the war. My tears were a mix of relief and anguish. Even though a part of me was glad the United States won the war, the Japanese part of me was speechless with grief and horror. I ran up to my room, fell on my bed, and sobbed. A few minutes later there was a soft knock on the door. My dearest classmate, Ellen, came in, sat on the bed beside me, gently put her arms around me and held me close as we both cried. Caucasian and Japanese together, we held on to one another until our tears subsided.

That evening in the dining room, the usual lively conversations were subdued. A classmate came up to me, put her hands on my shoulders, and whispered into my ear, "I'm sorry, Mary." The others hovered near, but were silent. I could tell from their woeful expressions that they didn't know what to say. I just nodded my head at each of them and said, "Thanks." Tears ran down my face.

Although Mama-san and Papa-san came to America by choice and stood by their decision against such terrible odds, I could imagine them staring silently at the news splashed across the internment camp newspaper. I knew they would be absolutely stunned by what they read. Japan was the land of their birth and both of them had family there. I imagined them sitting a long time with bowed heads, quiet, hands folded and clenched in their laps. I was sure Mama-san wept openly after the initial shock as the reality began to sink in. She would grieve for the suffering and the dead, but also for the implications for the future of the planet.

A letter came from Mama-san written on August 17. Her point of view was shared by many others who were born and raised in Japan.

> Japan is a small country but from a long time ago, she has never lost a single war. In order to defeat Japan, America took the sky for herself and tried to crush little Japan. They had a bad bomb that shouldn't be used in the world and used it to try to make Japan disappear. With this in the history of the world, the big dishonor remains. For us here, we do not talk about it. We might try to hide it but it cannot be hidden. This splendid America has done a very bad thing. We don't need to talk about it with others, but we must never forget that America did this kind of thing.

≈ ◎ ≈

The sacrifices that Yoneichi and other *Nisei* men made were eventually rewarded by Congress. On January 2, 1945, the government rescinded Executive Order 9066 after the Supreme Court ruled *Ex parte Endo* that "loyal" citizens could not be lawfully detained. In 1952, the Walter-McCarran Act repealed the Oriental Exclusion Act, permitting aliens like my parents to become naturalized citizens. Years later, some experts, including Senator Daniel Inouye of Hawaii, would attribute the outstanding record of the 100th and 442nd battalions as influential factors in the U.S. decision to confirm the statehood of Hawaii in 1959.

I believe another major benefit that resulted from the struggles of the war years is the change in Japanese-American status in our country. Instead of working primarily at low-paying, menial jobs, opportunities for positions in the professions and management became available. Japanese-Americans became teachers, professors in esteemed universities, lawyers, dentists, doctors—whatever they chose to do was open to them. Many used their GI Bill and went on to become professionals in their chosen fields, like my brother, Yoneichi. The time when *Niseis* could work only for their parents, or in primarily Asian districts, was over. The future for Japanese-Americans had changed profoundly, and I would never forget the courage of Yoneichi and the *Nisei* soldiers.

CHAPTER SEVENTEEN

HOME AGAIN

The official end of the war was on August 15, 1945, VJ Day, a time of great celebration around the country. We all hoped and prayed this would be the last world war.

Within the interment camps, the end of the war signaled the eventual end of internment and the closing of the camps, bringing mixed emotions. People still in the camps began leaving, most returning to the West Coast, even if they didn't have a home to return to. To them, that part of the country was still considered home despite hardships and racism they had endured.

The Umanis were among the first of our close friends to go back home to the Northwest. Several weeks later I heard from Mama-san in a letter dated August 30, 1945:

> On September 5th we will leave Minidoka and head for Vashon. After we arrive there, we will let you know how things are. Don't worry about a thing. The things that we needed to have done have been completed. It is amazing, with all of the work that we did, that we're finally going back home.

I later realized there were many things still unresolved, and Mama-san had written this to reassure me. Although Mama-san sounded optimistic, I imagined she was filled with both eagerness and fear. *What will she find when she returns to our farm?* I wondered. *She must feel both excitement and dread.* I felt similarly, and wanted to return with my parents, but I had to finish my nurses' training.

On September 5, 1945 my parents left camp with twenty-five dollars each from the U.S. government for travel expenses, arriving home two days later. Mama-san's letter to me written a few days after their arrival masked many emotions and details.

> It is September 9th. We left Minidoka on the 5th. We arrived in Tacoma on the 6th at 2:00. We stayed overnight at the Hirano-sans. The morning of the 7th Hisako-san and Jimmy-san took us to Vashon. The neighborhood

white folks don't seem to have changed much. The piano is here. The house doesn't look too bad. The strawberries look good. We have two acres. Mama.

My parents got home only a few weeks after the war ended. They immediately became engrossed in cleaning up the house and getting the yard in order. From our farm Mama-san wrote on September 14th:

It is now one week since we got home. Every day, every day, I am cleaning the house. Mack has taken care of it fairly well, so Papa-san and I are rejoicing. He painted the house. It looks fine. Mrs. Peterson and Mrs. McDonald brought a lot of vegetables. They're delicious. Our feelings are better than we had hoped. The strawberry plants are growing well. There are more Japanese people coming back to Vashon. They will come and stay at our place until they can find a place to live. It is wonderful, isn't it? The white people on Vashon, all of them, are very nice to us. Rejoice with us! Mama.

And I did rejoice! It was better than I could have imagined. According to the contract with the deputy sheriff, because my parents returned in September, the following year's crop would belong to them. However, my parents still had to deal with Deputy Sheriff Hopkins and the creditors. They decided to wait until Yoneichi returned from Europe to resolve the financial problems.

~◎~

I suspected Mama-san's mixed feelings about returning home were shared by the majority of *Isseis* who planned to return to the West Coast. Many could not forget the terrible injustices done to them prior to the evacuation. They feared resistance when they tried to return to their former homes. For those whose homes had been in California, and whose homes or businesses were already lost, their feelings of dread and fear were probably far more extreme. In some cases, those feelings turned out to be well justified. Returning home was painful and difficult for many Japanese-Americans. Years later some of their stories would be told in *Unlikely Liberators* by Masayo Umezawa Duus. Two of those stories haunted me when I read them.

In 1945, shortly after the end of the war in Europe, U.S. newspapers reported the tragic story of the family of Sergeant Kazuo Masuda, a *Nisei* hero who had been killed in northern Italy. The Masuda family was driven out of Santa Ana, California when they tried to return to their former house, despite their dead son's heroic war efforts. The situation would not change until six months later when General "Vinegar Joe" Stillwell, a war hero who fought in Asia, came to California on behalf of the military to honor the Masudas. The photograph of General Stillwell standing in front of the family's small, one-story, wooden house while pinning Sergeant Masuda's Distinguished Service Cross on this white-haired Japanese mother's chest aroused popular sympathy for the family.

Another painful story of racism against the Japanese after the end of the war took place in Hood River, Oregon. A national uproar was created when the local American Legion removed the names of sixteen Japanese-Americans from the honor roll in front of Hood River's city hall. Faced with criticism from the national headquarters and many other branches, they restored the names of the Japanese-Americans.

Even though their sons had died in the war, proving their loyalty to the United States, Japanese-American families still faced post-war prejudice. Yet, these stories also demonstrated how the *Nisei*, through their persistent courage and loyalty, finally succeeded in winning acceptance from the general public. It was important to me that Japanese-Americans be respected, and it was satisfying when that began to happen. When the *Nisei* combat battalions' wartime sacrifices became legendary I thought, *These incredible sacrifices have become the irrefutable demonstration of our loyalty to the United States.* Now I longed for a time when I could once again proudly be Japanese and American.

◁ ❀ ◁

While the war had been officially over in Europe since May, the men were still on guard duty in various places in Europe. Yoneichi wrote to Mama-san requesting Japanese pickles, *umeboshi* [sour plums], and *wasabi* [horseradish]. He wanted foods that reminded him of home, especially for Christmas 1945 when he would still be thousands of miles away.

That Christmas I was lonely, too. It was a typical snowy Iowa winter, both wondrous and desolate. We had completed classes for the quarter and most of my classmates who lived in the area had gone home for the holiday. Patients needed care and I was one of the students who stayed at the hospital.

One of my patients was an older gentleman who owned a major department store in Clinton. His wife had died the previous year, and he was lonely. I took extra time with him, listening to his memories of years spent with his beloved wife. He had many stories about the life they shared, their children, and how much he missed her. By listening to this man's sorrow and offering him comfort I felt better myself. A week later I got a letter from Mama-san that she wrote on Christmas Day:

Merry Christmas! The four of us had dinner together. I made a pie out of squash, made candied sweet potatoes, roast beef and baked biscuits. Putting Yoneichi-san's and your pictures on your chairs, we conversed with you as we ate our dinner. It was a wonderful meal. You couldn't come home for vacation so it must have been a very lonely Christmas. I think about that and feel apologetic but *shikata ga nai*.

My parents were busy throughout the winter with maintenance work on the farm. I could imagine them buying food and essential items on credit from local grocers who had known them for years and trusted them. They purchased fertilizer and supplies with money advanced by the National Fruit Company, a company they had sold crops to for years before the war. They could also buy strawberry plants from the man who owned the Vashon Packing Company. Despite little money to live on that winter, they persevered.

As spring 1946 came, my parents were anticipating Yoneichi's return from Europe, perhaps as early as that autumn. Mama-san sent me a letter describing an accident Papa-san had in early May while cultivating berries. He was adjusting the harness on our normally gentle horse, Dolly, and she kicked him, breaking several of his ribs. Papa-san managed to get back to the house and Mama-san immediately summoned our family doctor.

The doctor examined him and said that Papa-san could not do any outdoor work for several weeks. It was the worst time to receive such news—just as he was getting ready for the first harvest since returning home. Papa-san protested, saying he had to work. Yoneichi was in the army in Europe and there was no one else available.

The doctor adjusted the rib belt around Papa-san's chest to ease the pain and told him that he would give Papa-san some pills to help him rest easier. But the doctor was firm in his order. Papa-san was not to work, or he could risk puncturing a lung.

After all Papa-san and Mama-san had been through, it was intolerable to not be able to prepare for the first harvest. The doctor sensed Papa-san's dilemma and offered to place an emergency request with the local American Red Cross and ask that Yoneichi be released from his military duties right away. The doctor did not think this would be a problem because the war was over, and farming was an essential industry.

Mama-san pointed out that this way Yoneichi would come home much sooner. They agreed with the doctor's plan. When the doctor called the next day to check on Papa-san, he also told Mama-san that he had placed the request for Yoneichi's immediate release with the local Red Cross.

Mama-san's letter contained a surprise:

> Mary-san, you wouldn't believe what the doctor told us. The Red Cross worker who placed the call for Yoneichi-san's return was Mrs. Hopkins, the deputy sheriff's wife. I think it is the most wonderful thing that she should be the one to be here for us on this occasion. I'm sure she is a most gracious lady, to be doing this kind of work for our boys.

In her letter Mama-san sounded amazed by the coincidence that the person who advanced the request was the wife of the very person who had caused us such anxiety while we were held at the internment camp. After reading that, I thought, *In some inexplicable way, Mrs. Hopkins was fated to be the one to make Yoneichi's immediate release from the army possible so he could come home and rescue our parents and the farm.* Hope had burst through a blanket of doubt in humanity. The world did not seem quite as lonely.

It was not until much later that I finally understood why Deputy Sheriff Hopkins did not uphold his agreement with us to care for our farm. In October 1942 when we were held at the Tule Lake Internment Camp, Hopkins had visited us, an event I failed to remember due to my own troubles and because his business did not concern me. Hopkins met with Yoneichi and Papa-san with an offer he thought we could not refuse. He asked if we would sell our property to him. Yoneichi and Papa-san politely listened to his proposal, but firmly refused. Hopkins left empty-handed after a five-hundred-mile journey. I now believe his initial intentions in managing our farm were honest, but he gave in to the temptation to profiteer from our dire situation.

Yoneichi returned to the farm in mid-June 1946. He had to skip the victory parade in Washington, D.C., in July at which President Truman honored the 442nd Battalion for the seventh time. It was more important to be home in time to harvest the strawberries.

I was still in Iowa when Yoneichi got back, but imagined his homecoming as clearly as if I had been there. After the long journey from Europe back to Seattle, he called home. I am sure my parents eagerly examined the bus and ferry schedules for Yoneichi's arrival time. I am certain Mama-san impatiently paced the floor until it was time to walk out to the highway to meet her son. Undoubtedly Yoneichi had a broad smile as he alighted from the bus with his duffel bag. After a long embrace, the two of them must have walked arm-in-arm back to the house—a diminutive, gray-haired woman in work clothes beside her slightly taller, battle-weary son in his army uniform.

Once in the house, Papa-san must have extended his hand to greet his son while staying seated in his big chair in the living room, wincing from the sharp pain of broken ribs. Mama-san wrote that she prepared a sumptuous meal of hot rice, *sukiyaki* made of tender sliced beef and vegetables, and salad. Before eating, Mama-san said a prayer of gratitude for the safe return of her son. I wished so much I could have been there, too, to welcome home my brother. I'm sure Mama-san had a place setting for me at the table in front of my empty chair.

Yoneichi was home for only a week before he took matters into his own hands. He went to Seattle to talk things over with the lawyer who drew up the initial contract with the deputy sheriff in early 1942. The lawyer and Yoneichi discussed their options. One strategy was to sue Hopkins, if necessary, to force him to produce the money and the records of those four years' activities.

About a month later, Yoneichi returned to Seattle for a second meeting with the lawyer. Yoneichi looked over the record book that Hopkins had handed over. It was a mess—disorganized and obviously incomplete. There were a few receipts for income received and receipts for some of the expenses, but the dates were haphazardly recorded and the ledger was hard to follow.

"Hopkins brought me two thousand dollars in cash," the lawyer offered. "He said he was having trouble making ends meet and this is all he could come up with. It isn't much. If you want, we can go ahead and sue him and make him pay more. Do you want to sue him?"

Yoneichi considered this option for a long time, sitting thoughtfully. He figured the deputy sheriff probably owed him many times that amount. Finally he responded, "No, the money is not the issue, it is the principle. This has been a terrible time for our family, and the deputy sheriff added to our misery. I just want him to think about the dishonest way he's conducted himself and take ownership of his behavior. That's what I care about."

The lawyer nodded. "Okay, I'll write you a check for the two thousand dollars and we can close this case."

Later, Yoneichi would tell me he held up his hand and said, "No. I consider this blood money. I don't want it. No amount of money can make up for what our family went through. You helped us save our farm during a time when we really needed help. I'd like for you to accept this money. Thank you very much. I appreciate all you have done for us."

The lawyer stared, dumbfounded. "You can't be serious," he said. "How will you pay your debts?"

Yoneichi answered calmly, "It's only money. In time, we will earn more. Money should be exchanged honestly and willingly with respect for both sides. If I accept this money, our farm—and my family—will forever be tainted by the dishonor of how we forced him to pay." Yoneichi stood up, preparing to leave. "The important thing is that we still have our farm."

In retrospect, there were many reasons why Hopkins may have had difficulties. Pickers were in scarce supply during the war. He undoubtedly had many other responsibilities, including caring for other farms besides ours. Over time I decided Hopkins was more overwhelmed and unqualified to do the job than dishonest, but that did not excuse him for his lack of communication with us.

The end of my nurses' training was approaching. In addition to the white cap I had received in January 1945, I was now wearing a narrow black velvet band on my cap, signifying that I was a senior student. While on duty, I got to show the "probies," the probationary students, the ropes. But under the watchful eyes of the Director of Nursing, Miss Rinehart, and her assistant, Miss Schlapper, we seniors didn't have much opportunity to show off.

I finished nurses' training in July 1947. Before leaving for Des Moines to take my state board exam, I went into the nursing office to speak to Miss Rinehart. "I want to thank you and Miss Schlapper for all the help you gave me during my time here. I am sure you protected me from various problems that I don't even know about," I said gratefully.

"The people in this community had never seen a Japanese before, so you just stood out at first," Miss Rinehart replied. "But you and the other four Japanese nurses who came here were always so kind to the patients and took such good care of them that they came to respect all of you. I never received a complaint about you or any of the others once they got used to having you care for them."

I smiled back. "After I take the state boards, I'd like to get on the train and keep going west until I get home. I hope you will understand. I'd like to stay, but I'm afraid my parents need me too much to stay any longer. They have been through so much, I feel I must go home."

"I understand, and it will be fine if you do that," the director responded. "You have studied and worked hard here, and you have made a wonderful contribution to our community. I know your folks need you. We know how much they have needed you many times during these three years, and you have done admirably well. Go in peace. I know you will be a fine nurse wherever you practice." The war was over, there was no need for me to join the Army Nurse Corps.

Relieved and happy with that blessing, I headed for Des Moines with my classmates to take the final exam. As I sat down at my desk with the questionnaire in front of me, I said a little prayer. "Please, dear God, help me to relax so that I can reach into the recesses of my mind and find the right answers. I must pass this exam." When I looked at the first questions, I was relieved to see I knew most of the answers.

As soon as I finished the final exam, I boarded a train for home. It had been two and a half years since I had seen my family. On my long journey I had ample time to think about that first fateful train ride my family took on May 16, 1942. That train was so old and dirty, and the windows smoked over so we couldn't see out. This time the cars were clean, the seats were soft and comfortable, and the passing landscape ever changing and always interesting. Many times on that trip home I thought, *How my life has changed and how grateful I am.*

I could hardly wait to see my family. I wondered how the farm would look and what kind of changes had taken place. When I got to Seattle, I hurried to the bus station, called home, and got on the next bus that commuted via the ferry to Vashon Island. When I got on, I didn't recognize a soul. The ride across Puget Sound was the same as before, only the ferry had traversed the local waters thousands of times in the five years I had been gone. The blue summer sky was clear and as wide open as welcoming arms.

Once on the island I looked closely at all the houses and yards, the trees, and the familiar stores in little downtown Vashon. I wanted to note everything that had changed and everything that had remained the same. As we approached our road, I stood up and walked to the front of the bus. There was the familiar Matsuda mailbox and straight dirt road that led to our home. I almost ran down the road, gripping my footlocker. I arrived breathless in front of our home and stood for a moment looking at the farmhouse. Mama-san looked out of the kitchen window and immediately came out. We met in front of the porch and embraced. This was the second time we ever did this, and we smiled.

After years away, I heard my mother's wonderful, familiar greeting: *"Okaeri nasai."*

I responded, *"Tada ima kaeri mashita,"* words I had waited five years to say. I greeted Papa-san with the same words and with a slight bow, then a firm grip with my right hand. I took Yoneichi's hand with my right hand and hugged him in a long embrace with my left. I could hardly believe I was really home. I looked at each of them with tears in my eyes and they looked back with misty eyes, too. At last, we were all together again.

~ ◉ ~

Mama-san had prepared a delicious dinner of sushi and vegetables. As we all sat down together at the table, just as we had always done before, Yoneichi and I looked at Mama-san and said, *"Itadaki masu."* Mama-san replied, *"Dozo. Itadaki masho."*

The food tasted so good and the conversation flowed easily. None of us could stop smiling as we talked about the relief of being together again at our own table in our home.

During the meal I observed my parents when they weren't looking to see how they might have changed since I had seen them last. Their hair was a little whiter and Papa-san's was a little thinner in front. They had more wrinkles but a healthier, leaner look from working the farm. Aside from these superficial changes, their core values of love and respect for themselves and for Yoneichi and me were rock solid.

Yoneichi looked different. His youthful, carefree manner was gone. He talked less, looked at each of us and listened more intently. In addition to the lines on his face that were not there before, he looked more serious, stoic, and stone-faced. His usual light-hearted bantering and quick wit were replaced by thoughtful glances and a slow nodding of his head. The war had aged and hardened my brother.

Yoneichi never really talked about his war experiences, perhaps as a way to protect others, perhaps to protect himself. Perhaps he had to kill other people—he never said, and I never asked. Maybe close friends of his were injured or killed, he never said and I never asked. But that first night home I was so relieved and joyful that Yoneichi was alive, I did not fully consider what the war might have done to him. Not until years later would I realize he was tested and shaped by his war experience in ways only other veterans could understand.

That night at the dinner table I realized that I had changed, too. Although I left five years earlier a frightened, confused, angry girl, I now returned an independent young woman with professional skills to make my own way in the world. I had faced the trauma and contradictions of the evacuation and four internment camps, rising above the shock and depression to become a stronger person. I studied and worked hard to achieve my goal of becoming a registered nurse. When Yoneichi was overseas I had worked diligently to help my parents sort out and secure the legal documents they needed to return to the farm. Because I had lived independently from them while facing professional demands, I had developed my autonomy and ensured my self-sufficiency. But throughout the entire process, my parents taught me how to make their strengths my own.

☙ ❧

Mary at twenty-two years old in 1947, standing near Mama-san's roses.

After lingering over dinner, we went outdoors. I looked around for Frisky; he was not sitting in his usual place on the porch. "Frisky wasn't here when we got home," Mama-san said, wistfully. "Mack didn't know what happened to him. He suspects Frisky went off into the woods after we left and just died."

A big lump rose in my throat. "How sad! He died alone, maybe feeling like we had abandoned him. He had been with us for so many years—ever since I was four years old. I will really miss him."

Frisky was a medium-sized, black and brown mutt who had come to live with us in 1929. He and his master, Mr. Shereen, lived down the hill from us at Shawnee near the Sound. One day Papa-san learned that Mr. Shereen was gravely ill and had been hospitalized at Tacoma General Hospital. Papa-san caught the *Virginia V,* a passenger boat that made the rounds of the various docks along Quartermaster Harbor inlet and went to visit Mr. Shereen. When Papa-san greeted him, he could tell immediately that Mr. Shereen had lost a great deal of weight and was weak and frail. During the visit Mr. Shereen asked about Frisky.

"Would you like to see Frisky?" my father asked.

"Yes. I miss him very much."

Papa-san knew that Frisky had been Mr. Shereen's constant companion since his wife, Midge, died several years earlier. "I wish I could see him again before…." His voice trailed off.

Papa-san decided he would bring Frisky to the hospital. He returned to the island, got Frisky, and went back that same day. Papa-san discreetly walked past the pre-occupied nurses and slipped Frisky into bed with his master, then left them alone to say their final good-bye. After awhile Papa-san went back to the hospital room. Mr. Shereen thanked him, said his tearful goodbye, and sent Frisky home with Papa-san. Frisky became our loyal watchdog, and I became Frisky's admiring and loving friend.

"I asked Mack about Kitty," Mama-san said. "He didn't know. She also disappeared sometime shortly after we left. She probably went out into the woods to look for food."

"Where is Mack now?" I asked. "Does he still work for us?"

"No," she said, "he wanted to go down to California where it is warmer. He seemed so relieved to see us return to Vashon. He talked about how the harvest that first year after we left was so hard for him. He certainly looked thinner and more drawn."

"Yes," I said, "I can imagine the whole burden of running the farm must have been terribly difficult for him."

"He said it rained a lot and pickers were hard to find," Mama-san added. "Yoneichi-san used to go and bring the pickers here with the truck, but he wasn't here any more so some of the pickers couldn't get here. When we asked Mack where he sent the berries, he said, 'I continued sending them to the Vashon Packing Company that Mr. Dunsford took over when Masa Mukai had to leave, and that was okay. It was just hard without all of you here to work with.' I think he wore himself out working this place all alone."

"Yes, I can understand that," I added. "So you had a chance to thank him from all of us for all he did?"

"Yes, and Papa-san gave him a good bonus for being so faithful. He literally saved our farm for us. I am so thankful." Then we all grew quiet for awhile, each in our thoughts.

The air was balmy and peaceful my first day back home. The swallows dipped and soared, twittering as they streaked by. Mama-san and I walked along the eastern and southern boundaries of our farm. I thought about how frightened we were on that fateful day five years earlier as we took this same walk. Now we stopped and admired Mount Rainier off to the southeast, still looking majestic streaked in the sunset's pink reflections. We lingered by the orderly vegetable garden Mama-san had planted. The dark green, feathery carrot tops waved gently in the breeze. Bean stalks were still producing pods, ready to be picked and enjoyed. Tender lettuce and beets would be ready to harvest in the next few weeks, and nearby strawberry plants looked healthy. Fruit trees were loaded with maturing nectarines and apples. The pink and white carnations along the south and west sides of the house filled the night air with their perfume. All seemed right once again. Even the chickens clucking in the chicken yard, scratching for feed, sounded sweet.

While Mama-san and I walked back to the house, I thought, *Everything looks the same, and still wonderful. Only we have changed.*

CHAPTER EIGHTEEN

MAMA-SAN

The years following Yoneichi's return from the service were happy ones for him and my parents. The farm work picked up until it ran as productively as it had prior to the War. Pickers came during the harvest and at 10:00 every morning, Papa-san handed out three pieces of candy to each picker for a break. Every evening after dinner he sat in his big overstuffed chair in front of the oil stove, reading the newspaper until he fell asleep. Mama-san would awaken him for the evening snack, followed by a long, relaxing bath. After a good night's rest, the daily cycle would begin again. It was good to be home.

In 1954, both of my parents studied for and successfully passed the exam to become citizens of the United States of America. It was the fulfillment of their lifelong dream. Even though it took them so many years, it gave them great satisfaction and a sense that all of their sacrifice had been worth it.

Papa-san spent the rest of his life faithfully working the land with and for his son. Their roles changed, and Yoneichi became the head of the household. Although they always consulted each other regarding different decisions that had to be made, they both understood that Yoneichi was now in charge. That was the way things were done in the traditional Japanese family.

The career I began as a nurse's aide in Heart Mountain Relocation Camp led me to my life's work. I stayed at Vashon for only a few months in 1947 while I made future plans and reassured myself that everything was settled on the farm. Then I moved to Seattle and began my career as a registered nurse. While attending the College of Puget Sound to work toward my bachelor's degree, I met my future husband, Charles E. Gruenewald. We married in 1951, then moved to Boston, Massachusetts, where he completed his masters degree in Sacred Theology at Boston University School of Theology. During our time there, I worked for the Visiting Nurse Association.

After the completion of his studies, Charles and I returned to the West Coast where we served Methodist churches in Cosmopolis and Renton,

Washington, as well as Idaho Falls, Idaho, and Denver, Colorado. In Denver, while Charles worked on a doctorate degree, I worked with a team of private-duty nurses caring for patients of three heart surgeons during the early days of open-heart surgery. I found the work hard, exciting, and occasionally tragic when we lost a patient. As a minister's wife, I met many wonderful people and worked tirelessly to learn the many facets of that role. I also became a mother, bearing three children between 1954 and 1960.

⤳◉⤳

In the summer of 1965, my three young children and I visited the family farm on Vashon to help with the harvest, as we had every year. The harvest season was at its peak, and Papa-san and Yoneichi were in the strawberry fields daily with a host of pickers. Mama-san, seventy-three, had been struggling with stomach cancer during the previous year, and we knew her time was running short.

Each morning I would awaken the children at 6:00, fix their breakfast, and take them to Mama-san's bedside. Martha was eleven, and she was hesitant to get too close because Grandma looked quite emaciated. David was nine, and he looked at her intently as he approached her bedside and stood close to her. Ray was only five, and he snuggled up to her, in spite of her appearance. They all knew something was wrong, although Ray was too young to understand what it meant.

Mama-san would smile at them, nod, and say to me in Japanese, "They are a little afraid of me because I look so thin and different, aren't they? That's all right. Work hard, little ones, and help your mother, your uncle and grandpa, okay?" I translated her message to them. Once the children ran off to the fields to pick strawberries, I fixed Mama-san an injection of demerol and phenergan for pain. I gave her tea or okai, a thin gruel of rice or whatever she felt like eating. Then I bathed her, took care of her personal needs and helped her to settle comfortably for the next few hours.

One afternoon she opened the top drawer of her dresser. Silently she picked up her gold wedding band from its box. She slipped it on her thin ring finger, looked at it for a moment, and then returned it to the box. She looked content as she slowly got back into bed.

The following morning she looked especially alert, bright, and radiant. When I prepared her usual small dose of pain medication, she asked me to give her a larger one. As her eyes swept back and forth across the ceiling, she said, "Wherever I look, I see God as a glowing, white light beckoning me down this long corridor to come to Him. I am impatient. I want to go as soon as I can. Please give me a big dose of medicine so I may go as quickly as possible."

I was stunned by her request. It had been my life-long work as a nurse to save lives. Now Mama-san was asking me to end hers. It was hard enough for me to see her slipping away daily, but for her to ask me to give her a lethal dose of drugs to hasten her death was overwhelming. I swallowed hard, took a deep breath and said, "Mama-san, are you having a lot of pain and you want relief from that?"

"No," she said, "The pain is not that bad. God has given me a good life, and I know I will be going to a more wonderful, beautiful place. I want to go as soon as I can."

This was the way Mama-san looked at each new experience. She was always ready to take the next step. Now she was facing the end of her life with the same openness and faith that was so characteristic of her. I was utterly amazed and saddened beyond belief. Sounding more clinical than I intended, I said, "Mama-san, I cannot give you more than what the doctor ordered. It's against the law."

I forced myself to continue as tears welled in my eyes. "I can understand your desire to go to God because you have lived such a God-centered life." I stopped and struggled to continue with what was really in my heart. "I don't want you to leave us at all, but to hasten your departure is something I cannot do." I burst into tears, dropped to my knees beside her bed, put my head on her shoulder, and held her while I wept.

Mama-san gently stroked my head and softly said, "Mary-san, I understand. I shouldn't ask you to do that for me. It's all right."

We stayed that way for some time until my weeping eased. With one final attempt, I sat up and asked hopefully, "What would your answer be if a cure for cancer were to be found tomorrow? Would you be willing to stay?"

"No," she answered. "My work on earth is done. You and your brother are adults now. You both have families to care for, and it is time for me to leave."

She shifted her position in bed so she could face me directly. Mama-san paused and looked at me apologetically, then added, "But there are some things I must discuss with you. I can't erase from my memory that time in camp when I know Papa-san and I pushed you so hard when you had so many other burdens. And I am especially troubled by that time fourteen years ago when you asked for our blessing in marrying the *hakujin*, Charles. I owe you my deepest apologies for my rejection of him. In looking back, I should have accepted your choice and been glad for you. Please forgive us for what we did."

I was astonished that she could think about those things when she was so close to death. I put my hand gently on her shoulder as I replied. "I understood. I never blamed you for either of those things. I know it was hard for you when I first told you about Charles, but look how things have worked out. Charles is such an important part of our family now. And all the hard work we had to do during that very difficult time has really paid off. We have our farm back. It was worth all the effort. No forgiveness is necessary."

Mama-san smiled with a look of satisfaction on her face. I smiled back and silently took her pale, emaciated hand in mine.

From that moment on, as often as her strength would allow, we spent the next five days together reminiscing about our years together. We talked about my childhood triumphs and traumas, long-lost friends, and her hopes for my future. We recalled simple pleasures; a cool breeze on a hot day, the satisfaction of sharing ice cream bars with all of the pickers at the end of the harvest, of cooking meals together in the kitchen. A peace came over both of us.

I made it a point to check on her hourly. The morning of June 30, when I checked on Mama-san at 8:00, she was sleeping comfortably from the shot I had given her earlier. When I returned an hour later, Mama-san was lying motionless with a beatific look on her face. I held my breath as I crept closer. Her chest was no longer rising and falling.

I knelt by her side in the stillness, placed my hands on her hands, bowed my head and wept. I did not want to let her go. She was my strength, my inspiration, and my anchor. It did not make her departure any easier knowing that she had faith and courage in facing her final transition.

When I thought I had no more tears to shed, I got up and gathered a basin of warm water, clean towels, a fresh bar of Ivory soap and a bottle of Jergen's Lotion. Dipping a washcloth into the water, I carefully bathed and dried Mama-san's face, ears, and neck. I thought about how often she must have bathed me when I was young. Now I was bathing her body that had become thin and ravaged by cancer. My mother was always a petite woman but now she had become a mere shadow of her former weight. Her skin looked fragile and translucent.

I thought about all the other bodies I had bathed as a nurse, but it was nothing like bathing Mama-san's. Hers was the source of my life, the one that nourished me physically, mentally, and emotionally. My tears flowed as I washed her one last time. Carefully I rubbed the lotion on Mama-san's skin, then dressed her in a clean nightie. I combed her long gray hair, straightened the covers on her bed, and placed her hands in prayer on her chest.

Then I went out to the field to get Papa-san and Yoneichi. I approached them and without a word, they each knew what had happened. They came to the house with stricken faces. Papa-san looked briefly at her and, to my surprise, said, "She's just asleep." He promptly left the room. Yoneichi came into the bedroom, dropped down beside her, put his arm across her body and wept. I stood beside him and wept as well. We stayed that way for a long time.

Even though nothing had been said, word passed quickly among the pickers who were at the farm that day. Mama-san's illness was common knowledge and several people knew instantly what it meant when I summoned my father and brother. Many of the workers who knew her shed tears in the strawberry fields that day.

I called our doctor, and he notified the mortician, who arrived within the hour to pick up Mama-san's body. Soon the house was a hubbub of activity as the day's work ended and people began arriving in droves. I was only vaguely aware of the many people who came and went, expressing their condolences and offering support. My three children picked strawberries all day long and were unaware of their grandmother's passing. When they came in they were bewildered by all the activity and by seeing the empty bed where their grandmother normally slept. The two oldest took it upon themselves to comfort the youngest and explain what happened.

The next day the harvest continued as usual. Because Mama-san's death occurred during the height of the picking season, we requested that her remains be cremated and the ashes placed in the gravesite we had selected for her. We scheduled her memorial service for later in the summer, as she would have wished. Mama-san was a very sensible woman.

Papa-san eventually came to accept his wife's death, but he did so in the privacy of his own thoughts. I never saw him cry for her, but he did spend a great deal of time alone, working the fields. One day about two months after her death, I began talking about Mama-san in front of my father. He remarked with obvious pride that she had come from a long line of samurai. After that, something opened up inside Papa-san and he was able to reminisce about her. That was when I knew he had made his peace with her death.

In the weeks that followed, especially in the evenings, when the day's work was done and the children were asleep, I wandered around the yard that Mama-san loved so much, looking to the stars for some kind of answer to where she was. I remembered earlier in the year, when she was still well enough to venture outdoors, she planted peas knowing full well she would not be here to eat them. She started tomatoes she would never see ripen, and planted cuttings of chrysanthemums knowing that others would enjoy their beauty. Over the years I would come to know her wisdom and grace that would continue to flourish and bloom in my life in unexpected and mysterious ways.

Mama-san in the strawberry fields.

Just before our family was broken up at Heart Mountain in 1944 with each of us going in different directions, Mama-san suggested we imagine what it would be like twenty years in the future, looking back on our experiences. Ironically, her death occurred twenty years after that transcendent suggestion—and it was just as we had imagined. She helped us build a map for the future and allowed us to hope at a time when others might have despaired.

The stories I told my own children and grandchildren weren't Japanese fairy tales about Momotaro, Amaterasu, or Sentaro. Instead, I told them about the real-life bravery of their uncle Yoneichi, the calm strength of Papa-san, and especially the wisdom, courage and grace of Mama-san. It was her voice I heard during difficult times. She was the one who encouraged me, saying, *"Shikata ga nai"* or *"gaman suru."*

It was Mama-san's smile I would remember when an unexpected joy caught my attention and made me smile. And it was her strength that I would continue to carry with me every day, even while writing my memoir almost forty years after her death. While the internment experience was a tragedy, because of her I am at peace with it, and I am even grateful that I lived through it.

RETURN TO MINIDOKA

In the summer of 2004, I returned to Minidoka sixty years after I had left. I joined 130 *Niseis* and *Sanseis* nationwide to attend a special pilgrimage by former internees and their families to the site. Earlier, I had participated in meetings with National Park Superintendent Neil King and his staff, who were preparing to create a national monument memorializing the Minidoka Internment Camp.

When we reached Minidoka after a twelve-hour bus ride from Seattle, I was eager to see what the National Park Service had created after months of input from *Niseis*. At the first stop, I was surprised to find only a single barrack standing alone, with no gate or guard towers nearby. Most of the original buildings had been sold or moved away for use as storage buildings. However, I knew that later we would go to another site where we would see what remained of the original camp entrance.

At this first stop when I stepped onto the porch of a typical barrack and walked through the doorway of the end apartment, I was suddenly back in 1944. I put my hand to my throat and took a deep breath trying to relax the tightness in my chest. The wide gaps between the planks in the floor brought back memories of the frequent windstorms that whipped up dust through every crack and space in the floorboards, walls, and window frames. Automatically I closed my eyes as if to avoid the sting of the dirt and sand on my face, behind my eyelids, in my mouth, and between my teeth.

On that calm summer day in 2004 I once again felt suffocated, claustrophobic, terrified of being trapped again in the inescapable detention center. As if it were only yesterday, I still hated this place where I was held against my will. Once again, shame constricted my throat after all these years and I had trouble speaking to the people around me. Other Japanese-Americans, many of them third- and fourth-generation, wanted to learn about the evacuation and the imprisonment, and connect with the searing experience of their elders. Nearing my eightieth year, I knew I needed to tell

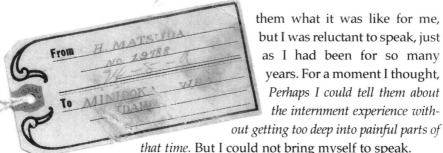

them what it was like for me, but I was reluctant to speak, just as I had been for so many years. For a moment I thought, *Perhaps I could tell them about the internment experience without getting too deep into painful parts of that time.* But I could not bring myself to speak.

Later in the day we went on a mile-long tour led by a guide. We walked through tall grass looking at the places where the National Park Service had started to recreate and label a small part of the original camp. We looked at what used to be the entryway adjacent to the military police building with its standing stone wall and a fireplace, all of the same basalt rock. I remembered this as a heavily guarded area, one that no one

Papa-san's luggage tag for the transfer to Minidoka.

could enter or leave without clearance from the military police. Now I walked freely around this area. I had the urge to fling my arms into the air and shout "Freedom!" but I kept a reserved demeanor.

Just inside the entrance I saw a terrible blank space. Once this public entryway had displayed a large wooden sign made and erected by internees, listing the names of the men from Minidoka Camp who served in the U.S. Army during World War II. My brother's name would not have appeared there, since he had departed for the war from a different camp, Heart Mountain.

Minidoka's Honor Roll had stood beside a Japanese-style garden made by an internee skilled in creating Japanese gardens of beauty and serenity. The honor roll was gone and no one seemed to know when or why it was removed, or by whom. I clenched my jaws. To remove this symbol of the ultimate sacrifice of our young men at a time of such hardship was unthinkable to me. I wanted to believe someone had carefully removed it and preserved it in some safe place for later recognition and honor. But I couldn't speak up and ask.

Still in a daze, I accompanied the others as we continued the tour to look at the original root cellar, which had been used to store root vegetables for the camp. Then we paused at the old swimming hole, now mostly hidden by a dense growth of trees and grass. *Yes,* I thought to myself, *life went on for us in the camps.*

The following day we returned to the Minidoka National Monument for a memorial service with flags and an honor guard by *Nisei* veterans. I thought of the mothers of these soldiers, such as Mama-san, who showed remarkable courage and sacrifice during those war years. Just like many other American parents, Mama-san had sent her only son off to risk his life in the fight for his homeland. But most parents didn't make that courageous decision from behind barbed-wire.

During lunch I sat with two women from Japan and another *Nisei* woman. In our conversation I mentioned that I had never visited Japan and had no interest in going. This resulted in startled looks, protests, and questions from the others. I explained that some years ago a *Nisei* friend of mine had taken a group of physicians and pathologists to Japan. Because he looked like a Japanese citizen, he was publicly ridiculed because he did not speak the language "properly." "I have never forgotten that," I said. "I am not willing to put myself into that position."

The ladies protested that Japan isn't like that any more, that attitudes have changed over the last twenty years. I was assured there are signs with English wording, and many Japanese understand English. They said I was missing out on an important life experience.

I had never explored the reasons for my reluctance to visit my parents' homeland. I later realized that it was one thing to be wounded by the rejection of American society during and after World War II. It was another to be haunted by the prospect that I could be rejected yet again—this time by the Japanese society of my ancestors.

The evacuation came at a time when I was struggling with my identity. The pressure to appear "loyal" to the United States caused me to bury my Japanese self for decades. This lunchtime discussion inspired me to begin to change my thinking and explore more of my life, especially the part of me that is Japanese. It has taken me sixty years to come to terms with who I am. The country of my ancestors is no longer my enemy.

After this three-day pilgrimage we headed back to Seattle. One of the coordinators extended an invitation to the *Niseis* on the bus to share their experiences of internment camps. I thought, *Maybe I should try again to speak up, one last time in spite of how hard it might be.* Once again my chest tightened, and my heart quickened. *I wonder if some of those Niseis out there will disagree with me?*

I had been saddled by feelings of paralyzing helplessness for so long. I wondered, *Once I open up and start talking, will I also cry? And if I do, will I be able to stop? And if I show any of my feelings, will I be ostracized for doing so?*

This time, instead of using my own words, I decided to read my mother's letters that I had brought with me. Maybe Mama-san, always eloquent, could reach across the seeming generation gap. I stood up and weaved my way to the front of the bus as it sped down the highway. I clutched the letters to my chest.

Sitting down in one of the front aisle seats, I turned to face the back of the bus and selected the first letter. Taking the microphone in my left hand, I looked up and saw all of the Japanese faces looking at me expectantly. Then I pictured Mama-san's smiling face, calm and steady, and this gave me strength.

September 3, 1944
Mary-san, I arrived in Ogden at 3:30. Please be relieved. After many, many miles of sagebrush, we finally arrived in Ogden. From the beginning to the end of our journey, it was sagebrush. It's beyond talking about— all this sagebrush along straight roads. It felt wonderful. I wish we could have been together, you and I. The image of your face in the bus window [when I had left her] remains with me. Please be sure and take care of your body.

As I read Mama-san's letters, all written in Japanese, I suddenly became aware that my voice sounded like hers. I paused where she would have paused. I emphasized the words she would have. It was her voice speaking to the third and fourth generations of Japanese-Americans who were listening. Together we were telling the next two generations our story.

I looked outside and saw the same sagebrush my mother described as she left Minidoka for the first time. Then I pulled out the next letter and began to read:

March 6, 1945
Mary-san, I am sorry for delaying so long to send you this letter. But I suspect you remain energetic and discharging your duty. Letters do not come from Yoneichi-san. It is really, really lonely. And you are so far away. Every day I think about you and Yoneichi-san. No matter how much I think about it or feel about it, and know that it is *shikata ga nai*, I can't keep from thinking about it. I think he has gone overseas. I had a very clear dream about him. Letters don't come to you from him either, do they?

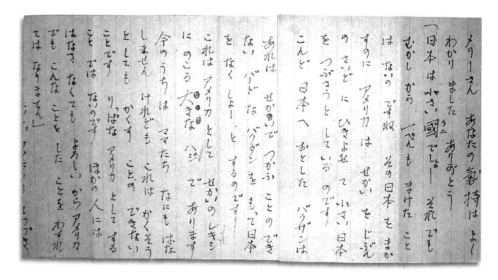

Mama-san's letter commenting on the atomic bomb.

I explained to the bus crowd, "I knew that my parents had sent their only son into battle knowing that he might die. That was the common philosophy among all Japanese." Taking a deep breath, I composed myself and continued. "The final letter I'm going to read was written after my mother heard about the dropping of the atom bombs on Japan. Most of you know our parents were never allowed to become citizens of the United States, so they were still citizens of Japan. My parents had chosen to come to America to live, and remained faithful to their dream, in spite of the betrayal of the principles of liberty for them. They never imagined that the war would end this way."

August 17, 1945
Japan is a small country, but from a long time ago, she has never lost a single war. In order to defeat Japan, America took the sky for herself and tried to crush little Japan...We must never forget that America did this kind of thing.

I looked down at the sea of mostly Japanese faces, everyone's eyes riveted on me. No one moved or said a thing. My hands trembled as I tried to focus on the letter. We all knew I said publicly what many Japanese-Americans had kept to themselves. In 1945 none of us dared to criticize America for dropping the atom bombs. After a few moments I stood to return to my seat in the rear of the bus. Two women sitting on either side of the bus near the front, gray-haired *Niseis* like me, stood up, put their hands out to touch me, and thanked me. They both had faraway looks on their faces. My mother's words—more powerful than mine—had reached across the divide.

Afterword

Several decades after the internment Japanese-Americans finally received a formal apology from the United States government acknowledging that "a grave injustice was done to both citizens and permanent residents of Japanese ancestry by the evacuation, relocation, and internment of civilians during World War II." President Ronald Reagan signed the Civil Liberties Act of 1988 into law on August 10. Each surviving internee received a letter of apology from the president and compensation of $20,000. The government also allocated funds for public education on the internment.

This legislation was a triumph of grassroots politics and the culmination of more than a decade of effort by a number of Japanese-American activists nationwide. At the recommendation of Senator Daniel Inouye from Hawaii, himself a decorated veteran of the 442nd Regimental Combat Team, the Commission on Wartime Relocation and Internment of Civilians was created to hold fact-finding hearings across the country. From July to December 1981, hundreds of *Nisei* testified before the commission and the national press, often telling their stories for the first time some thirty-five years later. Their heart-wrenching stories moved and shocked the nation, helping to sway public opinion in support of the redress movement. In many cases, this process also opened a dialog with third- and fourth-generation Japanese-Americans, some of whom had been unaware of the experiences that their own parents and grandparents had lived through.

For many Japanese-Americans, the redress process brought healing and a sense of legitimacy to their experience. When I received my formal apology dated November 21, 1989 and signed by President George H. W. Bush, I felt a sense of satisfaction but also regret that my parents and brother did not live to see the resolution of this terrible wrong.

The National Japanese-American Memorial to Patriotism in Washington, D.C. was built in honor of those who were interned and the *Nisei* soldiers who died during World War II. I attended the dedication in November 2000, along with a crowd of my peers—all of us with gray hair and wrinkles. The pent-up emotions that we *Niseis* had held back for fifty-eight years surfaced that day as many of us cried silently—alone and with each other.

When I looked up at the fourteen-foot bronze sculpture of two cranes—symbolizing happiness, good fortune, and longevity—enmeshed in barbed-wire, I was overwhelmed with contradictory feelings. I felt joy for the long-sought recognition of our suffering, sadness for those no longer with us to participate in the celebration, and heartache for all that the memorial represented. I wept for my family and for all peoples of all times who have suffered oppression and hopelessness in the face of overwhelming odds.

My parents would have wept, just as I did, but they would have felt a great deal of pride in the accomplishments of our people and would have known that they had contributed to the memorial's completion. The ceremony would have vindicated everything they ever believed about their adopted country. But they would have been even more proud if they knew about an honor that was bestowed upon me less than two years later.

The career I began as a nurse's aide in an internment camp would culminate in my being invited to the White House to speak with the president. For most of my career as a registered nurse I had worked at Group Health Cooperative, a healthcare organization in Seattle, Washington. In 1971 I founded the Consulting Nurse Service, which allows patients to consult by telephone with a registered nurse. The inspiration for this service came from fielding numerous patient phone calls in the middle of the night from people who were worried about urgent health problems. The Consulting Nurse Service, available twenty-four hours per day, has been replicated in hospitals throughout the country.

After I retired in 1990, I remained active with Group Health Cooperative as a volunteer, particularly in the Senior Caucus, a special-interest group. In May 2002, I joined a "March-On-Washington" for healthcare reform. About 230 delegates nationally, each one representing a healthcare organization, spoke to their elected representatives and senators on behalf of seniors who were Medicare+Choice consumers.

While in Washington, D.C., I returned to the National Japanese-American Memorial site with two Caucasian companions. As we approached the bronze sculpture surrounded by a curved wall listing all ten internment camps and the total number of Japanese-Americans who lived in each camp, I was again overcome by memories of those difficult times. Sixty years later and the tears still flowed. My friends put their arms around me. Again, I read the names of the *Nisei* men who had died in battle for our freedom and dignity. They had gone ahead courageously and paved the way for the rest of us. In front of the reflecting pool I pondered what Mama-san would think about this memorial. I could see her nodding and smiling, making the point that everything had worked out all right. We had all demonstrated *gaman*, been patient, and the difficult times had passed.

The next day I joined my colleagues at the White House and I briefly met and spoke with President George W. Bush in a carefully choreographed ceremony. I spoke for the healthcare reform legislation and urged swift action. Afterwards, I attended a press conference with President Bush, satisfied with my participation and overwhelmed with the spectacle surrounding the event.

That evening in my hotel room, when I was alone recording my thoughts, I came to a stunning realization: *My return to the memorial occurred exactly sixty years to the day after the evacuation from our Vashon home on May 16, 1942—and the very next day I met with the President of the United States of America.*

This synchronistic revelation swept over me. *How could it be that I would be in this place at this time?* I wondered. I didn't try to figure it out, I just bowed my head in thanksgiving for the mysteries of life—the mystery that brought me to such a place of fulfillment and completion sixty years later to the day. Mama-san was right. In my greatest moments of despair in the internment camps, she had asked, "What kind of memories will we want to have in twenty years of how we faced these difficulties now?"

⁓ ⊛ ⁓

Sixty years after the war, our strawberry farm is still in the family name, although its purpose has changed. The rows of strawberries have been replaced by fields of grass that are occasionally mowed for hay. My brother's wife still lives in our family home. The pond on which Yoneichi and I used to glide on our makeshift raft is still there with frogs that croak on warm summer evenings. Madrona trees still grow to the west of our property, but most of the evergreen trees are gone, logged and removed for commercial and residential use. The *osu* my father made from a large tree stump to make *mochi* for the New Year's celebration is still there. Mama-san's carnations on the south side of the house are gone, but her Silver Pine tree has grown tall and stately. Snow-capped Mount Rainier, ever constant as human history unfolds, is still spiritually stirring.

Papa-san lived out the rest of his days missing Mama-san but content, living in the home that he built and passed on to his son. After many years working the land that meant so much to us, Papa-san eventually became forgetful, at times wandering off, brought home by a kind neighbor. He peacefully slipped away in his sleep one night at the age of ninety-three.

After World War II, Yoneichi earned enough money to buy more land and equipment, eventually owning and farming fifty-two acres. In 1958, he married Marjorie Nakagawa and reared a family of four daughters. Tragically, Marjorie died from cancer in 1973. Four years later, Yoneichi married Miyoko Nishi.

Yoneichi taught social studies and the Japanese language for eighteen years at Ingraham High School in Seattle. He hoped the next generation would see the world through wiser eyes. After a full day of teaching classes, he took the ferry home to Vashon and prepared for the next day's classes, and then cultivated the strawberries in the dark, riding his tractor with the lights on.

Yoneichi decided to retire early because he had heard teachers don't live very long after retirement. He wanted to travel and had already made plans for an extended trip to Japan with his wife and daughters. One evening, less than three months after his retirement in 1985, Yoneichi was on his tractor cultivating strawberries when he had the first signs of a heart attack. He was rushed to the hospital, and despite receiving superb medical care, his condition deteriorated, and a week later he died, surrounded by family.

After his death, I wandered through my days, untethered, unable to believe that Yoneichi could really be gone. I felt cheated, anguished, and horribly disappointed that we never had our lengthy conversations about his war experiences. It would be years later while writing this book that I pieced together some sense of Yoneichi's war experience through my readings and by interviewing his war buddies.

I still visit Vashon and walk the family farm. Just down the road from our home is the Vashon Island Cemetery where my parents and brother are buried. Yoneichi had been one of the commissioners of the King County Cemetery District No. 1 for nine years. At the entrance to the cemetery, the county established a beautiful memorial garden for Yoneichi. Whenever I visit the cemetery, I pause at the memorial garden, gaze at the plaque and the garden's array of flowers. I have never stopped longing for my courageous brother who always worked to guide and support me, as he did others. In time I realized I would have to carry forward the family's courage. Telling my story would be my way.

Not until the 1990s did some *Niseis* begin to talk openly about their internment experiences, and yet even today, many of my contemporaries are still reluctant to discuss this time in U.S. history. Some *Sanseis*, the children of the *Niseis* who went through the internment, have asked, "Why didn't you fight back?" or "Why did you go like sheep to be slaughtered without any resistance?" Their questions made me rethink my experience and helped me realize the need to tell my story.

In my seventies I began to write down my story, reliving it all once again. Now, at eighty years, I am ready to tell the world my story of imprisonment. I have often thought that in these tumultuous, post 9/11 times, it is crucial that I tell my story. Perhaps if I share my experiences, this will be one more convincing piece of evidence against the possibility of internment camps in the United States ever happening again.

◇

New Year's Day 2005, my three grown children and my grandson were looking at the three jars of shells Mama-san and I had collected at Tule Lake more than sixty years ago. The old glass jars seem fragile with their slightly rusted, screw-on lids of different sizes. One has a faded, torn label that reads "Dill Pickles." Each of the jars holds a different kind of shell.

I keep these jars in a cabinet in my basement. Every so often I take them out. I run my fingers along the rough edges of the spiral shells and luminous white clamshells. Some are broken, yet still precious in detail. I scoop up handfuls of these delicate reminders of a bitter-sweet time. *Mama-san touched these shells too,* I say to myself, as I recall the simple pleasure of working side-by-side with her, collecting these shells that seemed to transport us far beyond that painful time in our history.

Recently my son counted all the shells in the three glass jars. Unknowingly, Mama-san and I had collected nearly 120,000 shells—about the same number of people interned in Japanese-American camps during the war.

As my children and I talk about the seashells and Mama-san, I hear her soft voice and see her face as she nods and smiles at us. While I received priceless gifts of wisdom and love from my parents, I have nothing tangible of theirs from the old country. What few treasures they brought from Japan were burned that evening in 1942 in a desperate attempt to avoid being identified with the enemy. Now these shells have become my family's new cultural treasures to pass on to future generations along with my story.

GLOSSARY

Arigato	thank you, appreciate.
Baishakunin	a matchmaker, marriage go-between.
Dozo	by all means, if you please.
Enryo	restraint, modesty, humility.
Fujinkai	a women's group.
Gaman	patience, perseverance, self-restraint.
Giri	duty, obligation to family or group.
Gochisosama deshita	it was very delicious.
Gomen nasai	pardon me, I apologize, sorry.
Haiseki	exclusion, prejudice.
Haji	shame , disgrace on family or other Japanese.
Hajime	begin, start.
Hakujin	a white person, a Caucasian.
Hapa	a mixed-race person.
Hina Matsuri	Girls' Day on March 3.
Ikebana	flower arrangement.
Inoru	to pray.
Issei	Japanese who immigrated to and settled in the United States.
Itadaki masu	I will eat now.
Itte kimasu	I am going.
Itterashai	please be on your way.
Kamisama	God, the creator.
Kibei	a Japanese born in America, educated as a child in Japan, and returns to America.
Konnichi wa	Good day, good morning.
Kowai na	fearful, dreadful, scary.
Mochi tsuki	to pound steamed rice into rice cakes.

Nikkei	a generic term applied to anyone Japanese.
Nisei	American-born second generation children of the *Issei*.
Oba-san	an old lady (woman); a grandmother.
Ochitsuite yo	be self possessed, calm.
Ohaiyo gozaimasu	good morning.
Okaeri nasai	welcome home.
Oyakoko	properly caring for one's parents.
On	one's debt or respect for one's parents or teacher; moral obligation.
Sabishi	lonely, desolate, solitary.
San	an honorific form of address, used after a person's name or nickname.
Sansei	third-generation Japanese-Americans, children of the *Nisei*.
Shamisen	a stringed instrument held like a guitar.
Shikata ga nai	it cannot be helped.
Shikkari suru	be strong, brave, steady.
Shinbo shimasho	let us be patient, persevere, bear, put up with.
Tada ima kaeri mashita	I have just returned home.
Tango no Sekku	Boys' Day on June 5.
Tenno Heika Banzai	"Long live His Majesty the Emperor."
Yoisho	yo-heave-ho, a worker's chant.
Yonsei and Gosei	fourth and fifth generation Japanese-Americans.

BIBLIOGRAPHY

Armor, John and Wright, Peter. *Manzanar,* Photographs by Ansel Adams, Commentary by John Hersey. New York, NY: Times Books, 1988.

Burton, J.F., Farrell, M.M., Lord, F.B., Lord, R.W. *Confinement and Ethnicity: An Overview of World War II Japanese-American Relocation Sites.* Tucson, AZ: Western Archeological and Conservation Center, 2000.

Chang, Thelma. *"I Can Never Forget": Men of the 100th/442nd.* Honolulu, HI: Sigi Productions, Inc., 1991.

The Commission on Wartime Relocation and Internment of Civilians. *Personal Justice Denied: The Commission on Wartime Relocation and Internment of Civilians.* Report. Washington D.C. and San Francisco, CA: The Civil Liberties Public Education Fund; Seattle, WA and London, UK: University of Washington Press, 1997.

Crost, Lyn. *Honor by Fire: Japanese-Americans at War in Europe and the Pacific.* Novato, CA: Presidio Press, 1994.

Denenberg, Barry. *My Name Is America: The Journal of Ben Uchida.* New York, NY: Scholastic Inc., 1942.

Duus, Masayo Umezawa. *Unlikely Liberators: the Men of the 100th and 442nd.* Tokyo, Japan: Bungeishunjusha, 1983.

Fugita, Stephen S. and Fernandez, Marilyn. *Altered Lives, Enduring Community: Japanese-Americans Remember Their World War II Incarceration.* Seattle, WA and London, UK: University of Washington Press, 2004.

Gorfinkel, Claire (ed.). *The Evacuation Diary of Hatsuye Egami.* Pasadena, CA: Intentional Productions, 1995.

Guterson, David. *Snow Falling on Cedars.* New York, NY and San Diego, CA: Harcourt Brace & Company, 1994.

Hill, Kimi Kodani (ed). *Topaz Moon: Chiura Obata's Art of the Internment.* Berkeley, CA: Heyday Books, 2000.

Hosokawa, William K. *Nisei: The Quiet Americans.* New York, NY: William Morrow and Company, Inc., 1969.

Houston, Jeanne Wakatsuki, and Houston, James D. *Farewell to Manzanar.* Boston, MA: Houghton Mifflin Company, 1973.

Inada, Lawson Fusao (ed.). *Only What We Could Carry: The Japanese-American Internment Experience.* Berkeley, CA: Heyday Books, 2000.

Inouye, Mamoru. *The Heart Mountain Story: Photographs by Hansel Mieth and Otto Hagel of the World War II Internment of Japanese-Americans.* U.S.A.: Cummings Printing Co., 1997.

Inukai, Harry. *Tule Lake Directory and Camp News.* Hood River, OR: Inukai Publishing, 1988.

Kashima, Tetsuden. *Judgment without Trial: Japanese-American Imprisonment during World War II.* Seattle, WA and London, UK: University of Washington Press, 2003.

Kafka, Franz. *The Trial.* Copyright 1937 and 1956 by Alfred A. Knopf, Inc., Schocken Books, New York, NY. First Schocken paperback edition published in 1968.

Kogawa, Joy. *Obasan*. New York, NY: Doubleday, 1981.

Levine, Ellen. *A Fence Away From Freedom: Japanese-Americans and World War II*. New York, NY: G.P. Putnam's Sons, 1995.

Matsuo, Dorothy. *Boyhood to War: History and Anecdotes of the 442nd Regimental Combat Team*. Honolulu, HI: Mutual Publishing, 1992.

Muller, Eric L. *Free to Die for Their Country: The Story of the Japanese-American Draft Resisters in World War II*. Chicago, IL and London, UK: The University of Chicago Press, 2001.

Okada, John. *No-No Boy*. Seattle, WA and London, UK: University of Washington Press, 1976.

Shimabukuro, Robert Sadamu. *Born in Seattle: The Campaign for Japanese-American Redress*. Seattle, WA and London, UK: University of Washington Press, 2001.

Shirey, Orville C. *Americans: The Story of the 442nd Combat Team*. Washington D.C.: Infantry Journal Press, 1946.

Sone, Monica. *Nisei Daughter*. Seattle, WA and London, UK: University of Washington Press, 1979. Originally published as an *Atlantic Monthly* Press Book by Little, Brown and Company, 1953.

Stanley, Jerry. *I Am an American: A True Story of Japanese Internment*. New York, NY: Crown Publishers, Inc., 1994.

Steidl, Franz. *Lost Battalions: Going for Broke in the Vosges, Autumn 1944*. Novato, CA: Presidio Press, 1997.

Tamura, Linda. *The Hood River Issei: An Oral History of Japanese Settlers in Oregon's Hood River Valley*. Urbana, IL and Chicago, IL: University of Illinois Press, 1993.

Tanaka, Chester. *Go for Broke: A Pictorial History of the Japanese-American 100th Infantry Battalion and the 442nd Regimental Combat Team*. Richmond, CA: Go for Broke, Inc., 1982.

Tateishi, John. *And Justice for All: An Oral History of the Japanese-American Detention Camps*. Seattle, WA and London, UK: University of Washington Press, 1984.

Uchida, Yoshiko. *Desert Exile: The Uprooting of a Japanese-American Family*. Seattle, WA and London, UK: University of Washington Press, 1982.

Weglyn, Michi. *Years of Infamy: The Untold Story of America's Concentration Camps*. New York, NY: Morrow Quilt Paperbacks, 1976.

Wilson, Robert A. and Hosokawa, William K. *East to America: A History of the Japanese in the United States*. New York, NY: William Morrow and Company, Inc., 1980.

Woodroffe, Pamela J. *Vashon Island's Agricultural Roots: Tales of the Tilth as Told by Island Farmers*. Lincoln, NE: Writers Club Press, 2002.

World Book Encyclopedia, Chicago, IL: World Book, Inc., 2005.

Yamada, Mitsuye. *Camp Notes and Other Poems*. Berkeley, CA: Shameless Hussy Press, 1976.

Yamada, Mitsuye. *Desert Run: Poems and Stories*. Latham, NY: Kitchen Table: Women of Color Press, Inc., 1988.

Yamaguchi, Jack. *This Was Minidoka*. Nagaoka, Japan: Nagai Printing Co. Ltd., 1989.

About the Author

Group Health Cooperative

In 2005 Mary Matsuda Gruenewald celebrated her eightieth birthday as well as the publication of her first book. She began writing her story in her seventies, no longer willing to stay within what she describes as "the self-imposed barbed-wire fences built around my experiences in the camps." With her book, Gruenewald breaks her silence as a *Nisei*.

During World War II Gruenewald entered nursing school and became a registered nurse. She worked as an R.N. for more than twenty-five years. She established the Consulting Nurse Service within the Group Health Cooperative in 1971, which has become a national model for numerous healthcare providers. In 2002 she was a medical delegate representing seniors on behalf of Medicare Plus Choice. At that meeting Gruenewald was selected along with ten other delegates to speak with President George W. Bush on healthcare issues.

Her articles on internment during WW II have appeared in major newspapers, and she has presented radio commentaries for NPR KPLU. Gruenewald was a consultant to the National Park Service during its establishment of Minidoka Internment Camp as a National Monument. She speaks regularly at schools, colleges, and universities, and students use her book as a class text nationwide. Gruenewald received an Asian American Living Pioneer Award in 2003.

Looking Like the Enemy was nominated by the American Library Association in 2005 for its list of "Best Books for Young Adults." Visit the author's web site at www.lookingliketheenemy.com.

OTHER BOOKS BY
MARY MATSUDA GRUENEWALD

*Young Reader's Edition of Looking Like the Enemy: My Years of Imprisonment in
    Japanese-American Internment Camps*
    (For readers 8 years and up)

Becoming Mama-san: 80 Years of Wisdom

OTHER BOOKS
BY NEWSAGE PRESS

One Woman One Vote: Rediscovering the Woman's Suffrage Movement
    an anthology edited by Marjorie Spruill Wheeler

Jailed for Freedom: American Women Win the Vote
    Doris Stevens, edited by Carol O'Hare

Montessori Learning in the 21st Century: A Guide for Parents & Teachers
    Shannon Helfrich

*Polar Dream: The First Solo Expedition by a Woman and Her Dog to the
    Magnetic North Pole*
    Helen Thayer

Women & Work: In Their Own Words
    edited by Maureen R. Michelson

*For a complete list of NewSage Press titles
visit our website: www.newsagepress.com,
or request a catalog from NewSage Press.*

NewSage Press
PO Box 607, Troutdale, OR 97060-0607

Phone Toll Free 877-695-2211
Email: info@newsagepress.com
Distributed to bookstores by Publishers Group West